Tennessee Williams
13 Essays

(Selected from *Tennessee Williams: A Tribute*)

EDITED BY JAC THARPE

188

UNIVERSITY PRESS OF MISSISSIPPI
JACKSON
1980

THIS VOLUME IS AUTHORIZED
AND SPONSORED BY
THE UNIVERSITY OF SOUTHERN MISSISSIPPI

Library of Congress Cataloging in Publication Data
Main entry under title:

Tennessee Williams: 13 essays

"Authorized and sponsored by the University of
Southern Mississippi, Hattiesburg."
  Bibliography: p.
  Includes index.
  1. Williams, Tennessee, 1911- —Criticism and
interpretation—Addresses, essays, lectures. I. Tharpe,
Jac. II. Mississippi. University of Southern
Mississippi, Hattiesburg.
PS3545.I5365Z847   812'.5'4   76-52971
ISBN 0-87805-032-9

TENNESSEE WILLIAMS: 13 ESSAYS

(Selected from *Tennessee Williams: A Tribute*)

for
Aunt Kate

Contents

Preface

THESE thirteen essays are selected from *Tennessee Williams: A Tribute*, published by the University Press of Mississippi in 1977. That large volume is now in a good many libraries across the land (presumably, since the original printing is nearly sold out). This volume attempts to meet the desires of those who found the original too expensive for personal libraries. Actually, we had planned a two-volume boxed set in 1977; but as costs of production rose, we had to find some way of reducing the price. One unfortunate result was that some readers unfamiliar with the preparation and publication of books thought they were getting too much for their money. My intention, insufficiently emphasized in the preface, had been to prepare a sourcebook of what I hoped would be readable and informative essays. The undergraduate seemed more in need than the scholar. I cut all the scholarly paraphernalia where possible and reduced it elsewhere. A bibliography was never a part of the project, as I did say with at least suggestive clarity. And the original documentation would have added another fifty pages, more or less, to the volume. But enough of that. Discussion of the numerous involvements of editing a volume would make a book.

The criterion for inclusion herein is approach: I have chosen some of those essays that deal generally with the work of Tennessee Williams and not with individual plays, themes, or contexts. One exception to interpretation is Leonard Quirino's excellent analysis of *A Streetcar Named Desire*. No matter what objections critics may have to his interpretation (and I have heard of none), Quirino presents Williams with the highest of compliments in reading one play so delicately and in crediting the playwright with a high artistry of fine detail.

*

The first essay is again that of Peggy W. Prenshaw, who tries to define the characteristics of southern culture as they affect the work of Tennessee Williams. The paradoxical world of the playwright reveals an artist strongly aware of the dichotomy between Cavalier and Puritan as well as that between frontier and genteel. One significant result for Williams is an ambivalence toward the past and especially the southern past. Within this setting, an ambivalence about both sexuality and the role of the artist has produced characters memorable for their struggles. Yet, these figures are frequently entrapped within the artist's paradoxical view and are therefore unable either to reconcile opposing forces in themselves or achieve a vision—either aesthetic or religious—encouraging transcendence.

Charles E. May studies "Three Players of a Summer Game" in depth as a way of analyzing the complexity of the later Brick in *Cat on a Hot Tin Roof*. The author talks of Brick's "tragedy" and of Williams' concentration on the ambiguous. The game of croquet in the short story is, the author feels, aesthetically significant, and his close study of "Three Players" makes that short story itself appear significant.

Glenn Embrey finds in *The Night of the Iguana* a level of meaning that undermines the claim of some critics that Williams affirmed life and thereby changed directions. The author suspects the apparently optimistic resolution of the action. Paradoxically, whatever the libertinism of the playwright, sex, the author suggests, is often the cause of the violence depicted in the plays.

George Niesen uses *Suddenly Last Summer*, in which the artist (also the main character) does not appear, and the most recent version of *The Two-Character Play* to frame his discussion of the artist's role in Williams' work. But in tracing his pervasive theme, he discusses numerous other plays.

John MacNicholas explains his title and his point in the second paragraph of his essay. The title has an ironic theological connotation related to a discussion of damnation and redemption in Williams' work. In a universe with a deus absconditus (hidden god), redemption depends upon humanity, according to the author's interpretation of Williams. The discussion of the artist-priest supplements Niesen's comments and leads to interpretations that offer insights into many of Williams' plays.

Judith Thompson discusses Williams' use of mythological allusions, archetypal figures, and ritual patterns in *The Glass Menagerie*, *The Rose Tattoo* and *Orpheus Descending* and finds the technique recurring in seven other plays. Williams both elevates and diminishes the protagonist's stature by moving him from "illusion" to "reality."

Charles Brooks some years ago outlined the comic aspects of *The Rose Tattoo*, *Cat on a Hot Tin Roof*, and *A Streetcar Named Desire*, to conclude that Williams' comic vitality was marred by sentimentalism (see bibliography). This new essay examines facets of Williams' comedy, the satire and the use of traditional comic types, and shows the complexity of characterization that derives from a realistic mixture of comic elements with other characteristics.

Leonard Casper discerns a technique "constructed of triangles" that Williams frequently employs. The idea here is used, among other purposes, to interpret the neglected *Kingdom of Earth* and *The Milk Train Doesn't Stop Here Anymore*. In Williams, the technique serves in varied ways for various purposes.

Albert Kalson's unusual essay begins with a discussion of the many references to movies and moviegoing then moves on to a study of the influence of specific movies in several plays and to a discussion of Williams' use of literal motion picture techniques. Well-chosen examples and perceptive comments make the essay much more than a study of a limited and specialized topic.

Norman Fedder's unassuming title heads an essay that severely assesses Williams as a working playwright. But the author also gives Williams credit for what he has done in creating dialogue and generally adding to the repertory of American theater.

William Free examines the shortcomings of *Small Craft Warnings* and *Out Cry,* in making an assessment of Williams' accomplishment in his *published* plays. A note at the end of the essay comments on the most recent published revision of *Out Cry* (re-named *The Two-Character Play*).

Donald Pease examines the relationship between Williams as man and Williams as artist. The opening paragraph succinctly presents the complexities of the relationships. A discussion of the forewords to the published editions of the plays and of major Williams characters gradually elucidates both title and subtitle of this unusual essay. Recent publication of *Memoirs* (1975), with its intermixture of art and autobiography, makes this essay especially pertinent.

*

As noted in the preface to *A Tribute,* citation of Williams is complex. References where possible are to the five volumes of *The Theatre of Tennessee Williams.* Variants occasionally cited are listed in a short bibliographical note, now abbreviated to provide only the information required to supplement internal documentation.

The Theatre is inconsistent in the use of typeface as well as typography. These matters and a few obvious errors or inconsistencies (use of hyphens, for example) in the collected edition of the plays are silently conformed. Williams' own frequent use of ellipsis points generally accounts for apparent inconsistencies in editing, though ellipsis points have occasionally been used in an attempt at clarity and of course to indicate omissions. To reduce costs of typesetting, italic used in stage directions in *The Theatre* is uniformly avoided, and parentheses are used instead of brackets. To reduce clutter, even lines of dialogue run into the text have but one set of quotation marks.

The renewed interest in Williams mentioned in the last paragraph of my preface to A *Tribute* was greater than I knew in detail. In addition to editing a collection of essays for Spectrum Books, Stephen Stanton was preparing *The Tennessee Williams Newsletter*, the first issue in the spring of 1979; and a revised edition of Signi Falk's *Tennessee Williams* was published by Twayne. Williams published a volume of poetry too late for us to consider it, and a new play, *Vieux Carré*. The *Newsletter* supplies details about other activity.

Whatever the shortcomings of A *Tribute* or this selection from it, those contributors here republished showed no strong inclination to revise their estimates of Tennessee Williams' performance over the years. Leonard Quirino still gives him credit for being a great artist, while William Free and Norman Fedder have doubts about his recent plays. Everyone takes him seriously. I never intended to function as critic and thus have no strong opinions to express. I regret that space and cost requirements prevent the publication of a larger selection of the original essays. And I personally feel the need for a study of European contexts and of Williams' influence on theater.

J.T.

TENNESSEE WILLIAMS: 13 ESSAYS

(Selected from *Tennessee Williams: A Tribute*)

specifically as the cause of Rose's loss of a potential husband and the beginning of her mysterious stomach trouble.

By Williams' own account and the evidence of repeated thematic motifs in his work, the conflict between the parents was irresolvable, lifelong, and irresistible as a shaping force on his imagination. Despite the detrimental psychological effect of the difficult early years— and we have much evidence that Williams' childhood was difficult— it was a productive coincidence that the contrarieties of experience, and especially the southern experience, should have been so fully and simply focused in his family. Largely as a result of this influence, I judge, an influence of manifold substantiation, by the way, arising as it did from every level of the playwright's experience—from parents, community, the whole region—Tennessee Williams has perceived and portrayed in his work a world of singular paradox. His characters and themes are built upon paradox. The exciting, sometimes brilliant, characters may oppose one another's values, both of which are arguable and tenable, but they are most affecting when they embody the opposition within themselves. Unlike the classical protagonists of flawed but admirable stature, the Williams protagonist, like most heroes of modern drama, derives from no fixed moral context. His challenge is not, however, the summoning of courage to live in the face of absolute uncertainty and loneliness, but rather in reconciling ancient claims of body and soul, the tensions of which dispose one to lonely separateness.

Perhaps the most striking feature of Williams' world view is his ambivalence of belief—in this he is less like William Faulkner than like Quentin Compson, and surely very different, at least in his early works, from the European Existentialists. He can neither disbelieve nor believe that life has significance, nor can he quite achieve either a classical detachment or a modern irony to deal with the conundrum. There are few Vladimirs or Estragons in the Williams canon and little of an unsparing irony that pities but finally repudiates the vision of Blanche or Alma or Kilroy. Rather, strangers build momentary communities; tenderness like "violets in the mountains" breaks the rocks (II, 527). Nonetheless, Williams and his characters speak repeatedly of life as solitary confinement within one's own skin. He says in his introduction to Carson McCullers' *Reflections in a Golden Eye* that the modern artist is afflicted with a sense of ineffable dread—reminiscent of Kierkegaard, though he does not make the explicit connection. But then he goes on, paradoxically, to explain the dread as "a kind of spiritual intuition of something almost too incredible and shocking to talk about, which underlies the whole so-called thing. It is . . . *mystery*" (p. xv). He might be getting at what Kurtz discovered in the jungle or even what Ahab suspected behind the whiteness of the whale, but the words he chooses suggest rather a Manichean vision, that of an unseeable Force that mercilessly destines man to entrapment by his dual impulses for good and evil.

Although Williams is a contemporary writer who understands and writes much about the modern affliction of meaninglessness, he is in many ways an old-fashioned moralist. He vacillates between opposing dogmas, however, never quite convinced of either Cavalier sensuality or Puritan transcendence. Arthur Ganz, calling him a "desperate moralist," writes: "Williams is passionately committed to the great Romantic dictum inherent in his neo-Lawrentian point of view, that the natural equals the good, that the great natural instincts that well up out of the subconscious depths of men—and particularly the sexual instinct, whatever form it may take—are to be trusted absolutely. But Williams is too strong a moralist, far too permeated with a sense of sin, to be able to accept such an idea with equanimity. However pathetic he may make the martyred homosexual, however seemingly innocent the wandering love-giver, the moral strength that led Williams to punish the guilty Blanche impels him to condemn Brick and Chance."[3]

The uneasy union of opposites characterizes all of Williams' work. When the tensions are perfectly balanced, the equilibrium is intellectually stimulating and aesthetically pleasing. But more often than not the center waffles, mainly, it seems, because Williams lacks the detachment necessary for a controlling vision. Despite the confused action of many of the plays, however, the brilliance of such characters as the Wingfields, Blanche and Stanley, Alma, the Pollitts, Hannah Jelkes and Lawrence Shannon commands attention. With varying intensity they and other Williams characters embody Williams' paradoxical view of life. Three paradoxes appear consistently: the effect of the past on the present, especially that of the southern past, the consequence of human sexuality, and the role of the artist.

As noted, Williams came to write of the southern myth of the plantation aristocracy out of his own experience as a Southerner. In his early *Battle of Angels* (1940), which years later was revised as *Orpheus Descending*, he creates in Sandra (Cassandra) Whiteside a decadent southern belle who can neither regain the assurance and power of her family's past nor give up the effort. Like Faulkner's Temple Drake she represents womanhood defiled, and like Temple of *Requiem for a Nun* she prophesies that the tensions between the old ideal of southern womanhood and the combined actualities of the moment and of the flesh at last exhaust the will. Her moral paralysis anticipates that of Brick Pollitt and Lawrence Shannon. She says to Val Xavier, whose name incidentally is a version of a Williams family name, Sevier, that they both are "things whose license has been revoked in the civilized world." She speaks of her own neuroticism, the result of blood "gone bad from too much interbreeding" (I, 45), and says that she has a guillotine inside her own body. She wears dark glasses to conceal eyes that hold disgusting secrets, but they seem only to enhance her fragile loneliness.

In Sandra, Williams exposes the desiccation of the old tradition. He also pinpoints its source, much as Faulkner does in *Go Down, Moses*. When the later generation is undistracted by plantation building and the ego trip of dynasty making, it finds it is caretaking a corrupt way of life, one that fiercely possesses the land and dispossesses the black laborers who work it. It finds it really has no ethical tradition to guide it, and so is faced with deriving one. Carol Cutrere, Sandra's counterpart in *Orpheus Descending*, explains to Val, who represents a kind of savior figure, her youthful effort to right the injustice she has seen. She was, she says, a "Christ-bitten reformer" who "wrote letters of protest about the gradual massacre of the colored majority in the county" (III, 251). She had put up free clinics with the money inherited from her mother and had protested the execution of Willie McGee—"he was sent to the chair for having improper relations with a white whore." Then she concludes: "I walked barefoot in this burlap sack to deliver a personal protest to the governor of the state. Oh, I suppose it was partly exhibitionism on my part, but it wasn't completely exhibitionism;

there was something else in it, too. You know how far I got? Six
miles out of town—hooted, jeered at, even spit on!—every step of
the way—and then arrested! Guess what for? Lewd vagrancy! Uh-
huh, that was the charge, 'lewd vagrancy,' because they said that
potato sack I had on was not a respectable garment. . . . Well, all that
was a pretty long time ago, and now I'm not a reformer any more.
I'm just a 'lewd vagrant'" (III, 252).

Predictably, she does not find absolution and renewal in her
effort to reform the world and so takes refuge in a self-pitying and
indulgent sensualism. She is like a Flannery O'Connor character
searching for the far country but cut off by pride. Her confession to
Val is that of the weary sinner who cannot feel guilt. Accordingly,
she concludes that all the past has to teach her is "Live, live, . . .
just live" (p. 252), but Williams shows that the simple lesson is
clearly inadequate for Carol.

When Williams comes in the same play to portray an alternative
to Carol's self-destructiveness, he creates Lady Torrance (Myra in
Battle of Angels), who is rescued by Val from the barrenness and
death represented by her dying husband. With heavy-handed symbolism, Williams suggests in her a Madonna figure—she is like a
barren fig tree that at last puts forth fruit, or a Christmas tree hung
with ornaments. In an ecstatic annunciation scene she cries out:
"I've won, I've won, Mr. Death, I'm going to bear!" (p. 338). But
shortly afterward she and Val die at the hands of her husband and
a mob of angry townspeople. The potential saviors, Val and Lady,
presumably are prevented from enacting their roles of renewal only
because of the murderous intolerance of others. But ironically, their
solutions, despite an overlay of religious hopefulness, are exactly the
same as Carol's—live, procreate. In *Battle of Angels* Sandra says to
Myra in the last act: "You've learned what I've learned, that there's
nothing on earth . . . but catch at whatever comes near you with
both your hands, until your fingers are broken!" (I, 100).

Like Sandra (Carol), Blanche, Alma (*Summer and Smoke* and
Eccentricities of a Nightingale) and even Laura of *Glass Menagerie*
represent the last of the southern ladies. Mothlike, sensitive, and
fragile in a way that is ultimately self-destructive, they are portrayed
as romantic idealists undone by a graceless and callous age. It is a
view echoed by Williams in the *Memoirs*: "Nowadays is, indeed, lit

by lightning, a plague has stricken the moths, and Blanche has been 'put away'" (p. 125). The crux of the paradox in the portrait of these characters is their innocence and moral purity. We are to understand that they are betrayed by the mortality that attaches to the flesh and to tradition alike but that salvation lies in a natural and healthful gratification of the flesh. Furthermore, the fastidious discrimination that raises them above the vulgar mass is at once a mark of quality and a harmful pretention. Williams ventures a similar portrait of his sister Rose, whom he exalts, as he does Laura, for her inescapable "difference." On the other hand, he locates the "true seat of Rose's affliction" as that of "a very normal—but highly sexed—girl who was tearing herself apart mentally and physically by those repressions imposed upon her by Miss Edwina's monolithic Puritanism" (*Memoirs*, p. 119). The morbid paradox is that disease is beautiful.

In *Summer and Smoke* when Alma comes to her senses and at last releases her subdued doppelgänger, she realizes her delicacy has "suffocated in smoke from something on fire inside her" (II, 243). To have clung to it would have meant dying "empty-handed," as the Alma of "The Yellow Bird" assuredly did not. But what Alma has at the end of the play is a stranger she has picked up. Her enormous dream is gone, and in its place she has a transitory affair that will be all of "Eternity" she is to know. She has searched for substance to fulfill her dream—or to replace the genteel hollowness of her life— and ends up feeling like a "water-lily on a Chinese lagoon" (p. 255). Jacob H. Adler, who regards *Summer and Smoke* as Williams' most revealing play about the South, calls it "an allegory of the Southern dilemma."[4] He sees Alma as the soul of the South, "daughter of a desiccated religion and of the sort of dementia that causes retreat into childhood" (p. 357). Retreating into the past produces a superficial grace but "a grotesque and childish ugliness" beneath the pleasant surface. The young doctor, John Buchanan, suggests a thoroughly contemporary South, cut off from its past. The violent murder of John's father, says Adler, is the result of these tensions and shows the failure of the South to know itself. "Thus Williams depicts a stale, poetico-idealistic culture, refusing to face reality, yet still partly beautiful; and unable to achieve, or to attract, power, until reality is faced" (p. 358). Adler concludes that the play is ironic

in its juxtaposition of culture and power, although he views its ultimate statement as that of a cautious hope for compromise, which
he interprets as more desirable than either sterility or violence.

An even more deeply ingrained irony in the portrait of Alma
bears directly on Williams' paradoxical view of southern history
and the effects of the past on the present. Alma's ancestry is at once
Cavalier and Puritan—her mother wears a plumed hat; her father
is a preacher. Alma cultivates social graces, romanticizes sex, and in
a manner dictated by her genteel code immediately sets out to
satisfy her desire for John. The forthright pursuit of self-satisfaction
that John urges on her is already present, implicit in her nature. At
the same time she admires Gothic cathedrals, has faith in a transcendent principle behind existence, and shows self-righteous assertiveness. Culture and power inhere in both traditions that have
produced Alma—and the South. At the end of the play she has not
so much tempered beautiful illusion with mundane reality as she
has shown herself ignorant of any historical perspective. Although it
is uncertain that Williams intended or even recognized the irony of
Alma's final action, her decision to take what gratification this
earth has to offer—giving little thought to the consequences—is a
playback of the South's history. All that is lacking is for her to
devise a new myth and ritual to justify her different circumstance.

Another level of the Alma paradox is her dual link with Edenic
innocence and civilization's corruption. She sings "The Voice That
Breathed O'er Eden" with an effeteness, a moral naiveté, that dissociates her from the ugly world. But her glory is civilization's hard-
won humanism—in *Eccentricities of a Nightingale* she dreams of
making Glorious Hill, Mississippi, an Athens of the Delta! The
realization that innocence, moral purity, is irrecoverable is nowhere
implied in Alma's actions. Such a realization would have forestalled
her effort to dump her past and start over, and thus to sacrifice the
accumulated wisdom of history in hopes of a new main chance. It
is John Buchanan, like Hannah Jelkes of *Night of the Iguana*, who
discovers what the most insightful of the Faulkner and Warren
heroes discover: that a stoic acceptance of the burdens of the past
is man's only chance for freedom and for the connectedness that can
allay loneliness. In short, they understand the impossibility of com-
muting between Eden and Athens. This knowledge eludes most

Williams characters from Cassandra Whiteside to Moise. They confuse "savage" and "aristocrat," viewing both as sensualists, which they both may well be, but they then impute to the sensualism an innocence controverted by history. They misunderstand that the nature of the freedom available before and after the Fall is of two radically different kinds. Thus Williams has Val Xavier grow up in a primeval swamp (Eden), discover the ecstasy of sex and the painful agony of separateness, and then with this knowledge ironically achieve a renewed innocence. Even Blanche goes to her end dressed in Della Robbia (Madonna) blue.

Thomas Porter has analyzed *A Streetcar Named Desire* for the paradoxes contained in the myth of the Old South as it is represented in Blanche.[5] He finds in her characterization an admiration of the tradition perfectly balanced by a rejection of it. The divisions of value and personality that operate within Blanche cause her madness and dissolution. They are divisions that obsessively engage Williams, appearing as we have seen in Cassandra, Laura, Alma and existing in some degree in many other characters—Amanda, Mrs. Stone, Brick Shannon, or more recently, Violet of *Small Craft Warnings*. Audiences and critics debate whether Blanche's demise is a victory or a defeat, depending largely on their view of Stanley, but in either case they view it as the inevitable passing of an old order. In one important respect, however, Stanley does not really represent an opposition to Blanche. The expense of will that built Belle Reve and the profligacy that lost it are in fact reborn in Stanley's vitality and assertiveness. He has a frontier rawness, to be sure, but that in time can be polished. What is lost on Stanley and to a large degree on Blanche herself is the tragic lesson of Belle Reve: the past has inescapable consequences for the present. Though Blanche tries, she cannot escape her past, either through nights with soldiers at the Flamingo Hotel or in a new start with Mitch. Blanche is most admirable when she turns backward—in her account of her selfless devotion to her dying relatives and in her self-condemnation for her cruelty to her young husband. Past prides—her own and that of a long family line—taint her life, but she earns her dignity in dealing with them (which is a confronting of *her* reality). Sadly, she does not recognize her moral strength, devalues it, and tries to recover her youth and innocence when she joins Stella. The ambiguities of *Streetcar* make it impossible to determine whether the play-wright sees Blanche's crucial flaw as her pretentions and illusions (which would oppose her to Stanley), or sees and wants us to see her failure of moral courage. If the latter, the position of Stanley and Stella is implicitly condemned; if the former, the "Southern myth" is trivialized and made meaningless. But in either case, Blanche DuBois is an immensely human, absorbing character.

In *Cat on a Hot Tin Roof* the grandeur of the plantation myth obviously suffers, but its foundations are more clearly shown than in *Streetcar*. Big Daddy's lusty aggressiveness could be that of any captain of industry. He is the crude but eloquent spokesman for the sensual life, a southern planter whose strength is power, not culture. Like an early settler he has built the plantation out of his magnificent will and "twenty-eight thousand acres of the richest land this side of the valley Nile" (III, 110) and has furnished it with boxcars of "stuff" from Europe's "big auction." Unlike Faulkner's Thomas Sutpen his design is not so much fulfilment of a cultural ideal as gratification of his raw appetite for power and pleasure. He is the spiritual progenitor of daughter-in-law Maggie, who is the sexual life force that can save husband Brick from "moral paralysis," a term Williams uses in a note of explanation about revisions he made in the play. Maggie admires Big Daddy because, she says, he "*is* what he *is*, and he makes no bones about it. He hasn't turned gentleman farmer, he's still a Mississippi redneck, as much of a redneck as he must have been when he was just overseer here" (p. 53). Although she comes from a "well-connected" family, she was poor and knows better than anyone that the elegant refinements of the plantation life depend upon having money.

Brick's despair over discovering his culpability in his friend Skipper's death comes from his feeling of guilt. Obviously, he is foolish to condemn himself for his sexuality, but if one is to consider him in some moral framework, then I judge Brick to be quite right in feeling responsible for his actions, sexual and otherwise. The thematic paradox in this play revolves not around the contemporary replay of the old plantation South—it is unambiguously exposed. What is ironic is that Big Daddy's vitality, untempered by moral compunction, is represented in Maggie as a saving grace, her success to be proved if she can get Brick to bed. The fusion of the natural and the ethical, the sensual and the materialistic, neutralizes the play's moral impulse. But as in *Menagerie* and *Streetcar*, the characters are compelling on the stage, indeed perhaps because they so fully express our culture's tensions, our contradictory yearning for both innocence and material success.

Williams has not often created characters who successfully resolve or learn to live with these tensions. John Buchanan in *Summer and Smoke* reaches an accommodation, but the effect of his moral progress is blunted in his secondary role to Alma. In the earlier characters, particularly in Tom Wingfield and Stella Kowalski, Williams explores the possibility for reconciliation of memory and desire. In *The Glass Menagerie*, which he calls a memory play, Tom searches the farthest reaches of the past's hold on him in his effort to free himself of it. At the end of the play he realizes the futility of his effort to put his family behind, but the knowledge forms no basis for action. In his concluding speech Tom reveals the ceaseless flight that has marked the years since he left home: "I descended the steps of this fire escape for a last time and followed, from then on, in my father's footsteps, attempting to find in motion what was lost in space" (I, 236–37). This perspective on the past is ultimately nostalgic and sentimental. It impels him to painful recollection, but it does not produce the weary and humble acceptance of one who has experienced tragedy. In fact, the play is a good example of the point Kierkegaard makes in his study of ancient and modern drama in *Either/Or*: that in classical tragedy, with its concept of fate, the sorrow is deeper and the pain less, whereas in the modern, the pain is greater and the sorrow less. In the recent *Out Cry*, which in some respects is like a sequel to *Glass Menagerie*, Williams creates an inversion of Tom's strategy of escape in the character of Felice, who never leaves the home that "has turned into a prison" (p. 55). Trapped inside their *Two-Character Play*, he and his sister Clare are as haplessly bound to their destined end as are Rosencrantz and Guildenstern.

Stella Kowalski, more emphatically even than Tom Wingfield, isolates herself from her family and the Belle Reve tradition. In her, as he had done with Myra Torrance, Williams tries to figure a spiritual rejuvenation in a pregnancy. But the fusion glosses the difficulty of redemption, whether ethical or religious.

Perhaps it is with Hannah Jelkes in *Night of the Iguana* that Williams most successfully resolves the problem of the burdensome legacy of the past, the "old order." Like that of John Buchanan, her role is secondary in the play, and we do not see her painful passage from innocence to knowledge except through her reflections. But as Shannon's mentor, she reveals how fully she understands that the past constrains an individual's action, even though the past turns out to be morally ambiguous and tainted with selfishness. In the earlier short story Hannah's background is southern and she is very much a southern lady, a product like Alma of the Puritan and the Cavalier strains. In her, as in so many of his characters, Williams sketches the same portrait of the divided southern mind that historian W. J. Cash has described: "The official moral philosophy of the South moved steadily toward the position of that of the Massachusetts Bay Colony . . . and this . . . coincidentally with the growth of that curious hedonism which was its antithesis. The two streams could and would flow forward side by side, and with a minimum of conflict." Cash goes on to say that the Southerner "succeeded in uniting the two incompatible tendencies in a single person, without ever allowing them to come into open and decisive contention" (pp. 59–60).

Precisely these forces come finally into open conflict in Williams' plays, however, forming in fact the chief contention of most of his work. In *Night of the Iguana* Hannah's internal conflicts have largely taken place before the action begins, but as a veteran who stood her ground and stayed for the battle, she can tutor Shannon in the art of fighting "spooks" and "blue devils," a way of remembrance and endurance. She accepts responsibility for her grandfather, though doing so is a costly sacrifice of independence. She supports herself, making whatever adjustments and compromises are necessary. Her unsparing demands on herself—her self-denial—produce in her a boundless capacity for tenderness and compassion toward others. A not quite emancipated Puritan, she understands and lives by the paradox that to win her freedom she must give up the self. By contrast, Shannon has spent years in a wearying rebellion against the restraints on him—against God, the bishops, the tour company he works for, the ladies on the bus, even the easygoing widow Maxine. Hannah helps him to cut free from his struggle by showing him that the ties to the past and to others cannot be repudiated. Shannon asks: "You mean that I'm stuck here for good? Winding up with the . . . inconsolable widow?" Hannah replies: "We all wind up with something or with someone, and if it's someone instead of just something, we're lucky, perhaps . . . unusually lucky" (IV, 365). She accepts limitations on her freedom and self-gratification more readily than on her delicate but tested idealism, and her acceptance delivers her from moral paralysis and disgust with life. To her own cri de coeur, she turns a pitiless deaf ear; it is a price very few of Williams' characters are able or willing to pay. For Hannah the result is an honorable humanism, which she expresses in the much-quoted line: "Nothing human disgusts me unless it's unkind, violent" (pp. 363–4). Although not many will choose her way, it at least reveals a valid and morally consistent solution to the plight expressed in Esmeralda's prayer in *Camino Real*: "God bless all con men and hustlers and pitch-men who hawk their hearts on the street, all two-time losers who're likely to lose once more, the courtesan who made the mistake of love, . . . the poet who wandered far from his heart's green country. . . . look down with a smile tonight on the last cavaliers, the ones with the rusty armor and soiled white plumes, and . . . oh, sometime and somewhere, let there be something to mean the word *honor* again!" (II, 585–86).

To consider Williams' paradoxical vision of sexuality is really to look only more deeply into his view of the past. In the stories and the plays sex is the repeated metaphor of the ecstatic life fully lived in the present moment, freed of all inheritances—secular or sacred. It thus has the positive and negative attributes of giving man pleasure and delight with little sacrifice of freedom, but of offering no means of transcending the amoral and mortal. Sexuality is transformed into salvation when it is seen as the only fulfilment this life has to offer. Chance Wayne expresses the view early in *Sweet Bird of Youth* to Alexandra del Lago, the aging movie queen: "the great difference between people in this world is not between the rich and the poor or the good and the evil, [but] . . . between the ones that had or have pleasure in love and those that haven't" (IV, 50). But to those sick of this world—its grossness and mutability—sexuality is the unmistakable symptom of rot. By the end of *Sweet Bird* Chance has come to pronounce the limits of the flesh: "Princess, the age of some people can only be calculated by the level of . . . rot in them. And by that measure I'm ancient" (p. 122).

In *Memoirs*, Williams expresses the pleasure and revulsion that have marked his attitude toward sex throughout the plays. For example, he writes of "the deviant satyriasis" which "happily afflicted" him (p. 53) during his early years in New York. An interesting reverse of the stereotyped Puritan (whose piety masks lust), Williams' satyriasis is betrayed by his judgmental streak: "Being a sensual creature—and why do I keep saying creature instead of man?—I will go on doing what I am doing while waiting" (p. 249).

Two early one-acts, *The Purification* and *Auto-Da-Fé*, illustrate very well self-condemnation and guilt that attach to sexuality, especially if anything is thought perverse or abnormal about it. In the first play, a verse drama in the manner of Lorca, Rosalio—son and brother—"purifies" himself in a ritual suicide for the violation of his sister. His love for her had made a normal life impossible, and it ultimately brought on her murder by her husband. Although he feels intense guilt for his actions, Rosalio is nonetheless portrayed as blameless—the innocent victim of "sangre mala." His mother defends him: "His ways are derived of me./I also rode on horseback through the mountains/in August" (p. 39). Similarly, in *Auto-Da-Fé*, Eloi atones for the sinfulness he recognizes in his obsession with some "indecent pictures" he has discovered in his job as a postal clerk. Unable to bring himself to report or burn the pictures, he locks himself in a burning house, thus cleansing the "infection" he has exposed. Realistically, the sin is nothing more than a sexual desire that he labels lust because of the prudish influence of his mother. But in Williams' symbolism Eloi, like Rosalio, serves as scapegoat for the world's corruption by the flesh, and his auto-da-fé is an act of faith and redemption.

To counteract the self-destructive consequences of shame and penance, Williams in some of his works takes the tack of D. H. Lawrence and makes a religion of sex. In *Battle of Angels*, with a heavy overlay of Christian symbolism, Val Xavier becomes the savior who restores to health and hope the frigid, barren and dying. The passion of the flesh and the Passion of Christ merge, and even poor Vee Talbot, the religious fanatic and primitive artist, translates her sexual desire for Val into a mystical anointment. In distorting her carnal impulse by perceiving it as spiritual, she is like a Flannery O'Connor freak in reverse. Of course, the consummate spokesman for the religion of sex is Serafina of *The Rose Tattoo*. To the priest Father De Leo she describes the pure relationship she had with husband Rosario Delle Rose: "I give him the glory. To me the big bed was beautiful like a religion" (II, 342). When she conceives, a rose matching her husband's tattoo appears on her breast as Annunciation. Although Rosario's death stills her passion for a time, the play's action concentrates on the arrival of Alvaro, who returns her to the world of the loving.

Such attainment of grace through sex is hard for Williams to maintain dramatically, though, for it nullifies one of his most affecting conflicts. Furthermore, the insistent religious metaphor paradoxically leads almost inevitably back to the Christian premise of the subjugation of body to spirit. Hence the reflective and sensitive characters never convincingly escape into natural joy. In fact, Williams is most successful in portraying worry-free sex when he spoofs the subject slightly in the comic *Baby Doll*. A perfect innocent, Baby Doll Meighan is, as husband Archie calls her, a U. W. (Useless Woman), except for one thing—her irresistible sexuality. When Vacarro, the operator of the new gin, takes up residence on the front porch, the "faunlike" lover and the nymph commence a breathless chase that leaves Archie and compunction far behind. The whole episode reminds one of a Eula Varner escaping the mechanistic Flem Snopes.

In the case of some characters, a tolerable sense of sinfulness for the acts of the flesh yields a kind of voluptuous suffering—an observation with which Hannah Jelkes needles Shannon: "Who wouldn't like to suffer and atone for the sins of himself and the world if it could be done in a hammock with ropes instead of nails?" (IV, 344). For most of the Williams characters of an artistic and philosophical (or religious) turn of mind, however, the "happy affliction" of carnality is the product of neither will nor chance, and is the source of neither remorse nor delight—but all of these at once. In *Eccentricities of a Nightingale* Williams parodies the Eden story in a serious little allegory of man's earthly circumstance. Alma's Aunt Albertine—wearing a plumed hat—had run away from the rectory with a bigamist, a mechanical genius named Schwarzkopf. They traveled about happily with a display of mechanical marvels, chief of which was Schwarzkopf's beloved masterpiece, a mechanical bird-girl who "smiled and nodded, lifted her arms as if to embrace a lover" (II, 87). Then suddenly one winter they made the mistake of mortgaging the Musée Mécanique to buy a snake. They had heard "Big snakes pay good," but the snake swallowed a blanket and died; and, rather than lose the museum to creditors, Schwarzkopf destroyed it and himself in flames. Albertine, grasping one of his buttons, was dragged from the building alive. " 'Some people,' she said, 'don't even die empty-handed!' " (p. 87).

The museum had been a blissful Eden but bloodless and soulless, and so, in wanting more, they "bought" the snake of phallic power and mortality. The loss of the warm, carefree nest sent one into fatal grief for what was irrecoverable, the other into gratitude for the little reminder of their original joy. Only in a fantasy such as the story "The Yellow Bird" does Williams manage to make the rewards of the sexual life commensurate with its delight. By contrast, in the realistic "Hello from Bertha," the aging prostitute dies "empty-handed" with only her few pathetic memories of her former lover, Charlie.

The fear, the near-fatal grief, that so many of the characters have for their incompleteness, their mortality or waning creative vitality, expresses itself in flight from the thoughtful to the sexual life. To Mrs. Stone the handsome young Romans arrest the "enormous drifting of time and existence" (p. 145). Alexandra del Lago and Flora Goforth can forget they are aging in body and in artistic power, if they can have the "distraction" of lovemaking. But such characters as Chance Wayne and Sebastian Venable, who live in the full paradox of their sexual natures, contending with the strain between desire and guilt, tire at last and yearn to be freed. Williams obviously attempts to represent in them what he describes in the foreword to *Sweet Bird* as the only chance man has to "rise above his moral condition, imposed upon him at birth and long before birth, by the nature of his breed"—the "willingness to know it, to face its existence in him" (IV, 6).

When Chance comes finally to say at the end of the play, "Something's got to mean something" (p. 121), he is like Joanna Burden in *Light in August* who decides after her orgiastic affair with Joe Christmas that it is "time to pray." Chance's surrender to Boss Finley's gang is his auto-da-fé. Similarly, Sebastian in *Suddenly Last Summer* at last renounces his corruption in an act of self-sacrifice. In recounting his story after his death, Catharine gives it the coherence and inevitability of a morality play.

Sebastian for years viewed the world as mercilessly naturalistic, imaged in the scene of the Galapagos turtles that were prey to ravenous birds. His "Poem of Summer," a hymn to such a world, aggrandizes—and mitigates—it by transforming the violence and pain into poetic metaphor. Traveling each year with his mother Violet, who helps him turn his gaze "out, not in," he keeps up his poetic pretensions and homosexual affairs until fear and revulsion overtake him. He sees in cousin Catharine the moral discrimination so lacking in Violet: Catharine condemns her violator and judges the ugliness and corruption that surround her. Thus on his last journey he takes Catharine, not Violet, to Cabeza de Lobo and exposes the degradation so long masked by youth and graceful refinement: "Suddenly, last summer Cousin Sebastian changed to the afternoons and the [public] beach" (III, 410). Although Catharine regards herself as having tried to save him from completing some "terrible image" of himself, she actually enables him to do so. That summer, for the first time, Sebastian "attempted to correct a human situation" (p. 419), and having introduced judgment into his world, he inevitably has to judge himself. Catharine describes with horror how at last he climbed the steep street and delivered himself to a "band of naked children," who like a flock of birds pursued and devoured him.

In his most reflective characters Williams creates a model of man's body-and-soul dilemma that suggests an aerialist suspended perilously on an unsteady wire. Alternately it is jerked taut from the physical and spiritual poles, each of which holds a perch that offers both island of refuge and hostile territory. In *Period of Adjustment* Ralph says that "if you took the human heart out of the human body and put a pair of legs on it and told it to walk a straight line, it couldn't do it. It could never pass the drunk test" (IV, 241). Lovers of life are thus like the lovers in John Crowe Ransom's "The Equilibrists," who burn "with fierce love always to come near" until "honor [beats] them back and [keeps] them clear." Employing a paradoxical image that Williams too has frequently used, Ransom writes: "Their flames were not more radiant than their ice."

Williams' strategy for escaping the "torture of equilibrium" is like that of the narrator of the poem, through the detachment of art. But rarely, if ever, do even the artists in Williams' works escape the paradox; thus, they never arrive at the ironic stance of the poem's narrator, who smiles pityingly at the intense lovers and chides them for their simple dialectic. In the recent novel, *Moise and the World of Reason*, for example, the narrator describes a "beautiful blonde acrobat" who "performed a metaphor" between two tall buildings, but he interprets the act with no trace of irony as a dramatic death dare.

Most often in Williams' work, art functions ideally in a direct way to release the artist from his animal passions and mortality and to offer a chance for victory over anarchy and time (the "sailing to Byzantium" theme). Interestingly, for both the playwright and his characters the attitude toward art is decidedly modern and chiefly therapeutic—what art can do for the artist. But the problem here is that viewing art as an extension of the artist, either for what he is or what he needs, leads solipsistically back to the mortal and flawed being that the artist seeks to transcend. Thus the artistic creation is constantly endangered by the "personal lyricism" that Williams talks so much about. At the most extreme, art simply distracts the artist from his self-destructiveness, as in Sebastian's case, and the distraction, or creation, is extremely tenuous, "as thin and fine as the web of a spider," says Violet (III, 408). In both his expository and his dramatic writings, Williams implies that the "poet's vocation" is the road to truth, but at the same time he refutes the conviction, suspicious that art is simply the "truth" of an illusionist —or theatrical showman. The young writer of "The Lady of Larkspur Lotion," or even Tom Wingfield, casts a magical web over experience, transforming the ordinary and ugly, and even painful, into a thing of beauty. But undermining their transformations of life into art is their (and their creator's) lurking doubt that the vision is wholly truthful or that it is sufficiently beautiful to outlast mortality.

Thus in Williams' world the artist's defeat of time is uncertain, probably illusory. Alexandra del Lago escapes the "withering country" of time only to the extent that her art is admired. (A has-been-who-never-was, like Chance Wayne, never has a hope of salvation through art.) Alexandra is like Sabbatha, one of the eight mortal ladies possessed, whose slipping talent and prestige constantly threaten her hope of victory, which is even further threatened by her medium, that of acting. In the *Memoirs*, Williams writes that his goal in writing has been to "capture the constantly evanescent quality of existence" (p. 84), but as an artist he seems to subvert his goal and whatever satisfactions it might bring by his introspective focus on "evanescence" and the paradox it holds for the artist. To the writer-narrator, Moise says, "Evanescent, you're evanescent by nature. Infinitely variable as the snake of the Nile . . ." (p. 170). Williams' view that such a nature gives the writer the knowledge and empathy necessary to the creation of art and at the same time the flaw that makes his creation specious is the worrisome paradox, I suspect, that has eroded his artistic power. His latest works reveal clearly the entrapment in self-consciousness.

In the earlier works the role of the artist is like that of Byron in *Camino Real*. He is aware of his limitations but is not paralyzed by them in his goal to translate *"noise* into *music,* chaos into—*order"* (II, 507). What the artist, and even a scientist like John Buchanan, sees when he looks outward is part anarchy and part order, but as long as his gaze is outward, he can reconcile these opposites in an artistic creation. When like Sebastian he looks inward, he apparently must forget his art and tend to his soul or make of his art a dialogue of the self. *Out Cry* illustrates such a dialogue, with characters reminiscent of Roderick and Madeline Usher. The doppel-gänger symbol of the cripplingly divided nature of the human psyche is more overt than Poe's, however, and the action even more static. Sister Clare's attempt to escape the playhouse, which is like an "empty vault," carries little of the shock of Madeline's return from the grave, and only a muffled revelation of the play's subject: the destructiveness of radical self-consciousness and the futility of escape.

Philosophical rather than dramatic, the play is among Williams' closest approaches to the European drama. Unfortunately, it is so far refined from the outward world of particularity that the characters lack substance and appeal. Even the question of the murder-suicide of the parents never creates suspense because the knowing is impossible and inconsequential. The epistemological motif of an illusion locked within an illusion, as old as Narcissus, has long intrigued writers, especially modern ones. But when a relentless preoccupation with the universal circumstance overwhelms the preoccupation with the particular, which has not often happened to southern writers, including Williams, the result is a thin, anemic art. And of the character, or artist, who is trapped inside his own image, one can never know whether he has defeated time or is frozen in timelessness.

At the beginning of this essay, I suggested that Williams' disposition to see the world in paradoxical terms and to embody the paradoxes in memorably concrete and human characters aligned him closely with the writers of the modern South. That some of his plays, especially the later ones, show a declining concern with the society that surrounds the characters and a consequent declining vitality bears out an observation that Lewis Simpson has made in a recent study of southern literature. He writes that the southern literary renaissance seems to have occurred in two stages: the first roughly from 1920 to 1950, and the second perhaps still not completed. In the earlier period the writers sought to understand the full meaning of the past, to go beyond the romanticized, pastoral view that had for so long paralyzed the South's will to face up to its present. Of course, Williams' career begins in this period, and we see in such plays as *Glass Menagerie*, *Streetcar* and *Summer and Smoke* his preoccupation with the effects of the past and the great difficulty of penetrating the illusions to get at the truth about it. Although his view of history is far less complex than that of a Faulkner or Warren—or Chekhov—he shows a similar historical impulse. The second stage of Williams' career coincides interestingly with the second period Simpson describes. In it, the writers record their failure to gain an understanding of the past and suggest that they have lost trust in the power of their own vision—"suggest, moreover, that the process of the destruction of memory and history within the literary mind symbolized by Poe in 'The Fall of the House of Usher' cannot be halted; that inauguration of any attempt to establish a new literary covenant with the past is futile and that the only meaningful covenant for the latter-day writer is one with the self on terms generally defined as existential."[6]

Perhaps the ultimate paradox of Williams' Southern-ness is that he is caught between two Souths of the literary imagination. (Even *Out Cry* is set in the "deep Southern town" of New Bethesda, the end of the line for Clare and Felice.) Even so, the "southern matter" of his work, invigorated by his own ambivalence and tense effort to reconcile the oppositions within the tradition, has furnished the source of his most affecting characters. They loom unforgettably, even when they are appallingly self-ignorant, in their embodiments of the "heart in conflict with itself."

The sexual-spiritual duality of man has, like the southern matter, formed a chief strain of ambiguity and conflict in Williams' works. The ancient body and soul struggle shows no waning in its power to obsess and little susceptibility to resolution in his "sensual-romantic" vision. Nonetheless, he tries to create in some characters a capacity for innocent sexuality, untainted by Puritan repressions (Baby Doll, Rosa delle Rose, Alma of "Yellow Bird"), or a heightened, mystical sexuality that can be a saving grace (Lady Torrance, Serafina, Maggie). But the most serious protagonists, those who count most in Williams' world, suffer the division that Leona describes of Violet in *Small Craft Warnings*: "Her mind floats on a cloud and her body floats on water. And her dirty fingernail hands reach out to hold onto something she hopes can hold her together. . . . Oh, my God, she's at it again, she got a hand under the table" (V, 284).

Williams expresses the dilemma in dialogue, of course, but he also represents it in a cluster of images which he draws on repeatedly. To simplify greatly, the color blue serves as a metaphor of spirituality, roses of carnality, and birds as a fusion of the two impulses. Blanche wears "Madonna blue"; Myra Torrance in her reborn state buys a dream of "ecstasy blue"; Elena in *The Purification* is the "blue" girl. Rosalio, Rose Comfort, Rosa delle Rose, Rosario, and a host of other roses, human and floral, are linked with sexuality or earthliness and occur throughout the works. And the yellow bird named Bobo is only one of many otherworldly messengers who bear enigmatic or paradoxical meaning for anxious mortals. Similarly, Williams' combination of realism and Expressionism serves as apt theatrical metaphor for the conflict of body and spirit. Flannery O'Connor once remarked that the writer whose world view is deterministic will produce tragic naturalism, whereas the writer who believes that life is essentially mysterious will use concrete detail in a more drastic way, the way of distortion.[7] I suspect that Williams' alternation between the two outlooks accounts in part for his continual alternation between the realistic and expressionistic modes.

Insofar as his vision is directed to this world, he sees transcendence of the self as available only through art: "all we have to do is remember that if we're not artists, we're nothing" (p. 22), says Felice in *Out Cry*. Characters from the plays and the fiction, as well as the playwright himself, according to his account in the *Memoirs*, engage life with "Blue Jay" notebook always at hand. Sebastian's poem, nevertheless, goes unfinished, and Nonno at age ninety-seven barely manages to complete his poem before he dies. The uncertainties and fragmentation that plague existence also threaten art, and even the artist's truth. With neither art nor God to depend upon, the yearning of the heart for transcendence can never be assuaged. "For me," Williams writes in *Memoirs*, "what is there but to feel beneath me the steadily rising current of mortality and to summon from my blood whatever courage is native to it[?]" (p. 249). In Williams' plays the paradoxes of this life provoke in the characters their bitterest frustrations, and their quandaries are those of their creator. Lacking the resources to encompass paradox in some larger perspective, Williams is frequently trapped inside, and the result is melodrama, inadvertent comedy or intellectual myopia. But the view from inside can also be charged with all the danger that goes with personal risk. When this view is transmuted on the stage into an evocative Laura or Amanda, Blanche, Alma, Maggie, or Big Daddy, we are likely to be held in our seats, transfixed in blood and glands, if not in brain. In their compelling pathos, they resemble, finally, the birds in Wallace Stevens' "Sunday Morning" in making "Ambiguous undulations as they sink,/Downward to darkness, on extended wings."

Notes to Peggy W. Prenshaw, "The
Paradoxical Southern World of Tennessee Williams"

1. C. Hugh Holman, *The Roots of Southern Writing* (Athens: University of Georgia Press, 1972), p. 1.
2. Cleanth Brooks, *The Well Wrought Urn* (New York: Harvest-Harcourt, Brace, & World, 1947), p. 3.
3. Arthur Ganz, "The Desperate Morality of the Plays of Tennessee Williams," in

American Drama and its Critics: A Collection of Critical Essays, ed. Alan S. Downer (Chicago: University of Chicago Press, 1965), pp. 216–17.

4. Jacob H. Adler, "The Rose and the Fox: Notes on the Southern Drama," in *South: Modern Southern Literature in Its Cultural Setting,* ed. Louis D. Rubin and Robert D. Jacobs (Garden City, N.Y.: Dolphin-Doubleday, 1961), p. 353.

5. Thomas E. Porter, *Myth and Modern American Drama* (Detroit: Wayne State University Press, 1969), pp. 153–176.

6. Lewis P. Simpson, *The Dispossessed Garden: Pastoral and History in Southern Literature* (Athens: University of Georgia Press, 1975), p. 71.

7. Flannery O'Connor, *Mystery and Manners* (New York: Farrar, Straus, & Giroux, 1962), pp. 41–42.

The Cards Indicate a Voyage
on A *Streetcar Named Desire*

LEONARD QUIRINO

"Art is made out of symbols the way your body is made out
of vital tissue."

Tennessee Williams[1]

" 'They are the souls,' answered his [Aeneas'] father
Anchises,
'Whose destiny it is a second time
To live in the flesh and there by the waters of Lethe
They drink the draught that sets them free from care
And blots out memory.' "

Description of the inhabitants of Elysian Fields
in Book VI of the Aeneid.[2]

So MUCH HAS been written about A *Streetcar
Named Desire* in terms of its theatrical presentation as interpreted
by a specific director and set of actors[3] and so much concern has
been lavished on the social attitudes and psychological constitution
of its characters[4] that the author's primary intention as revealed in
his use of mythic symbolism and archetypal imagery to create a
dialectic between soul and body to depict universally significant
problems such as the conflict and mutual attraction between desire
and death has been generally obscured or denigrated as pretentious.[5]
My own intention in this essay is to consider the play neither as
interpreted in any specific production nor as it may embody a
study of satyriasis, nymphomania, or reconstruction in the South,

29

but, rather, as it constitutes what an examination of its symbolism reveals to be Tennessee Williams' intention: a tragic parable dramatizing existence, the fact of incarnation, itself. Far from wishing to dissolve Williams' carefully constructed characters and theatrical effects into illustrations of archetypal figures or myths devoid of the author's particular "signature," I shall try to suggest how Williams' special use of two very ordinary symbols—the cards of destiny and the voyage of experience—aesthetically patterns the mosaic of his literary and theatrical imagery in *Streetcar*, investing the play with an artistry and meaning that transcend the mere theatricality and sensationalism with which it has so often been credited and discredited.

"Catch!" (I, 244) says Stanley Kowalski throwing a bloodstained package of meat to his wife, Stella, at the opening of the first scene of *A Streetcar Named Desire*. Laughing breathlessly, she manages to catch it. "This game is seven-card stud," reads the last line of the play. In between, much of the verbal and theatrical imagery that constitutes the drama is drawn from games, chance and luck. Williams had called the short play from which *Streetcar* evolved *The Poker Night*, and in the final version two of the most crucial scenes are presented within the framework of poker games played onstage. Indeed, the tactics and ceremonial of games in general, and poker in particular, may be seen as constituting the informing structural principle of the play as a whole. Pitting Stanley Kowalski, the powerful master of Elysian Fields against Blanche DuBois, the ineffectual ex-mistress of Belle Reve, Williams makes the former the inevitable winner of the game whose stakes are survival in the kind of world the play posits. For the first four of the eleven scenes of *Streetcar*, Blanche, by reason of her affectation of gentility and respectability, manages to bluff a good hand in her game with Stanley; thus, in the third scene Stanley is continually losing, principally to Mitch the potential ally of Blanche, in the poker game played onstage. However, generally suspicious of Blanche's behavior and her past, and made aware at the end of the fourth scene that she considers him an ape and a brute, Stanley pursues an investigation of the real identity of *her* cards. As, little by little, he finds proof of what he considers her own apishness and brutality, he continually discredits her gambits until, in the penultimate scene, he caps his winnings by raping her. In the last scene of the play, Stanley is not only winning every card game being played onstage, but he has also won the game he played with Blanche. Depending as it does on the skillful manipulation of the hands that chance deals out, the card game is used by Williams throughout *Streetcar* as a symbol of fate and of the skillful player's ability to make its decrees perform in his own favor at the expense of his opponent's misfortune, incompetence, and horror of the game itself.

Equally as important as the symbol of the card game in *Streetcar* is the imagery connected with the mythic archetype of the voyage which Williams portrays both as quest for an imagined ideal and as flight from disillusioning actuality. "They told me," says Blanche in her first speech, "to take a streetcar named Desire, and then to transfer to one called Cemeteries and ride six blocks and get off at— Elysian Fields." Putting together the allegorical names of these streetcars and their destination at Elysian Fields with Williams' portrayal of Blanche as resembling a moth, traditionally a symbol of the soul, we find in her journey a not too deeply submerged metaphor for the soul's disastrous voyage through life. Caged in a body that it attempts to transcend but cannot escape, the moth-soul yearns for the star (Stella) and for rest in the isles of the happy dead; it finds, instead, the flaming "red hot" milieu of the primal blacksmith ("Stanley" or "stone-lea" suggests the Stone Age man and "Kowalski" is Polish for "smith") and a world even more blatantly dedicated to "epic fornications" than its native Belle Reve, a world that shows every sign of prevailing. We are not surprised to learn that the agent of Blanche's journey to Elysian Fields, her school superintendent, is a Mr. Graves, and we can understand the implications of Blanche's statement late in the play, "The opposite [of death] is desire," to be more than merely sexual. Shuttling between yearning and frustration defines the basic rhythm of life itself for Blanche. Opening with her arrival in the land of life in death, the play chronicles the human soul's past and present excursions in the only vehicle that fate provides her, the rattle-trap streetcar of the body; the play closes with the soul's departure for incarceration in another asylum, another kind of living death.

Because the play, so rich in effects, is made to cohere largely by means of Williams' use of the imagery and symbolism of the voyage and the ceremonial and jargon of card games, a detailed exploration of *Streetcar* focusing on these two textural and structural principles might prove rewarding in assessing its artistic achievement. The ultimate aim of such an examination of the symbolism of the play, of course, is to demonstrate that the proper sphere of *Streetcar* is not the socio-clinical one to which it is so often relegated, but the realm of the tragic-universal which is more often than not denied it.

The epigraph to A *Streetcar Named Desire* is taken from Hart Crane's "The Broken Tower":

> And so it was I entered the broken world
> To trace the visionary company of love, its voice
> An instant in the wind (I know not whither hurled)
> But not for long to hold each desperate choice.

Besides focusing attention on Williams' positing of *two* broken worlds, both Belle Reve and Elysian Fields, and on the vision of life as a making of desperate choices, the epigraph introduces Williams' theme of the soul's quest for ideal love in the most unlikely of places —the broken world of actuality. Both the broken worlds which Williams compares and contrasts in the play bear wish-fulfilling names, but neither of these worlds fulfills Blanche's dreams of the ideal and of romantic love.

Blanche's first speech provides the introduction to Williams' treatment of her journey in the universal terms of life (desire) and death (cemeteries). In depicting her destination, Elysian Fields, which proves unwelcome and unwelcoming to Blanche, Williams continues to fuse and juxtapose images of life and death. In the ninth scene, for example, which takes place on the evening of Blanche's birthday (and shortly before the expected birth of the Kowalski child) a Mexican crone hawks "flores para los muertos" through the Elysian Fields offering her funeral "corones" to Blanche. In the previous scene, during the ghastly celebration of her own birthday, Blanche had been presented with a bus ticket back to Laurel (a name which ironically suggests wreaths of immortality) where she is even less welcome than she is in Stanley's domain. The birthday gift is a death sentence, and the soul on its desperate journey through existence finds destinations that are progressively horrifying. "Travelling," Blanche confesses, "wears me out."

Elysium, the paradise of the happy dead for the Greek poets, becomes in *Streetcar* a street which "runs between the L & N tracks and the river." Its flanks themselves suggest voyage although only the train ride, like the journey by streetcar, connotes horror for Blanche: "Out there I suppose is the ghoul-haunted woodland of Weir!" "No, honey," Stella replies, "those are the L & N tracks" (I, 252). But for Blanche whose mental landscape is haunted by her dead husband, the allusion to Poe's "Ulalume" in which the memory of a dead love haunts the narrator of the poem is extremely appropriate. Although she is fearful of further locomotive journeys of desire, Blanche regards the prospect of voyage by water with pleasure. She dreams of cruising the Caribbean on a yacht with Shep Huntleigh (whose first name suggests a pastoral swain and whose last name suggests aristocratic sport) and, in the last scene, even looks forward to death on the sea: "I can smell the sea air. The rest of my time I'm going to spend on the sea. And when I die, I'm going to die on the sea" (p. 410). Throughout the play, Blanche's addiction to water and to the baths which make her feel "Like a brand new human being," her hydrotherapy as she calls it, seems to be connected with the geography and function of the Elysian Fields as represented both in myth and in Williams' play.

In myth, the dead who entered the Elysian Fields were made to drink of the water of the river Lethe to forget all traces of their mortal past. And in Book VI of the *Aeneid*, Vergil depicts Lethe as a kind of watery purgatory where the dead are cleansed of all taint of memory and desire before they can be considered fit for reincarnation. In his adaptation of the concept of Elysian Fields for *Streetcar*, Williams, until the very end when he allows her the refuge of madness, denies the memory-haunted Blanche the full powers of the river Lethe. He depicts Stella, on the other hand, as one of the happy dead: after a night in bed with Stanley, "Her eyes and lips have that almost narcotized tranquility that is in the faces of Eastern idols" (p. 310). While Stella can bridge the two worlds of Belle Reve and Elysian Fields, Blanche is unwelcome in both.

This distinction is important to note because too many critics have made oversimplified, sociologically oriented interpretations of the conflict in *Streetcar* as a representation of Williams' nostalgia for vanished, decadent southern aristocracy and his horror of vital industrial proletarianism. Other critics, noticing that Williams *com-*

pares as well as contrasts Belle Reve with Elysian Fields, claim that his presentation of social conditions is ambivalent and confusing. But Williams, usually little interested in sociology beyond its reflection of the human predicament of survival, does not use Blanche's pretentious cultural standards—which he exposes as pitiful—to measure Belle Reve against Elysian Fields; rather, he emphasizes the uninhabitability of both for his supremely romantic heroine to the extent that she symbolizes the soul. The vitality and "raffish charm" of Elysian Fields is outweighed by its brutality; the fabled graciousness of Belle Reve by its debauchery. The former world with its brawling, bowling cocks-of-the-walk is male-dominated; the latter as its grammatically incorrect name (feminine adjective modifying masculine noun) suggests is a female-oriented, effeminate world whose scions, as symbolized by Blanche's young husband, are apt to be disinclined to propagate. Blanche's remark to Stella about Stanley early in the play, "But maybe he's what we need to mix with our blood now that we've lost Belle Reve . . ." proves, in the light of his (and even Mitch's) rough treatment of her, ironic. There can be no copulation or reconciliation between the world of the "beautiful dream" and the world of death in life actuality that will be mutually and ideally satisfactory. Stella's erotic will to life at any cost, her ability to shut one eye to the claims of the ideal and the other to the horrors of the actual, Williams portrays not as an easy truce between the two worlds but as a "narcotized," quasifatalistic commitment to survival that resolves none of the existential problems it poses.

Elysian Fields, the world that has replaced Belle Reve, will do, Williams seems to be saying, for the insensitive Stanley and the pragmatic Stella just as it provides satisfaction for their upstairs neighbors, the Hubbells, whom he names Eunice (literally "good victory") and Steve (literally "crown"); but it can only further the process of destroying Blanche which Belle Reve had begun. Its amusement-park thrills, its desperately gay and feverish music provide sufficient fulfilment only for the undemanding. The spirit of the whole place is characterized by the name of one of its nightspots, the "Four Deuces"—the poorest of the best hands in poker.

The introduction of Blanche's homosexual husband, Allan Grey, into the design of *Streetcar* has seemed gratuitously sensationalistic to some critics. Mary McCarthy, for example, found Blanche's story of the marriage so "patently untrue" that she took it upon herself to vouch for its incredibility to others: "the audience thinks the character must have invented it" (p. 134). Openly hostile to Williams' symbolism and incapable of interpreting it fairly (she insists on comparing Blanche to a typical sister-in-law—whatever that may be). Miss McCarthy failed to realize that Allan Grey, the deviate poet of Laurel and Belle Reve, is presented as the extreme opposite of the "gaudy seed-bearer" of Elysian Fields, that Blanche's attraction to him is as credible as is her abhorrence for Stanley, and that Blanche's relationship with her young husband proves mutually destructive because Williams' intention was to portray the impossibility of ideally consummating any union in which the body is involved. In Blanche's marriage Williams portrayed the futility of the romantic preoccupation with trying to achieve fulfilment with an epipsychidion or soul mate; in Blanche's intimacies with strangers and with Stanley he portrays the alternative to, and dramatizes the consequences of, that futile quest for fulfilment. "After the death of Allan—," Blanche tells Mitch, "intimacies with strangers was all I seemed able to fill my empty heart with. . . . I think it was panic, just panic, that drove me from one to another, hunting for some protection—here and there, in the most—unlikely places—even, at last, in a seventeen-year-old boy . . ." (p. 386). Throughout the play we are aware of Blanche's being ghoul-haunted by the suicide of her husband and we witness her interlude with the young newsboy whom she envisions as a prince out of the Arabian Nights. Her last attempt to settle for rest with Mitch is thwarted: she has misjudged even that simple soul and is denied even the small demands she makes of this love. All her intimacies have been with strangers to her deepest yearnings. Only when we realize this can we fully appreciate the irony, pathos and horror of her last line in the play: "Whoever you are—I have always depended on the kindness of strangers."

There can be salvation for Blanche neither in the pretentious world of Belle Reve from which she has salvaged only a trunk full of artificial goods and a head full of nightmares nor in the sex-glutted death in life of Elysian Fields because in *Streetcar* Williams has devised a conflict for her which only annihilation can resolve. As a symbol of the soul pitted against and in thrall to the body which fetters it, her natural state, like the moth's, is frustration.[6]

In the fourth scene of *Streetcar*, the following colloquy takes place between Stella and Blanche about the satisfactions of the flesh:

> STELLA: But there are things that happen between a man and a woman in the dark—that sort of make everything else seem—unimportant.
> BLANCHE: What you are talking about is brutal desire—just—Desire!—the name of that rattle-trap streetcar that bangs through the Quarter, up one old narrow street and down another . . .
> STELLA: Haven't you ever ridden on that streetcar?
> BLANCHE: It brought me here.—Where I'm not wanted and where I'm ashamed to be . . . (p. 321).

The banging of the tired old streecar up and down the narrow streets simulates Blanche's view of intercourse just as, in the very first scene, Stella's breathless laughter upon catching the blood-stained package of meat that Stanley throws her simulates *her* reaction to sexuality. In neither case does Williams portray sexuality, which he views as part of a cruel life force, in an attractive light. When Blanche says of Desire "It brought me here" we may take her to mean not only the streetcar that bore her to Elysian Fields, the land of the living dead, but human desire which brought her into existence. Incarnation is what she is ashamed of, and the flesh is what she has abused in her self-punishment for submitting to its importunate demands. "A man like that is someone to go out with," she tells Stella, "—once—twice—three times when the devil is in you. But live with? Have a child by?" (p. 321). Blanche has been conditioned to believe that the anarchy of the flesh must, whenever possible, be transcended in the interests of family and culture; Williams, however, dramatizes the futility of attempts to transcend the limitations of the human animal.

At the end of this fourth scene, imploring Stella to leave Stanley, Blanche delivers a harangue which in its cadence and hysterical rhetoric betrays her desperation and vulnerability. Describing Stanley as the amoral mortal enemy of humanistic aspiration, she says: "He acts like an animal, has an animal's habits! . . . Thousands and thousands of years have passed him right by, and there he is—Stanley

Kowalski—survivor of the Stone Age! Bearing the raw meat home from the kill in the jungle! . . . Night falls and the other apes gather! . . . His poker night!—you call it—this party of apes! . . . Maybe we are a long way from being made in God's image, but Stella—my sister—there has been *some* progress since then! Such things as art—as poetry and music—such kinds of new light have come into the world since then! In some kinds of people some tenderer feelings have had some little beginning! That we have got to make *grow*! and *cling* to, and hold as our flag! In this dark march toward whatever it is we're approaching. . . . *Don't—don't hang back with the brutes!"* (p. 323). Williams frames this speech, just before it begins and immediately after it ends, with the sound of two trains running like the old rattle-trap of Desire: at the same time, he has Stanley enter, unheard because of the noise of the trains, and remain to listen unobserved to Blanche's speech. Her two destroyers, desire and Stanley Kowalski, are thus made to hover like fateful accomplices over Blanche as she implores Stella to join with her in battle against them. That Stanley is placed in the strategically superior position of the unobserved viewer of the scene forecasts his eventual triumph over Blanche. To emphasize the inefficacy of Blanche's appeal and struggle against her fate, Williams ends the scene with Stella's embracing Stanley "fiercely"—joining the "brutes"—as Stanley grins at Blanche in victory. From that point on, Stanley begins to gain the upper hand in the struggle with Blanche.

Though in her long speech Blanche, characteristically rhapsodic, views the main struggle of existence as one between culture and brutality, the context of the play provides the struggle with wider, metaphysical significance. As a soul subjected to existence and hence to a body, her quarrel is not only with apes and brutes but with the apishness and brutality of matter with which she herself is involved and by which her mothlike flightiness is crippled and doomed. She herself has been unable to resist brutal treatment of her husband and she herself has ridden, without discernible satisfaction, on the streetcar of desire whose tracks, unlike the rungs of Plato's ladder of love, pointed to no great destination. Quite the contrary, for Blanche the desire and pursuit of the whole has proved, in practice, to lead to further disintegration.

While Stella and even Stanley would not, by any theological

standards, be considered devoid of a soul, Williams prefers to dramatize the soulfulness of Blanche at their expense because he conceives of the soul not in dogmatically theological but in ideal terms. For Williams, the soul appears to be that impulse in humanity which aspires to transcend the natural corruption and propensity to declivity that he constantly portrays as the informing principle of matter. Whereas he presents Stella and the earthy Stanley as the living dead narcotized by sex, gaming and comic books, characters contentedly buried in what Strindberg in *The Ghost Sonata* called "the dirt of life," Williams portrays Blanche as guiltily drawn to water and baths and as claiming, preciously, that she would die of eating an unwashed grape. The soul, for Williams in this play, seems to be that entity which produces and is sustained by culture but is not synonymous with it. It is that entity which, desiring the Good, is yet powerless to attain it by reason of the inexorable baseness of the matter that incarnates it. When Stanley, overpowering Blanche at the climax of the play says, "We've had this date with each other from the beginning," Williams is portraying what he views as the fated culmination of the soul's struggle against the body. The words "from the beginning"—in the mythic context of the drama—suggest the origins of the human race itself. All of Blanche's mothlike rushing and dashing about, which the stage directions call for her to do, cannot save her from the flame with which she has flirted. Though she was able to frighten Mitch away by shouting "Fire!" she collapses when faced with this more powerful flame to which her treacherous body draws her.

The predominating conflict of flesh and spirit modifies and includes all the other conflicts—sociological, psychological, moral, cultural—which A *Streetcar Named Desire* presents. It would be an oversimplification, as I have stated above, to see Belle Reve and Elysian Fields merely as opposites when Williams has subtly pointed out their similarity and the shortcomings they share in fulfilling the claims of the ideal. And it would be simpleminded to call Williams' presentation of both the attractiveness and failure of these two ways of life as ambivalence and to claim that it mars the play. By pitting the sterility of Belle Reve against the fertility of Elysian Fields, the weakness of Blanche against the insensitive stolidity of Stanley, her cultural pretensions against his penis-status, her sorority-girl vision of courtship and good times against his "colored-lights" orgasms, the simulated pearls of her lies against the swinish truth of his facts, her uncontrollable epic fornications against Stanley's own, less hysterical mastery in this area of experience, Williams attempts to dramatize the inevitable succumbing of the former to the greater power of the latter. If he seems to favor Blanche, it is because she is the weaker and because, at one time, as Stella attests, she showed great potential for tenderness and trust, the qualities of a typical victim. Only her stifled potential and her futile aspirations to transcend or mitigate the harshness of actuality—to cover the naked light bulb with a paper lantern—seem to qualify her, in Williams' eyes, as a symbol of the trapped soul. Not even her moral code, "Deliberate cruelty . . . is the one unforgivable thing . . . the one thing of which I have never, never been guilty," admirable as far as it goes, qualifies her as a symbol of transcendence so much as her pitiful attempts to combat actuality do. And, ironically and tragically enough, it is her very preference for soulful illusion and for magic over actuality which paves the way for her voyage to the madhouse.

Aware of the pity and terror of Blanche's world, Williams is not blind to the same qualities in the world that abides by Stanley's "Napoleonic Code." Stella and Mitch, for example, as creatures less hard than Stanley must nevertheless abide by his rules and even his lies (such as his denial of raping Blanche) if they are to survive in his domain. Though the furies of retribution visit Blanche for her hubris in making too many impossible demands of the "broken world" of mortality, they do not seem powerful enough to affect her antagonist, Stanley. In a way, the plot of *Streetcar* is modeled on the legend of Tereus, Philomela and Procne—the rape of the visiting sister-in-law by her brother-in-law in the absence of his wife—but Blanche's sister does not cut up her baby and serve it to Stanley for dinner as Procne served her son to Tereus; instead, Stella refuses to believe the story of the rape in order to go on living with Stanley and to provide a home for their child. Nor do the gods enter and transform the triangle into a trio of birds. And, while Mitch appears to believe that Stanley raped Blanche, he is powerless to overthrow his old master sergeant whose code of morality he must continue to endure just as, in the past, he was influenced by it in his treatment of Blanche.

While Williams dramatizes the plight of the incarnated, incarcerated soul primarily in terms of her futile voyage in quest of fulfilment—or, failing that, of peace and rest—he portrays the roles that fate and luck play in existence primarily in images of gaming. And the master of games in *Streetcar* is Stanley Kowalski. By reason of his amoral fitness for survival in a world which, in Williams' Darwinian view, is geared to the physically strongest at the expense of the meekly vulnerable, Stanley has an "in" with the fates. Though the intrusion of Blanche into his world rattles Stanley and threatens to undermine the self-confidence that sustains his power, he systematically allays his own fears at the expense of aggravating Blanche's. Though he loses at the poker games played in scene three, he wins at those played in the last scene of the play.

Introducing fate into his play by way of luck at games, Williams pits Stanley's chances of survival against Blanche's. When Williams summed up the moral of the play as, "If we don't watch out, the apes will take over" (quoted in Tischler, p. 137) he expressed the same view of existence that he delegated to Blanche in her speech denouncing the poker players as "a party of apes." That the tone and strategy of the play reveal it not merely as a cautionary drama but as a tragedy of the futility of attempting to flee the apes, I have stressed above. What the play really demonstrates is that, willy-nilly, the apes *must* take over since apishness is presented throughout as the natural, unavoidable condition not only of survival but of existence itself. A close examination of the Poker Night scene displays Williams' remarkable use of mythic and symbolic imagery to orchestrate both the "moral" of the play as he is reported to see it and the wider context in which I have been placing it.

Williams describes the poker players in scene three, Stanley, Steve, Pablo and Mitch, as "men at the peak of their physical manhood, as coarse and direct and powerful as the primary colors" of the kitchen setting (p. 286). As the scene opens, Stanley is losing and Mitch, who is shortly to meet Blanche, has been winning and is no longer in the game. They have apparently been playing games in which specific cards are "wild," games that depend to a greater extent on luck (read "fate") than on skill. In the game which we witness, "One-eyed jacks are wild." The rule of this game seems to describe the wild players themselves both as knaves and, in the mythic context of the play, as Cyclopes who, like these players, dwelt apart in caverns, observed no social, moral or legal order and existed by advantage of rude, savage strength unhampered by culture or intellect. By the end of the scene, we will be made witness to their apishness, particularly Stanley's (who as "Kowalski" is linked metaphorically with the Cyclopes who worked as smiths for Vulcan), and we will observe in action the caveman attraction he exerts for Stella whom he carries off to bed with him in their flat which is described as cavelike in the stage directions. Much is made, at the opening of the scene, of Mitch as a mamma's boy. He is playing in a game whose ultimate victors will not be the gentler giants attached to mothers, dead fiancées and flighty moths, but the rougher giants who survive and prevail by means of their brutishness and sheer brag.

The symbolic name of the second game played in this scene, "seven-card stud," is, of course, obvious in the context of these Elysian Fields where values are based on studmanship. While the cards for this game are being dealt out, Steve tells a joke about hens and roosters: the animalistic view of existence is underlined to contrast with Blanche's unsuccessfully transcendental one. As the joke ends, Blanche and Stella, the hens of the household, appear. They are unwelcome intruders in the masculine game. The scene then continues in twin focus on the card game in the kitchen and on Blanche's flirtation with Mitch in the bedroom.

Immediately before Blanche's first conversation with Mitch, Stanley had decided to play "Spit in the Ocean," a game which demands the pushing of one's luck. The name of the game suggests Stanley's attitude to Blanche's dream of ocean voyage and her addiction to the purgative and healing functions of water and, in line with the mythic context of the play, recalls the ancient superstition, popular with the Greeks and Romans, of spitting in the ocean to ward off enchantment and enchanters. The game played by Stanley in the kitchen provides an aptly ironic accompaniment to the game Blanche plays in the bedroom where, in her red satin wrapper, she flirts with Mitch, smokes his "Luckies," has him put up her paper lantern, dances to the music of a Viennese waltz, and tries to create the kind of "enchantment" that is unwelcome in Stanley's world. The romantic bedroom scene is abruptly terminated with Stanley's going as wild as a one-eyed Jack, or Cyclops, breaking the radio, striking Stella, and battling the other apes. Stanley's destructiveness, which Stella fondly rationalizes in the next scene as part of his passionate nature, is also part of the gaudy seed-bearer's physical potency. It is described by Blanche as "lunacy" but Williams ironically emphasizes its normalcy in context of the view of nature he presents in the play, and he has Blanche, instead, carted off as a lunatic at the end.

The poker night scene ends when Stella, unable to resist Stanley's "howling," "baying" and "bellowing" for her, returns to him: "they come together with low, animal moans. . . . [Stanley] lifts her off her feet and bears her into the dark flat." Outside the apartment, terrified, Blanche flits and rushes about like a moth looking "right and left as if for a sanctuary" (p. 307). She is calmed and comforted by Mitch.

Throughout the play, images drawn from gaming, chance and luck compete in number with those suggesting water and voyage. The sixth scene, for example, renders Mitch's marriage proposal to Blanche within the framework of imagery suggesting the game of chance which Blanche is desperately playing with him and with survival. The scene opens with the return home of Blanche and Mitch from their unsatisfactory date. "They have probably," the stage directions tell us, "been out to the amusement park on Lake Pontchartrain, for Mitch is bearing, upside down, a plaster statuette of Mae West, the sort of prize won at shooting galleries and carnival games of chance." At the door to Stanley's flat, Blanche says, "I'm looking for the Pleiades, the Seven Sisters, but these girls are not out tonight. Oh, yes they are, there they are! God bless them! All in a bunch going home from their little bridge party." The presence of the Pleiades in the sky seems to comfort Blanche; her reference to them as bridge ladies not only aligns them with the imagery of existence as a game of chance, but the familiarity with which Blanche treats the seven nymphs who, even as stars, must constantly flee the mighty, devastating hunter, Orion, suggests mythically and cosmically, a parallel to her own danger, pursued as she is by Stanley's vital lust for domination and destruction. The scene ends with Blanche's pathetic belief that Mitch's proposal is a sign that the gods have furnished her with an earthly protector. "Sometimes—," she says, "there's God—so quickly!" The name "Mitch" or "Mitchell," incidentally, is derived from "Michael" and means "someone like

God," but the godlike figure in this play is shown to be less powerful than—indeed in thrall to—the primal savage force represented by Stanley.

Generally, the two major image patterns concerned with voyage (particularly as escape from fate by means of water) and with games (as the framework of human chance and destiny) are only very casually suggested; occasionally they are even joined in a single speech as when Blanche, for example, explains to Mitch why she has come to Elysian Fields: "There was nowhere else I could go. I was *played out*. You know what played out is? My youth was suddenly gone up the *water-spout*, and—I met you . . ." (my italics, p. 387). In the last scene of the play, Williams more forcefully calls attention to his two most important image patterns in a superbly executed finale that boldly juxtaposes them.

Scene eleven opens with these two stage directions:

"It is some weeks later. Stella is packing Blanche's things. Sound of water can be heard running in the bathroom.

The portieres are partly open on the poker players—Stanley, Steve, Mitch and Pablo—who sit around the table in the kitchen. The atmosphere of the kitchen is now the same raw, lurid one of the disastrous poker night" (p. 403). The first words of dialogue in this scene are spoken by Stanley, the ultimate victor in the game between flesh and spirit: "Drew to an inside straight and made it, by God." "*Maldita sea tu suerto!*" says Pablo. Stanley, accustomed to winning by taking unfair advantage of whoever is weaker or of what he cannot understand, says, "Put it in English, greaseball." During the play, Stanley himself has been described in the stage directions as "grease-stained" and even by Stella as "greasy"; now, however, as the vanquisher of Blanche, he lords it over the socially inferior, Spanish-speaking Pablo just as, previously, Blanche and Stella, "a pair of queens," had condescended to him. "I am cursing your rutting luck," says Pablo whose choice of epithet aptly describes the reason for Stanley's power in the Elysian Fields, his fabulous rutting. Stanley, "prodigiously elated," then explains his view of luck: "You know what luck is? Luck is believing you're lucky. Take at Salerno. I believed I was lucky. I figured that 4 out of 5 would not come through but I would . . . and I did. I put that down as a rule. To hold front position in this rat-race you've got to believe you are lucky." The combination of physical and sexual potency together with his knowledge of the odds and his capacity for thinking positively assures Stanley, as Williams pictures him, survival in any war or race, human or rat. Mitch, unable to countenance Stanley's self-assurance, blurts out: "You . . . you . . . you. . . . Brag . . . brag . . . bull . . . bull." Even apart from the way Mitch apparently means the terms "brag" and "bull" here, he is appropriately summarizing Stanley's major claims to success. As a noun, *brag* is the name of a card game in which the players *brag* about holding cards better than those that have been dealt them. And *bull*, of course, suggests the awesome fertility that is geared to the successful cowing of other players in any game of seven-card stud.

After introducing the theme of the fatal card game as an analogue of earthly existence, the last scene of *Streetcar* shifts to focus on Eunice and Stella as they prepare Blanche for another journey. Speaking from the bathroom which has been her refuge throughout the play, Blanche asks, "Is the coast clear?" As Eunice and Stella assist her to dress, Blanche treats them like two handmaidens preparing her for a romantic ocean voyage. With "faintly hysterical vivacity" she concerns herself with her clothes and appearance. In having Blanche ask for a bunch of artificial violets to be pinned with a seahorse on the lapel of her jacket, Williams portrays her insignia: the violet which traditionally symbolizes innocence in flower language together with the creature whose natural habitat would be water—not land.

When Blanche meets the doctor who has come for her and sees that he is not Shep Huntleigh, the stage directions read, "There is a moment of silence—no sound but that of Stanley steadily shuffling the cards." As Blanche tries to escape the doctor, "The Matron advances on one side, Stanley on the other. Divested of all the softer properties of womanhood, the Matron is a peculiarly sinister figure in her severe dress. Her voice is bold and toneless as a firebell." When the matron says, "Hello, Blanche," "The greeting is echoed and re-echoed by other mysterious voices behind the walls, as if reverberated through a canyon of rock" (p. 415). The cold, peculiarly sinister figure of the matron whose firebell voice subsumes and awakens echoes of the other voices which have haunted Blanche in the play may be seen as the archetypal embodiment of disaster for her. When Williams states that the matron's greeting must sound like the reverberations in a canyon, we are reminded of Blanche's speech to Mitch about being "played out" which I quoted above and which introduces the image of the world as a rock: "I thanked God for you, because you seemed to be gentle—*a cleft in the rock of the world that I could hide in!*" (my italics, p. 387). However, Blanche's journey has provided her no canyon to hide in and now the hoped-for canyon itself is portrayed as reverberating with inescapable memories of horror. The theatrical image presented by Blanche's "retreating in panic" from the matron on the one hand and Stanley on the other suggests, in the mythic context of the play, the moth-soul trying to evade the grasp both of a cold, earthy, mother-figure (portrayed in imagery that suggests a harsh view of mother nature herself) and that figure's ally described earlier in the play as a type of "gaudy seed-bearer." Blanche's two antagonists here form a theatrical icon of incarnation and existence that graphically summarizes the wider significance of her plight throughout the play.

Only when the old doctor becomes courtly and addresses Blanche gently does her panic abate and does she allow herself to be escorted from Elysian Fields. Blanche's last speech about her continual dependence on the kindness of strangers, though terrifying in context of what these strangers have subjected her to, allows her the dignity of repudiating, by implication, what her relations have done to her. At the same time, since the audience knows that Blanche is being conducted to the madhouse and, possibly, to her death there, the dignity of her repudiation is gained at the expense of the so-called sanity and brutal vitality of Elysian Fields, the Darwinian state of existence.

As Blanche leaves the scene, Eunice places Stanley's infant son in Stella's arms. Again, the images of destruction and creation are juxtaposed. Stella is sobbing and Stanley comforts her in the only way he knows how: "He kneels beside her and his fingers find the opening of her blouse." Echoing the sinister matron's attempts to subdue Blanche with the words, "Now, Blanche!" Stanley "voluptuously, soothingly" consoles Stella with "Now, honey. Now, love. Now, now, love. . . ." The play ends with the "swelling music of the 'blue piano' and the muted trumpet" as Steve says, "This game is seven-card stud."

Throughout *A Streetcar Named Desire*, Williams used every device of theatrical rhetoric to portray and orchestrate existence as a stud game. From the desperate gaiety of the tinny "Blue Piano" which Williams says in his first stage direction "expresses the spirit of the life which goes on here" to the brawling of the Kowalskis and their neighbors, from the cries of the street vendors ("Red hot!" and "Flores para los muertos") to what Elia Kazan called the "ballet" of the passerby in quest of money or sex, Williams created in *Streetcar* a frenetic dramatization of spiritual frustration and physical satiation alike, of life fraught with death (Blanche) and of death burning with life (Elysian Fields). Though not without its quieter moments and lyrical interludes, the play might best be characterized as a syncopated rendition of what Williams views as the basic rhythm of physical existence: tumescence and detumescence, desire and death.

While Williams appears to be primarily concerned with sexuality in *Streetcar*, his symbolic depiction of desire transcends merely sexual passion to include existence itself as its ultimate referent. One need not necessarily accept Freud's theory of the libido as the basic life force to appreciate what Williams means by equating, as Blanche does, desire with life. With more restraint than Williams in *Streetcar*, Paul Valéry in an essay on Flaubert makes much the same equation of desire (and frustration) with life that Williams dramatizes in the play. Variously calling desire "greed," "temptation" and "lack" Valéry writes: "In Nature the root of the tree pushes towards wet ground, the summit towards the sun, and the plant thrives by changing unbalance into unbalance, greed into greed. The amoeba deforms itself in approaching its tiny prey, obeys that which it is going to convert into its own substance, then hauls itself to its adventuring pseudopodium and reassembles itself. This type of mechanism is characteristic of all organic life; the devi, alas! is nature itself, and temptation is the most obvious, the most constant, the most inescapable condition of life. To live means to lack something at every moment—to modify oneself in order to attain it—and hence to aim at returning again to the state of lacking something."[7] It is on this basis that Williams identifies desire with the nature of existence itself and on this basis that he contrasts Blanche's continuous frustration with the narcotized, makeshift fulfilment that prevails in the Elysian Fields of the play.

To point out the symbolic, mythic and tragic implications of the literary and theatrical imagery in *Streetcar* is not to deny that the play is often as jazzy and comic as the vision of existence it depicts (though close inspection reveals that the jazz is usually desperate and the comedy often very cruel). Elements of melodrama, frequently present in tragedy, are also evident in its structure—to such an extent that they have sometimes blinded viewers to its other qualities. Even the usually perspicacious Susan Sontag wrote in her controversial essay of 1964, "Against Interpretation," that *Streetcar* should be enjoyed merely as "a forceful psychological melodrama . . . about a handsome brute named Stanley Kowalski and a faded mangy belle named Blanche DuBois . . ." and that any *other* interpretation of the play would be unwarranted.

What I have tried to do in this essay, however, is to avoid rehashing the most blatantly realistic aspects of the play and to view it, instead, in terms of Williams' persistent concern with creating universal and "timeless" worlds in his plays. In play after play, Williams has consistently (albeit with varying degrees of success) employed symbolism and the mythic mode to universalize the significance of the realistic action he posits, not only, apparently, because he thinks of symbolism and universality as essentials of art, but also because these qualities seem to be characteristic of his personal reactions to life in general. For example, speaking years later of the autobiographical genesis of *Streetcar*, Williams said that whenever he stayed in New Orleans, he lived "near the main street of the [French] Quarter which is named Royal. Down this street, running on the same tracks, are two street-cars, one named DESIRE and the other CEMETERY. Their indiscourageable progress up and down Royal struck me as having some symbolic bearing of a broad nature on the life in the *Vieux Carré*—and everywhere else for that matter."[8]

Read in the light of Williams' personal and aesthetic predilections, all the images, symbols and allusions, even what appear to be only the most casual or realistic of details in *Streetcar*, combine to reveal a tragic parable of the pitiable and terrible fate of the human soul. Incarnated in treacherous, decaying matter, the soul, it appears, has been destined to voyage continually from one broken world to another, the only kinds of environment open to it in a flawed universe. Seeking union with the stars (themselves, whether symbolized as

Stella or the Pleiades, in a precarious situation), or, failing that, at least repose in the extinction of memory and cares in the Elysian Fields, the moth-soul finds, instead, only another broken world, another Darwinian environment in which the brutally fittest rule. As Tennessee Williams dramatizes his vision of existence in A *Streetcar Named Desire*, we see that "from the beginning" the cards of destiny have indicated a seemingly endless voyage for the human soul through progressively disastrous worlds, and the name of the game is tragedy.

Notes to Leonard Quirino, "The Cards Indicate a Voyage on
A *Streetcar Named Desire*"

1. Introduction to Carson McCullers, *Reflections in a Golden Eye* (New York: New Directions, 1941), p. xiii.

2. Vergil's *Aeneid*, trans. Patrick Dickinson (New York: New American Library, Mentor, 1961), p. 140.

3. The best examples of reviews concerned with the effect of production and acting on the interpretation of *Streetcar* are Harold Clurman's "Review of A *Streetcar Named Desire*," in *Lies Like Truth* (New York: Macmillan, 1958), pp. 72–80 and Eric Bentley's "Better than Europe?" in *In Search of Theatre* (New York: Alfred A. Knopf, 1953), pp. 84–8.

4. See especially Harry Taylor's Marxist view of *Streetcar* in "The Dilemma of Tennessee Williams," in *Masses and Mainstream* 1 (April 1948), 51–8 and Robert Emmet Jones's sociological analysis of Blanche DuBois in "Tennessee Williams' Early Heroines," *Modern Drama* 2 (December 1959), 211–19.

5. For the best example of denigration see, of course, Mary McCarthy's review, "A Streetcar Called Success," in *Sights and Spectacles 1937–1956* (New York: Farrar, Straus and Cudahy, 1956), pp. 131–5.

6. This Neoplatonic dialectic of body and soul or of flesh and spirit is one of the most persistent concerns of Williams. In *Summer and Smoke*, the revision of an earlier play called A *Chart of Anatomy*, Williams developed this dialectic in morality-play fashion; Williams evades resolving the conflict he creates for Alma and John by having each defect, too late, to the camp of the other. While appearing to embrace D. H. Lawrence's gospel of the identity of body and soul, Williams constantly reveals his own fundamental lack of trust in the impertinent body and its power to transcend such physical limitations as age and illness—predicaments which he emphasizes in play after play. Even in his paean to the undying spirit of D. H. Lawrence, *I Rise in Flame, Cried the Phoenix*, Williams depicts Lawrence at a time when, deathly ill, the body he so celebrated was betraying him.

7. Paul Valéry, "The Temptation of (Saint) Flaubert," trans. Lionel Abel, *Partisan Review Anthology*, ed. William Phillips (New York: Holt, Rinehart and Winston, 1962), p. 55.

8. Quoted in Tischler, p. 62. For further elucidation of Williams' preoccupation with universality in life and art, see especially his essay, "The Timeless World of a Play," preface to *The Rose Tattoo*, II, 259 ff.

Brick Pollitt as Homo Ludens:
"Three Players of a Summer Game" and *Cat on a Hot Tin Roof*

CHARLES E. MAY

Iᴼ Mᴀɢɢɪᴇ ᴛʜᴇ Cᴀᴛ is one of Tennessee Williams' most dramatically engaging characters, her husband, Brick Pollitt, is one of his most metaphysically mysterious. Brick's enigmatic detachment in *Cat on a Hot Tin Roof* has been the subject of more problematical commentary than either Maggie's feline restlessness or the spirit of mendacity that dominates the thematic action of the play itself. With his cool ironic smile and relative immobility (suggested both by his literal crutch and by the crutchlike liquor cabinet from which he never strays very far), Brick is, by contrast, the ambiguous center for all the characters in *Cat* who dance about on the hot tin roof of their "common crisis." Because Brick's detachment is thus so crucial, and also because Williams makes him so teasingly mysterious, the central question of the play that has always puzzled critics, a question still unanswered, is: What, apart from its function as catalyst for the dramatic action, does Brick's detachment mean?

In his "Note of Explanation" in the published version of *Cat*, Williams makes it quite explicit that for him Brick's "moral paralysis" is central to the play, a "root thing" in Brick's "tragedy." In fact, Williams felt Brick's problem was so basic to his own conception of *Cat* that of the three changes Elia Kazan urged him to make in the Broadway version of the play, the alteration in Brick's character in the third act is the change to which he devotes most of his ex-

49

planation. Williams complains that such a dramatic progression tends to obscure the meaning of Brick's tragedy, for no matter how revelatory the conversion, it never effects such an immediate change in the "heart or even conduct of a person in Brick's state of spiritual disrepair" (p. 168). Indeed, Nancy Tischler says that as a result of the change in Brick in the third act of the Broadway version, audiences may leave the theater suspecting that the "whole truth" about him has not been told (p. 210).

However, even those critics who consult Williams' original third act, included in the published version of the play, complain that the meaning of Brick's tragedy remains obscure. Williams' own commentary offers no clarification. He is well aware of the mystery of Brick's personality, and he wishes to leave it that way. "Some mystery should be left in the revelation of character in a play, just as a great deal of mystery is always left in the revelation of character in life, even in one's own character to himself" (pp. 114–15). Although everyone familiar with the play is aware that Brick's disgust with life and resultant detachment has something to do with his homosexual relationship, latent or otherwise, with his friend Skipper, most readers sense that this is not the whole truth. Again, Williams encourages rather than clarifies the ambiguity. As Brick and Big Daddy "timidly and painfully" try to discuss the "inadmissible thing that Skipper died to disavow," Williams comments that the "fact that if it existed it had to be disavowed to 'keep face' in the world they lived in, may be at the heart of the 'mendacity' that Brick drinks to kill his disgust with. It may be the root of his collapse. Or maybe it is only a single manifestation of it, not even the most important" (p. 114).

Throughout the published version of *Cat*, Williams' comments suggest that Brick's problem is spiritual or metaphysical in nature, not simply psychological, and therefore not so liable to "pat" conclusions or "facile definitions which make a play just a play, not a snare for the truth of human experience" (p. 115). What Williams says he wishes to capture in the play is not the solution of one man's psychological problem, but rather the "true quality of experience," the "interplay of live human beings in the thundercloud of a common crisis" (p. 114). However, since much of this "common crisis" is the result of Brick's disgust and detachment, many critics have argued that Brick himself should be more adequately explained. As Benjamin Nelson says, "A true quality of experience cannot be grasped when the situation and characters involved are left unexplained" (p. 211). Signi Lenea Falk even goes so far as to suggest that "Williams writes as if he himself did not know the physical and moral condition of his hero and the reason for his collapse" (p. 107).

Nelson, Falk, and other critics who have accused Williams of obscurantism in regard to Brick have done so precisely because they do not see that Brick's problem is not simply psychological and therefore not solvable by "facile definitions." What is wrong with Brick is rather metaphysical in nature and thus not "knowable" or "explainable," at least not in the way that Nelson and Falk expect when they use those terms. Brick's mysterious disgust can perhaps best be approached by comparing it to the problem of a similar disgust in *Hamlet* as it is analyzed by T. S. Eliot. As Eliot says, although Hamlet's disgust may be occasioned by his mother, she is not an adequate "objective correlative" for it. Similarly, Brick's disgust exceeds the so-called homosexual problem with Skipper. As a result, he, like Hamlet, is unable to understand the cause of his dilemma. In one of the stage directions in act two, when Brick tries to explain himself to a skeptical Big Daddy, Williams describes Brick as a "broken, 'tragically elegant' figure telling simply as much as he knows of 'the Truth' " (p. 122).

The "true quality of experience . . . , that cloudy, flickering, evanescent—fiercely charged!—interplay" (p. 114) that Williams wants to catch in *Cat on a Hot Tin Roof*, does not stem from a psychosexual problem, but rather from the metaphysical implications of some "inadmissible thing" that Williams attempts to objectify by means of Brick's "homosexuality." If the objectification is inadequate, it is not because Williams does not know what the problem is but because it is simply not knowable or explainable in psychological or sexual terms. However, since the psychosexual answer is such an easy if not completely satisfactory one, it has been used to account for Brick's malaise just as Hamlet's disgust has been explained as a reaction to his incestuous desires for his mother. Similar explanations have been given for Claggart's mysterious hatred for Billy Budd in Melville's novella and Gustave Aschenbach's degeneration in Mann's *Death in Venice*. In fact, much of the metaphysical mystery of the so-called southern Gothic school of literature, a group in which Williams is often placed, has similarly been attributed to suppressed homosexuality, incest, pederasty, and other sexual "perversions."

That such explanations miss the point quite a bit more than they hit it is suggested by Williams in his introduction to the New Directions edition of Carson McCullers' *Reflections in a Golden Eye*. In this mock dialogue with a puzzled representative of the "everyday humdrum world" in which Williams compares the southern Gothic writers to the French existentialists, he also gives us a clue to the metaphysical mystery of Brick Pollitt. The true sense of dread in life, says Williams, is "not reaction to anything sensible or visible or even, strictly, materially, *knowable*. But rather it's a kind of spiritual intuition of something almost too incredible and shocking to talk about, which underlies the whole so-called thing. It is the incommunicable something that we shall have to call mystery." Brick's detachment is an existential leveling of values that makes no one thing more important than another. It is the result of an awareness of absurdity that, as Albert Camus says, can come at any time with no discernible cause and that resists any attempts at psychological explanation. Like Hamlet who senses that the rottenness in Denmark reflects a rottenness at the heart of existence, Brick is existentially aware of the universality of the mendacity on Big Daddy's plantation kingdom, and in face of it he too would wish that his too solid flesh would melt.

However, whereas Hamlet cannot find anything to do that is adequate to resolve the disgust he feels, Brick no longer tries to do anything. This withdrawn impassivity, Brick's refusal to act, even to think, makes his basic situation difficult for the reader to understand. When a fictional character faces a problem that he cannot articulate, a problem that evades attempts to conceptualize it, perhaps the only way the artist can communicate the nature of the problem is to show how the character attempts to deal with it. Thus, the "inadmissible thing" that lies at the heart of *Oedipus* cannot be presented directly. Rather, the play unfolds as a series of attempts by Oedipus to resolve a problem which, while symbolically objectified by the plague, truly hides within metaphysical mysteries that evade all "pat conclusions" and "facile definitions."

Ernest Hemingway, who was always concerned with the artistic problem of finding objective correlatives for the sense of metaphysical dread that Williams calls an "incommunicable something that we shall have to call mystery," also found that he could best present it by objectifying the attempts of his characters to deal with it. For example, in "A Clean, Well-Lighted Place," there is no objective correlative adequate to the old waiter's sense of nada which has seized him. However, the clean, well-lighted place itself is a communicable symbol of a way to live with that sense of nada. Similarly, the mysterious fear and dread that have taken hold of Nick Adams in "Big Two-Hearted River" is not adequately objectified by the "tragic" nature of the swamp, but the way to deal with the dread is adequately communicated by the detailing of Nick's fishing activities that make up the story.

However, in *Cat on a Hot Tin Roof*, because Brick makes no effort to deal with his problem, we are given no clues as to the nature of Brick's problem via an objectification of a possible solution or even, as in Hemingway's stories, a possible palliative. The click in his head that Brick drinks to achieve seems merely an intensification of his already withdrawn state. It gives no hint of why he wishes to withdraw. And, as noted, Brick's disgust seems to exceed its ostensible cause as objectified by the relationship with Skipper. The result is that while a great deal of action goes on around Brick in the play, action which reveals the motives of the other characters, Brick remains inactive and thus unrevealed.

I suggest that Williams does not have Brick make any effort to resolve his problem in *Cat on a Hot Tin Roof* because in an earlier fictional account of the dilemma Brick does make such an effort, the only kind of effort that can be made, and it is inevitably doomed to fail. Tom S. Reck, in an essay on the relationship between Williams' stories and plays, suggests that "Three Players of a Summer Game," published in *The New Yorker* only two years before Williams wrote *Cat*, may come closer to the "whole truth" (p. 147) about Brick than the play does. However, Reck makes no more effort than any of the other critics to determine what that whole truth is.

The truth is certainly not to be found in the ostensible cause for Brick's disgust given in the story, for that is left even more mysterious than in the play. Williams' story-telling narrator says only that his "self-disgust came upon him with the abruptness and violence of a crash on a highway. But what had Brick crashed into? Nothing that anybody was able to surmise, for he seemed to have everything that young men like Brick might hope or desire to have" (*Hard Candy*, pp. 13–14). The only strictly "knowable" thing suggested in the story that might be the cause of Brick's "dropping his life and taking hold of a glass which he never let go of for more than one waking hour" (p. 14) is, as it is in *Cat*, a sexual problem—in this case, his emasculation by his wife Margaret and a consequent sexual impotence. This is hinted at in Brick's drunken monologue to the house painters in which, "explaining things to the world," he is, as he also is in *Cat*, "like an old-time actor in a tragic role," telling as much as he knows of the Truth: "the meanest thing one human being can do to another human being is to take his respect for himself away from him. . . . I had it took away from me! I won't tell you how, but maybe, being men about my age, you're able to guess it. That was how. Some of them don't want it. They cut it off. They cut it right off a man, and half the time he don't even know when they cut it off him. Well, I knew it all right. I could feel it being cut off me." A bit later Brick continues the castration allusion by explaining how he is going to solve his drinking problem. "I'm not going to take no cure and I'm not going to take no pledge, I'm just going to prove I'm a man with his balls back on him!" (pp. 21–6 passim).

The irony and seeming contradiction of trying to prove one's masculinity by learning to play what Brick himself calls the "sissy" game of croquet should be hint enough that Brick's problem is not emasculation and impotence in the psychosexual sense in which we usually understand such terms. Rather as in *Cat*, Brick's problem is a more basic and pervasive one for which his sexual dilemma is merely a symbolic objectification. The complexity of the problem can best be seen by examining the way Brick seeks to deal with it, that is, by examining the summer game itself—both the purely aesthetic game of croquet and the psychological game Brick plays with the other two players, the young widow Isabel and her daughter Mary Louise. Brick's impotence is not a reaction against the emasculating Margaret, but rather a revolt against the flesh itself. His flight into the chaste, because death-purified, arms of Isabel is the search for Truth in its Keatsean equation with Beauty. It is an attempt to escape from flesh into art, to escape from the intolerable, because contingent, real into the bearable, because detached and fleshless, ideal of artistic form.

However, this attempt to escape the contingency of existence by means of aesthetic patterning and idealizing is doomed from the start, for Brick's hoped-for ideal relationship with Isabel as well as his effort to play the superior game of art and form with human beings as counters comes crashing against the "real" fleshly and psychological needs of the other two players. The problem is similar to the one facing Aschenbach in *Death in Venice*. He, too, wishing for the form and detachment of Beauty, finds that unless it is embodied in the flesh it is inhuman; but if it is human, it must therefore be fleshly and consequently be that very thing from which he wishes to escape. It is this intolerable aesthetic and metaphysical dilemma that destroys him.

Tennessee Williams offers several suggestions throughout "Three Players of a Summer Game" that this indeed is the inadmissible, because unnamable, thing that so plagues Brick. At the end of the major events of the story, after Brick has realized the impossibility of his summer game and no longer comes to the widow's house, the narrator says, "The summer had spelled out a word that had no meaning, and the word was now spelled out and, with or without any meaning, there it was, inscribed with as heavy a touch as the signature of a miser on a check or a boy with chalk on a fence" (p. 41). Any attempt to "spell out" the problem, even the attempt the story itself makes, is inadequate to get at the Truth. However, even as the attempt to escape from life through art is the subject of the story, art is the only means to present such a subject; for it is a subject that must be presented obliquely and metaphorically through symbolic objectifications.

At the very beginning of the story the narrator establishes the metaphor that identifies the summer game with the nature of the art work, and he does so in language that Williams later uses in *Cat on a Hot Tin Roof* to refer to that "fiercely charged!—interplay of live human beings" that he wishes to capture in the play—"flickering, evanescent" (III, 114). The game of croquet itself, says the narrator, "seems, in a curious way, to be composed of images the way that a painter's abstraction of summer or one of its games would be built of them. The delicate wire wickets set in a lawn of smooth emerald that flickers fierily at some points and rests under violet shadows in others, the wooden poles gaudily painted as moments that stand out in a season that was a struggle for something of unspeakable importance to someone passing through it, the clean and hard wooden spheres of different colors and the strong rigid shape of the mallets that drive the balls through the wickets, the formal design of those wickets and poles upon the croquet lawn—all of these are like a painter's abstraction of a summer and a game played in it" (p. 9).

Likewise the characters in the story become images and abstractions, not so much real people as stylized gestures which are pictorially woven within the lyrical narrative that make up the "legend" of Brick Pollitt. The narrator is well aware that he is playing the game of detachment of form, the rule-bound ritualized game of arranging images in a formal design that both reveals and conceals, the game of art. "These bits and pieces, these assorted images, they are like the paraphernalia for a game of croquet, gathered up from the lawn when the game is over and packed carefully into an oblong wooden box which they just exactly fit and fill. There they all are, the bits and pieces, the images, the apparently incongruous paraphernalia of a summer that was the last one of my childhood, and now I take them out of the oblong box and arrange them once more in the formal design on the lawn. It would be absurd to pretend that this is altogether the way it was, and yet it may be closer than a literal history could be to the hidden truth of it" (pp. 11–12).

This engagement in the formally-controlled, ritualized patterning of the art work that one plays to deal with the incongruity and contingency of life is of course the same game Brick wishes to play. The croquet game means the same kind of control to Brick that the fishing trip does to Nick Adams in "Big Two-Hearted River." As Brick explains to the painters and thus to the world, croquet is a wonderful game for a drinker. "You hit the ball through one wicket and then you drive it through the next one. . . . You go from wicket to wicket, and it's a game of precision—it's a game that takes concentration and precision, and that's what makes it a wonderful game for a drinker" (p. 26). The game for both Brick and the narrator of "Three Players of a Summer Game" is thus an Apollonian means to deal with the Dionysian drunkenness and incongruity of raw existential reality.

Although the relationship between the process of art and the process of game has often been noted, it has perhaps been given its most profound treatment in Johan Huizinga's *Homo Ludens: A Study of the Play Element in Culture*. Huizinga says that engagement in both play and art involves the assertion of freedom, the abolition of the ordinary world, and the participation in an action that is limited in time and space. In both the game and the art work, something invisible and inchoate takes form and transcends the bounds of logical and deliberative judgment. As Huizinga says, "All poetry is born of play. . . . What poetic language does with images is to play with them. It disposes them in style, it instills mystery into them so that every image contains the answer to an enigma" (pp. 129, 134). However, as Huizinga suggests, it is not the psychological meaning of the action that reveals the answer to the enigma, but rather the ritualized pattern that is formed from the bits and pieces, the actions and images, that make up the art work. It is this spatializing of the temporal, the transforming of the historical into myth, that the narrator of Williams' story says may come closer to the hidden truth of Brick Pollitt's summer game than a literal history.

That the summer game Brick plays with Isabel and her daughter is bound up with his own aesthetic search for detachment and form, his search for an escape from the temporal into the spatial, can be seen in what he desires of the relationship with Isabel. Williams must have had Keats stirring about in his mind when he wrote "Three Players of a Summer Game," for Keatsean aesthetic motifs echo throughout. Even the name Isabel and the fact that Isabel's husband's illness begins in a shocking way in which "An awful flower grew in his brain like a fierce geranium that shattered its pot" (p. 16) suggests Keats's Isabella and her beloved but gruesome pot of basil. Just as in Keats's poem, in Williams' story, hoped-for love and beauty germinate in death itself and remain inextricably tied to the horrors of the flesh.

Brick is initially drawn to Isabel because her actual encounter with the contingency and horror of flesh reflects his own metaphysical encounter. As together they watch the young doctor die, "God was the only word she was able to say; but Brick Pollitt somehow understood what she meant by that word, as if it were in a language that she and he, alone of all people, could speak and understand" (p. 16). After Brick pumps the death-delivering contents of the hypodermic needle into the doctor's arm, he and Isabel consummate their communion of metaphysical despair by lying together chastely in bed, "and the only movement between them was the intermittent, spasmodic digging of their fingernails into each other's clenched palm while their bodies lay stiffly separate, deliberately not touching at any other points as if they abhorred any other contact with each other, while this intolerable thing was ringing like an iron bell through them" (p. 17). The summer game thus becomes, says the narrator, a "running together out of something unbearably hot and bright into something obscure and cool" (p. 17); it is the running out of the hot, unbearable world of existential reality into the cool, obscure world of the art work.

However, when Brick realizes, as does Gustave Aschenbach, that form must inevitably become involved and entangled with the reality of flesh, he finds himself caught on the horns of an unresolvable metaphysical dilemma. Thus, in "Three Players of a Summer Game," the ideal game of art as Huizinga describes it becomes enmeshed with the real game of existential reality as it has recently been analyzed by Eric Berne in *Games People Play*. Because two other players are involved in Brick's game, players who have real fleshly, emotional, and psychological needs, the game is contaminated when it must be played at the expense of Isabel and Mary Louise. Brick's motive for his game, concealed by its metaphysical and inchoate nature, results in the "real world" of the story in what Berne calls an "ulterior transaction" in which others are exploited by the player. Thus, the artistic game, at the same time that it is the most noble and ideal of all games, becomes a "substitute for the real living of real intimacy" as Berne says most of our social games are (p. 18).

The exploitation is made quite clear in its effect on Mary Louise, lonely already because of the "cushions of flesh" which her mother promises will "dissolve in two or three more years" (p. 31), who is made even more lonely during the summer by being shut out of the house when Brick is there. However, as the summer passes, it also becomes apparent that Brick's need to play the artistic game of inhuman form is not satisfying to Isabel either. Although the conflict between Brick's ideal and Isabel's flesh is suggested in various ways in the story, the scene that makes it most obvious occurs one evening when, after setting up the croquet set, Mary Louise stands beneath her mother's bedroom window and wails for her and Brick to come out and play: "Almost immediately after the wailing voice was lifted, begging for the commencement of the game, Mary Louise's thin pretty mother showed herself at the window. She came to the window like a white bird flying into some unnoticed obstruction. That was the time when I saw, between the dividing gauze of the bedroom curtains, her naked breasts, small and beautiful, shaken like two angry fists by her violent motion. She leaned between the curtains to answer Mary Louise not in her usual tone of gentle remonstrance but in a shocking cry of rage: 'Oh, be still, for God's sake, you fat little monster!'" (p. 30). The imagery of flight into an unexpected obstruction and the breasts like fists suggest the frustratingly unyielding obstruction her own flesh has met in Brick's gauze-like ideal.

The contrast between that ideal of the frozen art work that Brick desires and the real physical life that he must live with is perhaps indirectly suggested by an incident the narrator relates about a visit he and Mary Louise pay to an art museum. The scene may have more than accidental significance since it did not appear in the original version of the story in The New Yorker, but rather in the revised version that was published the following year in Hard Candy. When the two children enter a room with a reclining male nude entitled the "Dying Gaul," Mary Louise lifts the metal fig leaf from the bronze figure and turns to the narrator to ask, "Is yours like that?" (p. 19). Since the added incident has nothing directly to do with the problem of Brick, it may be another of the bits and pieces that reflect Brick's basic dilemma—being caught between the ideal Greek beauty of idealized body and the real and therefore ugly flesh of physical body .

Williams adds another passage to the Hard Candy version of the story. In the concluding description of Brick's being driven through the streets of town by Margaret, much the way a captured prince might be led through the streets of a capital city by his conqueror, Williams has the narrator describe him as the handsomest man you were likely to remember, adding significantly, "physical beauty being of all human attributes the most incontinently used and wasted, as if whoever made it despised it, since it is made so often only to be disgraced by painful degrees and drawn through the streets in chains" (p. 44). Thus, what Brick and the narrator learn in the story, although they learn it only in an inchoate and oblique way, is that when one uses human beings in an effort to play the game of art and reach the beauty and detachment of form, the result is the inevitable disgrace of the flesh. The beauty of the art work alone can remain pure, but only because of its inhumanness, its noninvolvement. Ike McCaslin's attempts to realize the Keatsean equation of Beauty and Truth in Faulkner's *Bear* by relinquishing all claims to the world and the flesh meet with the same ambiguous and inescapable paradox.

When Brick realizes the hopelessness of his aspiration, he is transformed from tragic actor to clown. The croquet lawn becomes a circus ring. Brick's tragicomic efforts come to a climax one night when he turns on the water sprinkler, takes off his clothes, and rolls about under the cascading arches. No longer the Greek statue, Brick is now "like some grotesque fountain figure, in underwear and necktie and the one remaining pale-green sock, while the revolving arch of water moved with cool whispers about him" (p. 33). The degeneration of the tragedy can also be seen in what the narrator calls a conclusion "declining into unintentional farce" as Isabel and Mary Louise carry on trivial conversations in the face of Brick's absence from the house. The conversation about the ice that Mary Louise uses to ease her mosquito bites is the culmination of a pervasive motif of frozen coolness interwoven throughout the story. A game that began with a running out of something hot into something obscure and cool, a game that took place among frozen stylized figures on the cool, dark lawn of a house that has the appearance of a block of ice, has now become a banal banter between "two ladies in white dresses waiting on a white gallery" (p. 35) in which the ice is reduced from its symbolic significance to the practical utility of cooling Brick's drinks, easing Mary Louise's mosquito bites, and putting in the ice bag for Isabel's headaches.

This analysis of how Brick attempts to deal with his problem in "Three Players of a Summer Game" should make clearer the metaphysical mystery of Brick's detachment in *Cat on a Hot Tin Roof*. The basic tension between the ideal and frozen art work and the unbearable hot tin roof of reality is the tension of both the story and the play. Even the "Person-to-Person" preface which Williams writes for *Cat* contains a clear reference to the problem of the Keatsean equation of Truth and Beauty that he is concerned with in the play. However, because Williams sees that such an equation is possible only in death or in the deathlike art work, the poem he chooses to reflect the dilemma is not from Keats, but from Emily Dickinson. In "I Died for Beauty," it is only in the grave that Beauty and Truth recognize that they are "brethren."

Perhaps one of the reasons for Williams' often expressed admiration for Maggie the Cat is that she alone in the play seems to realize what Brick's desire is. However, she also realizes that it means death and rejects it in her famous cry, "Maggie the cat is—*alive! I am alive, alive! I'm . . .—alive!*" (p. 60). Against Brick's protestations she tries to explain that she made love to Skipper only because of Brick's detachment, only because he refused to return the love of those who cared for him. "Skipper and I made love, if love you could call it, because it made both of us feel a little bit closer to you. You see, you son of a bitch, you asked too much of people, of me, of him, of all the unlucky poor damned sons of bitches that happen to love you . . . you—superior creature!—you godlike being!—And so we made love to each other to dream it was you, both of us! Yes, yes, yes! Truth, truth!" (pp. 55–6). Maggie insists she does understand about Brick and Skipper, knows "It was one of those beautiful, ideal things they tell about in the Greek legends. . . . Brick, I tell you, you got to believe me, Brick, I *do* understand all about it! I—I think it was—*noble!* Can't you tell I'm sincere when I say I respect it? My only point, the only point that I'm making, is life has got to be allowed to continue even after the *dream* of life is—all—over . . ." (p. 57).

It seems obvious that what Brick hoped to achieve in his games with Skipper is the same thing he aspired to in his croquet game with Isabel and Mary Louise, and it is also obvious that his effort fails for the same metaphysical reasons in both the story and the play:

human needs always interfere with purely ideal aspirations. As a result, in *Cat* Brick stops playing altogether, or at least thinks he does; however, the click he waits to hear in his head is a metaphoric echo of the click of the croquet mallets that can be faintly heard offstage in act one. Maggie understands Brick's game-playing posture when she tells him he has always had a detached quality as though he were playing a game without much concern over whether he won or lost. Now that he has quit playing, she says he has the "charm of the defeated.—You look so cool, so cool, so enviably cool" (p. 30).

However, everything is not so cool for Brick, or else he would not continue to drink and wait for the click in his head; he would not stare out the window at the moon in act three and envy it for being a cool son of a bitch. Brick continues to try to play the ideal game in which the goal is not to win or lose, but rather to carry the game through. This time, though, he tries to play it alone. As Huizinga says, the essence of play can be summed up in the phrase, "There is something at stake"; yet this something is not the material result of the play, but rather the "ideal fact that the game is a success or has been successfully concluded" (p. 49). Now, however, Brick's problem is that the human games of others are always breaking in on the ideal game of cool withdrawal he wishes to play. If it is not what Maggie calls the "cardsharp" games of Gooper and Mae as they use their children as counters to win the legacy of Big Daddy, it is Maggie's own game of attempted seduction of Brick. The most pervasive game, however, that surrounds the action of the play and threatens to shatter Brick's detachment, is summarized in an offhand phrase by the insensitive Reverend Tooker as a game of life and death in which "the Stork and the Reaper are running neck and neck!" (p. 72).

In *Cat on a Hot Tin Roof*, Brick's game of detachment is as destructive and exploitative as his more directly involved game in "Three Players." This time Brick preserves his "charming detachment" by that "simple expedient" of not loving anyone enough to disturb it. Consequently, he damages Skipper, Maggie, and Big Daddy, all who need his love and involvement. However, as much as Brick realizes these needs, he can do nothing to satisfy them without entangling himself in the chaos of that real life that so disgusts him. He intuits that love of another human being not only is insufficient to fulfill the ideal demands of the human spirit; by its very nature such a love negates the possibility of such fulfilment. Perhaps it is this realization that made Williams object to the change Kazan wanted effected in Brick in the third act. In the original version of the play, when Maggie makes her announcement that she is pregnant, Brick simply keeps quiet, not as an attempt to save Maggie's face, but rather as a result of his own continued indifference. In the stage version, Brick actively supports Maggie's false claim, as if it truly makes a difference to him. His last words in the Broadway version are: "I admire you, Maggie" (p. 214). The implication is that he has found a solution to his problem and will henceforth be "alive" as Maggie says she is. The conclusion to the original version of the play is more ambiguous. As Maggie turns out the lights in the bedroom and the curtain begins to fall slowly, she says to Brick, "Oh, you weak people, you weak, beautiful people!—who give up.—What you want is someone to—. . . take hold of you.—Gently, gently, with love! And—. . . I *do* love you, Brick, I *do!*" Brick's final words before the curtain falls are uttered with that charming sad smile still on his face: "Wouldn't it be funny if that was true?" (pp. 165–6). This final question of the play is not just in response to Maggie's declaration of love, but rather it is a fittingly enigmatic and ironic response to Maggie's claim that all such people as Brick need to resolve their metaphysical dilemma is for someone to take hold of them with love. Brick's final skeptical query then bears a striking resemblance in its hopeless ambiguity to Jake Barnes' reply to Lady Britt at the conclusion of Hemingway's *The Sun Also Rises*: "Isn't it pretty to think so?"

It is thus with Brick's mysterious metaphysical problem still unresolved that Tennessee Williams wished to end his play, for it is a problem that is not knowable by any ordinary epistemology nor solvable by any ordinary psychology. In "Three Players of a Summer Game," Isabel is obliquely referring to Brick when she responds to Mary Louise's question about why the sun goes south: "Precious, Mother cannot explain the movements of the heavenly bodies, you know that as well as Mother knows it. Those things are controlled by certain mysterious laws that people on earth don't know or understand" (p. 36).

The Subterranean World
of *The Night of the Iguana*

GLENN EMBREY

Most of Tennessee Williams' characters eventually discover there is no fate worse than sex; desire maims and kills, often in the most violent fashion. Val Xavier is burnt to death, Blanche DuBois is raped and driven insane, Chance Wayne waits to be castrated, and Sebastian Venable is torn apart and devoured by children—all because of sexual drives. Many other characters in Williams' plays are destroyed by their passions, only in less physical and sensationalistic ways.

The idea that sex is fatal is not always easy to catch in the plays, for it is usually not developed explicitly. Instead, it lurks in the background, like a vague but persistent nightmare that affects the shape of whatever else the plays have to say. Also, it contradicts some of the popular notions about Williams. After all, his heroes and heroines often openly revel in their sexual exploits. He is considered the champion of the promiscuous, the passionate, the deviant. When these characters are destroyed, they appear to be the victims of an insensitive or sadistic world that will not tolerate their differences, especially their sexual differences; they seem to be brutalized not by their own desires, but by cruel, external forces. Blanche DuBois, for example, is assailed by a crude society that has no room for her sensitivity, her ideals, or her need to find comfort in sexual encounters. But this view of Blanche is only half true. There is in *Streetcar* what

Shannon would call a "subterranean" or "fantastic" level. On this level, the play is really a dramatization of how Blanche and her delicate nature are devastated by the promiscuous behavior her sexual nature drives her to, a fate paralleling the way her family's plantation was lost through the "epic fornication" of their ancestors. When Stanley ravages her mind and body at the end of the play, he is not so much an agent of the real world as he is a symbol of the sexual drives that have ravaged her throughout her life.

The main character of *The Night of the Iguana* seems to escape the violent fate usually in store for Williams' heroes. True, desire has been ruining Shannon's life for the past ten years, but at the climax of the play he manages to form what promises to be a lasting sexual relationship with a mature woman. This optimistic ending appears to make *Iguana* very different from the serious plays that precede it; for the first time hope breaks across Williams' bleak world. But appearances are deceptive, for there is a "subterranean" world within *Iguana*, as there is in *Streetcar*, and this world makes *Iguana's* optimism naive and unjustified, and makes the play just another variation on the theme that haunts all of Williams' works—that sex kills, that it is disgusting and dangerous. The conflict that exists between the different levels of *Iguana* is also typical of the playwright's works, and the play provides a clear example of how they collapse into confusion because unacknowledged fears of sexuality undermine their more overt and positive levels.

Shannon arrives onstage in the condition of the typical Williams hero—on the verge of going to pieces. Emotionally, physically, psychologically, financially, in almost every possible way, he is at the end of his rope, just like the frantic iguana. The play provides a surfeit of explanations for his imminent breakdown. One is simply his bizarre lifestyle: he roams about the world, towing his unsuspecting tour groups after him, in search of the most horrifying and disgusting scenes he can find. The understandable complaints posted by his parties, along with his seductions of the youngest ladies of the groups, get him fired from one travel agency after another. He is currently employed by the sleaziest of the agencies, and none is left to hire him if he is fired again.

Another reason for his collapse is that he is so preoccupied with himself he is cut off from everyone else. Despite his busloads of companions, some more intimate than others, he is abjectly lonely. In his conversation with Hannah during the second act he explains what has led to his miserable way of life. Ten years before, his brief career as a minister ended after he committed both fornication and heresy in the same week. A young Sunday school teacher had come to the rectory and wildly declared she loved him. When he knelt with her to pray for guidance, they suddenly found themselves making love. Afterwards, he slapped her and called her a tramp; when she went home she tried to commit suicide. On the following Sunday, facing a congregation expecting an explanation and apologies, he suddenly threw away his prepared remarks and shouted an impromptu sermon that drove the people from the church. The gist of his outburst was that he refused to conduct services for the kind of God he felt they believed in: a *"senile delinquent,"* "a bad-tempered childish old, old, sick, peevish man" (IV, 303–4).

He was locked out of his church and committed to an asylum to recover from his apparent nervous breakdown. When released he became a tour guide, and his itineraries show he never fully recovered from whatever had possessed him. On each of his tours he clearly reenacts the dual sin of fornication and heresy. He seduces one or more of the youngest members of the party, afterwards treating them as abusively as he did the Sunday school teacher. The tours themselves are a continuation of his heretical sermon, for on them, he tells Hannah, he is trying to "collect evidence" of his own "personal idea of God" (p. 304), evidence that attacks his congregation's notion of God. And the results are just the same: he is fired by his tour groups as he was fired by his congregation.

Shannon's concept of God needs some explaining for it seems at odds with the kind of evidence he gathers. He is primarily interested in examples of the disgusting misery of human life. The story that Hannah finds nauseating about the aged filthy natives crawling about a mound of excrement looking for bits of undigested food to eat epitomizes what Shannon collects. So does the iguana. Jerking about desperately and uselessly against its noose, destined to become Maxine's dinner, the iguana is a metaphor not only for the major characters of the play but also for all human beings, creatures made grotesque by suffering and terror, frequently forced to live in the most degrading of conditions.

Shannon's God provides quite a contrast to these images. He is personified as a "terrific electric storm"; he is the "God of Lightning and Thunder" and of blazing, apocalyptic sunsets. Shannon's descriptions recall the Old Testament God of overwhelming majesty and righteous wrath. And although this is the kind of God he really believes in, he overtly rejects the idea by arguing that his God is in no way interested in punishment or suffering.

The key term in Shannon's theology is "oblivious"; when he points out the nearing thunderstorm to Hannah, he says, "That's him! There he is now! . . . His oblivious majesty" (p. 305). According to Shannon traditional theologies see suffering as purposely sanctioned by God as an opportunity for men to atone for their sins and rise to him, but Shannon feels that suffering is simply the result of the world's "faults in construction." They are architectural imperfections, God's accidents, and men do suffer because of them; but no divine plan lies behind the misery. To claim design, as Western theologies do, says Shannon, makes God either a cruel child or a sadist; Shannon refuses to conduct services for such a God. The logic connecting human degradation and divine majesty is somewhat tenuous. Apparently Shannon's twisted thinking runs along these lines: God is awesome, powerful, majestic (this idea is a product of his childhood, and he never seems to question it; it is a given). But a God who is all these things could not possibly be aware of man's extreme misery and let it continue to exist; therefore God must be unaware of it. Thus, the more examples of suffering Shannon can collect, the more he is demonstrating that God is oblivious, and consequently the more he is proving God's majesty.

Williams takes the explanations of Shannon's crack-up a step further in the third act, when Maxine uncovers the psychically damaging events that eventually led to the eruption of Shannon's double offense. She recounts to Shannon, surely for the audience's sake rather than his, what she once heard him telling her deceased husband. His problems supposedly began when his mother caught him masturbating; after spanking him she said his behavior made God even angrier than it made her and that if she did not punish him, God would, and much more severely. Maxine continues, "You said you loved God and Mama and so you quit it to please them, but it was your secret pleasure and you harbored a secret resentment against Mama and God for making you give it up. And so you got back at God by preaching atheistical sermons and you got back at Mama by starting to lay young girls" (p. 329). A simplistic psychological explanation, to be sure, but one that Williams apparently intends us to take seriously, for none of the characters or Shannon's actions contradict it. On the contrary, his theology and behavior are perfectly in tune with it. It reveals, for example, the origin of his belief that God is awesome, threatening, and by extension, majestic; this is his adult version of his mother's warning that God was angry and ready to punish him severely. It also explains why fornication is always linked with heresy. He was told that he would have to suffer for his sexual pleasure; thus, to ward off the punishment he has earned whenever he indulges his sexual desire, he must immediately assert that God is actually oblivious to mankind. Sex becomes safe if he can deny his mother's idea of God, so he tries to collect evidence for this denial.

Maxine's comments also explain the sudden, powerful emergence of his sexuality that occurred that day on the rectory floor. Fear of punishment caused the young Shannon to repress his sexual nature; the consequences of his repression are the same as those suffered by other Williams characters. Driven underground for whatever reason, sexual urges grow more powerful and more threatening. The vicious circle in which repression causes a strengthening of the desire repressed, which in turn causes renewed effort to repress, can end only disastrously when desire breaks through its restraints. By this time it has grown so powerful that it is virtually uncontrollable and blasts away the character's former life. This pattern appears in the lives of Blanche in *Streetcar* and Alma in *Summer and Smoke*. The dangerous energy that repressed desire takes on is manifest in Stanley Kowalski and John Buchanan, menacing sexual supermen who are really the women's sexual alter egos. Since that first incident, Shannon has learned what Blanche and Alma learned. Initially he was able to smother his sexual nature so thoroughly that he became not only a minister of the God who opposed his sensual pleasure; he also became what he calls "the goddamnedest prig" imaginable.

Desire burst free while he was kneeling with the Sunday school teacher and has remained irrepressible ever since. His continual seductions are not so much a way of getting back at his mother, as Maxine suggests; they are something he is driven to, in spite of his conscious reluctance, by his voracious sexual appetite.

And he obviously has a great deal of reluctance. I have said that his initial trauma explains Shannon's wanting to make God oblivious and unvengeful, but it should be clear by now that all his efforts in this direction are a case of his protesting too much. Shannon is afraid that God is full of righteous wrath, and naturally he is terrified about what his uncontrollable passion will bring down upon him. His panic and anxiety are very understandable in this light. No doubt even his feeble efforts to avoid God's wrath by preaching about a different kind of God aggravate his guilt and fear—he is aware rebellion will not escape notice or punishment.

There is plenty of evidence that Shannon still believes in the God he pretends to dismiss. We have his latest lover's word that he continues to feel as guilty about sex as he did after his first transgression: "I remember that after making love to me," Charlotte tells him, "you hit me, . . . you struck me in the face, and you twisted my arm to make me kneel on the floor and pray with you for forgiveness" (p. 298). An oblivious God would hardly be interested in forgiveness. Shannon's continuing fantasy that he will write to his former bishop and be reinstated as a minister suggests how ineffectual his efforts have been to break away from the God his mother warned him about. He dreams of giving up his heretical and sexual offenses and being forgiven by one of God's agents. In effect, he wants to become a good boy again.

Shannon's parody of Christ's crucifixion is the most blatant evidence of his failure to get free from this God. He is so far from truly believing that God is oblivious to suffering and atonement that he plays at being God's son. In the third act when he has finally cracked up, Maxine has him tied in a hammock to keep him from drowning himself. He struggles melodramatically against the rope, and Hannah, a quick-sketch artist who specializes in accurate psychological portraits, accuses him of being a perverse Christ figure engaged in a self-indulgent passion play: "There's something almost voluptuous in the way that you twist and groan in that hammock—no nails, no blood, no death. Isn't that a comparatively comfortable, almost voluptuous kind of crucifixion to suffer for the guilt of the world, Mr. Shannon?" (p. 344). How useless all his evidence has been. Afraid of being punished for his sins, he tries to stave off God's wrath by "suffering" like Christ, to atone for his offenses. Ironically, he is never totally free from either his dread of God or his sensual nature; each aspect of his personality corrodes the other. His guilt and fear keep him from ever enjoying sex fully, and his sexual instincts manage to corrupt his attempts to suffer for his sins since he derives sensual pleasure even from his suffering.

Caught between his sexual drives and his religious fears, between his need to deny God and his yearning for forgiveness, Shannon can find momentary relief from this tension, from his "spook," only in periodic crack-ups. During such times he loses control of himself and can no longer be held accountable for his sins.

Williams captures Shannon's predicament brilliantly in a brief and wordless scene in act three, after Shannon has lost the last vestiges of control over his touring party. He stands onstage wearing a few pieces of his ministerial garb; suddenly, he "with an animal outcry begins to pull at the chain suspending the gold cross about his neck" (p. 340). He jerks savagely back and forth on it, slashing himself. His actions illustrate how he is tied to his warped theology, just as the iguana is tied to the stake. He shows how his religious beliefs make him suffer, how his efforts to free himself from them are useless and only make him suffer the more. And he shows how willingly he punishes himself.

This masochistic pantomime ends in a very significant way, and this is where *Iguana* begins to differ from Williams' prior works. Hannah rushes over to help him and soon frees him from his chain and his self-laceration. During the rest of the play, she will accomplish in actuality what she does here symbolically—she frees him from his obsessive, self-destructive notions so that he can move completely out of the previous pattern of his life, find a measure of peace, and establish a healthy sexual relationship. To underline Hannah's triumph, at the end of the play Williams has Shannon give his cross and chain to her.

Hannah begins her therapy by pointing out to him how self-indulgent and voluptuous his struggles actually are. Then she focuses on the problem of his miserable loneliness. He has been so obsessed with himself and his fears, she tells him, that he hasn't been able to see that people might help him. Even his sexual escapades have been cold and lonely, she says, and isolate rather than connect him with others. Her initial advice echoes Big Mama's plea in *Cat*: "we just got to love each other an' stay together" (III, 157). Hannah tells Shannon he needs to find relief in "Broken gates between people so they can reach each other, even if it's just for one night only . . . communication . . . A little understanding exchanged between them, a wanting to help each other through nights like this" (IV, p. 352). People must struggle to break through the walls that keep them apart and come together, even if only momentarily, with understanding, kindness, and sympathy. Hannah reinforces her advice by becoming an example of what she is talking about. She reaches out to him with compassion and respect. And her advice and example are very effective; he is finally able to put aside his obsessions and establish a healthy connection with another human being, Maxine.

Hannah also makes two other important suggestions. She tells him he must learn simply to endure the tension and terror that are part of his life. Later she advises him to go beyond endurance to acceptance; after recounting the two bizarre incidents that comprise her "lovelife," she tells him "the moral is Oriental. Accept whatever situation you cannot improve" (p. 363). It's no accident that "the moral is Oriental" for the play creates a definite contrast between East and West, in which the Eastern attitudes of stoicism and fatalism are offered as a positive alternative to the Western preoccupations with guilt and suffering.

Iguana conveys the superiority of East over West in a number of ways. For example, near the end of the play Hannah tells Shannon how moved she was by the peaceful deaths of the poor in Shanghai: their "eyes looked up with their last dim life left in them as clear as the stars in the Southern Cross. . . . Nothing I've ever seen has seemed as beautiful to me" (p. 356). In this respect, Nonno's calm resignation before death is "Oriental," as Hannah makes clear, and is in stark contrast to the terror and hysteria the approach of death usually evokes in Williams' characters. The East-West theme is also established visually. Close to the beginning of the third act Hannah puts on a Japanese Kabuki robe, so that when she later manages to free Shannon from his cross and chain her exotic Eastern attire makes her look a world apart from the neurotic minister. She wears the robe throughout the act, reminding us of the source of her compassionate advice.

The Fahrenkopfs provide an even more vivid contrast to the Oriental Hannah. In their Rubensesque proportions and Wagnerian exuberance they represent the culmination of Western civilization. Their boisterousness and frenetic activity counterpoint Hannah's demeanor, and as Nazis they epitomize the cruelty and violence of the Western world.

Williams even manages to have Maxine reinforce the theme—in her characteristically crude way. Early in the third act, in an effort to soothe Shannon's nerves, she tells him her cook's philosophy of life, one she appears to share: "The Chinaman in the kitchen says, 'No sweat.' . . . 'No sweat.' . . . All the Chinese philosophy in three words, 'Mei yoo guanchi'—which is Chinese for 'No sweat'" (p. 330). And at the very end of the play, in a surprising transformation, Maxine *becomes* Oriental; in a stage direction Williams writes: "It is apparent that the night's progress has mellowed her spirit: her face wears a faint smile which is suggestive of those cool, impersonal all-comprehending smiles on the carved heads of Egyptian or Oriental deities" (p. 373). No doubt this metamorphosis is a major reason Shannon can accept her at the climax of the play.

This climax sets *Iguana* apart from Williams' other serious works. Shannon survives. He attains some measure of peace. He is neither returning to the ministry nor continuing his rebellion against it and his mother. Instead, he has been led beside the "still waters" of the Costa Verde Hotel. Much more than this, he enters what is apparently a healthy sexual relationship. Other Williams characters have found momentary stays against despair in brief, casual encounters with strangers, but Shannon seems to be entering into something more lasting with Maxine. His decision to stay with her fulfills both parts of Hannah's advice: he is finally reaching outside of himself, and he has decided to accept Maxine and his present situation. He leaves the play chuckling happily, with Maxine "half leading half supporting him" (p. 374). Anyone familiar with the bulk of Williams' work can appreciate how unusual, how positive this description of their relationship is.

Shannon's loosing the iguana at the end of the play is obviously a symbol of the optimistic resolutions that are simultaneously occurring. The lizard is set free at the same time Nonno is set free from his poem and his life, at the same time Hannah is unburdened of her dying grandfather, and at the same time Shannon escapes from his God, his mother, and his loneliness.

Unfortunately, the ending isn't as believable as it is formally pleasing and optimistic. Even according to the overt level of the drama, the ending sounds suspiciously like the product of wishful thinking. For one thing, it comes rather suddenly and unexpectedly; an hour's exposure to human compassion, a cup of poppy tea, and a bit of Oriental wisdom hardly seem sufficient to eradicate habits and attitudes hardened over the past ten years. For another, the advice Hannah gives him doesn't really speak to the main sources of his problems: terrible guilt, fear of God, and an overpowering sex drive. The two characters never mention these things, much less work through them during their conversation. Hannah could conceivably convince him that human contact is worthwhile, but she never points out or tells him how to combat those feelings that have made human contact so difficult for him. The optimistic conclusion simply ignores the psychological portrait Williams works out so carefully during the course of the play.

And if the ending isn't entirely convincing on the overt level, it is completely incompatible with some less explicit, subterranean elements which work like an undertow to suck the mood of the play back into bleakness and despair. The difference between acceptance and endurance is a key to the nature of the shadow side of the play. Acceptance is a more positive notion. A person is able to accept an undesirable situation by putting aside his own needs or expectations and seeing beyond the negative aspects to find something positive he can embrace. Endurance is more pessimistic. It implies that the unsatisfactory situation remains exactly as it seems—painful, destructive, threatening, or whatever. Nothing redeeming is to be found in it. Maggie in *Cat* provides an example of this notion. Tense and frustrated by her husband's physical and emotional rejection of her, she wonders what victory a person who feels like "a cat on a hot tin roof" can achieve; she decides, "Just staying on it, I guess, as long as she can . . ." (III, 31). Endurance implies that the roof never cools down; the cat merely grins fiercely and bears it. This is the implication of Hannah's remarks when she tells Shannon she showed her own spook "that I could endure him and I made him respect my endurance." Shannon asks how and she replies, "Just by, just by . . . enduring" (p. 353). Though she will later speak of *acceptance*, much in the play makes this concept out of the question for Shannon and indicates he is in a situation he can barely endure.

In a way, we have Williams' own word for this point. In an interview during the rehearsals for *Iguana* he said the theme of the play is "how to live beyond despair and still live" (Funke and Booth, p. 72). The context makes clear that *beyond* means not *without* but *in a state worse than* (despair). Many elements of the play itself reinforce this feeling of utter bleakness. Nonno's poem, his best, coming as it does at the climax, is a poetic commentary on what the play is about. Implicit pessimism in the first stanza is emphasized because the penultimate stanza is almost identical:

> How calmly does the orange branch
> Observe the sky begin to blanch
> Without a cry, without a prayer,
> With no betrayal of despair (p. 371).

The implication is clearly that there is a great deal of despair—however, the tree heroically refuses to give any sign of it, much as Hannah tries to keep hers under control with her deep breathing.

But what is it that can only be endured, that is the cause of this vast despair? The poem suggests initially that it is death, or the ageing or ripening accompanying it. But the fourth stanza carries a much more important idea. According to the poem, when the fruit grows ripe it falls to the earth where it must suffer

> An intercourse not well designed
> For beings of a golden kind
> Whose native green must arch above
> The earth's obscene, corrupting love.

This is an accurate description of the basic dilemma of most of Williams' major characters: they are sensitive idealists forced to indulge in sexual activity, which they find corrosive and obscene. The assumption that sex is disgusting and threatening is the real motive for Shannon's behavior; in fact, the play itself seems to foster the same feelings about sex. It is this underlying fear that makes Shannon's final situation at best only endurable.

What makes this attitude hard for the audience or reader to catch is that it is never explicitly discussed by any of the characters, much less identified as the basis of Shannon's problems. As we've seen, all three main characters offer a variety of other plausible explanations, and these keep us from seeing this one clearly. It is a very real part of the play, nonetheless, and makes itself felt in a number of ways. We sense, for example, that much more than either guilt or rebellion accounts for Shannon's sexual behavior. At the end of the play he speaks of "Always seducing a lady or two, or three or four or five ladies in the party, but really ravaging her first by pointing out to her the—what?—horrors? Yes, horrors!—of the tropical country being conducted a tour through" (p. 369). It is as if for a select few the last stop on his repulsive itinerary is his own bedroom. Sex for him is on a par with the other ravaging horrors he subjects himself and his tours to.

His penchant for the very youngest ladies suggests that he is afraid of more mature women. His attitude toward Maxine reinforces this idea and reveals his feelings of disgust as well. Whenever she makes sexual advances, he draws away vehemently, uncomfortably, or cruelly. At the beginning of the play, he disgustedly tells her she looks as if she's "been having it" and then pleads with her to button up her blouse so she will look decent. Later he suggests she has turned into a pig. At another point he says she is "bigger than life and twice as unnatural" (p. 270). His fear of her is apparent in his calling her a "bright widow spider" (p. 317), referring to an insect that proverbially devours her mate after intercourse. The audience itself tends to see her in much the same way. Nothing whatever in the play suggests that Shannon is incorrect about her, that his feelings are a product of his demented imagination. On the contrary, the playwright seems at pains to validate this vision of Maxine. In a stage direction at the beginning she is described as "rapaciously lusty" (p. 255). We are quickly made aware to what excess her sexual appetite runs—she has hired not one but two young Mexicans to serve her desires. Williams' description of her constantly recurring laugh emphasizes her animallike nature: "*Maxine* always laughs with a single harsh, loud bark, opening her mouth like a seal expecting a fish to be thrown to it" (p. 255). Throughout the play she is coarse and suggestive, and at one point she tells Shannon that her interest in him is primarily sexual: "I know the difference between loving someone and just sleeping with someone—even I know about that. We've both reached a point where we've got to settle for something that works for us in our lives—even if it isn't on the highest kind of level" (p. 329). Even her name, Maxine Faulk, is unattractive: her first name suggests that she is manlike, aggressive, and her last name is a crude pun. Given all this, the audience has little chance of regarding her in a way fundamentally different from Shannon's.

The central symbol of the play also points up the frightening nature of Maxine's desires. The iguana scrambling frantically at the end of its rope represents all the main characters, but it has a special affinity with Shannon. Not by coincidence is it supposed to become Maxine's dinner—its intended fate reinforces Shannon's fears that she will devour him, too. He may free the lizard at the end of the play, but he himself is tied more closely than ever to the "bright widow spider." The director of the original Broadway production must have sensed how inappropriate optimism is in the conclusion, for when Shannon returned to the stage after cutting the iguana loose, he was wearing the rope around his own neck (see Adler, "Night," p. 63).

No wonder, then, that Shannon feels threatened by Maxine, this female version of Big Daddy Pollitt. The wonder is that at the end of the play she can abruptly change, somehow, somewhere offstage, into a mellow Oriental goddess. To be believable such a radical transformation requires much more than the stage-direction and the few lines of dialogue Williams supplies. As it stands, the ending comes as quite a jolt. A character we have been forced to see as vulgar, aggressive, and menacing suddenly acquires alluringly soft edges. More than this, throughout the play Shannon has drawn away from the rapacious widow in apprehension, an apprehension the play helps the audience to share; now in a bizarre about-face he willingly agrees to live with her. Blanche DuBois might as easily become more receptive to the sexual overtures of a Stanley who has become suddenly more gentle and solicitous. (The arrangement Shannon and Maxine come to at the very end makes the conclusion even more outrageous. He agrees not only to live with Maxine but also to cater to the sexual needs of the female guests of the hotel. Incredibly, he "chuckles happily" at the thought—this from a man who previously has been obsessively guilty about, disgusted by, and terrified of sex. Their interchange—at least his response—violates the seriousness of the play and of Shannon's problems. This interchange ought to be dismissed simply as a momentary lapse, or as one of the occasions on which the playwright falls victim to his popular reputation of being obscene and shocking.)

Even Hannah, the most positive and sympathetic of the main characters, contributes to the underlying feeling that sex is dangerous or dirty. In stage directions, Williams describes her as appearing "androgynous" (p. 266) and as having "a fastidiousness, a reluctance, toward intimate physical contact" (p. 348), a description made concrete when she hesitates to touch Shannon to find his cigarettes. She admits to Shannon that sex is definitely not a part of the "broken gates" between people that she sees as an antidote to loneliness. She has clearly never accepted or enjoyed her own sexuality. Her lovelife consists of two pathetic incidents in which she was hardly a willing participant and which, in spite of her protest to the contrary, add to the suspicion that sex is degrading. The only lasting relationship she has formed is the very safe, asexual one with her grandfather. She quickly and surely squelches Shannon's suggestion that the two of them travel together, even after they have grown close through their compassionate nighttime exchange. There is obviously a very definite boundary to her willingness to communicate and share: it comes to a complete halt this side of the physical. In effect, Hannah creates in the audience the impression that withdrawing from sex is positive or healthy, since we tend to see all the behavior of an admirable character as admirable, unless something indicates we should feel otherwise. And nothing in this play indicates that her sexual reluctance is a problem.

Hannah's attitude, however, adds to the improbability of Shannon's final decision. Why would his feelings toward the sexually voracious Maxine turn around after a conversation with this sexless spinster? In fact, it seems likely that a major reason he is able to communicate with Hannah to any degree is that she *is* sexless; since she does not arouse his desires, he does not have to be afraid of her. In this regard *Iguana* reflects a pattern typical of Williams' works:

a character can offer or find either love or sex, but not both. The underlying attitude toward sex explains why this dichotomy occurs: love is an ideal, something only "beings of a golden kind" can attain; sex is obscene and corrupting and so must be kept separate from the ideal. Thus Hannah can give Shannon a momentary glimpse of what it means to love only by being asexual; and Maxine's sexual drives keep her from being able to offer him real love.

A glance at the play as a whole shows how everyone in it contributes to the feeling that human desire is obscene and fearful. Not a single sexually healthy character appears; no figure can define for the others (or for the audience) what sexual normalcy is, or give any hope that such a state can even be attained. (Where in any of Williams' work is such a figure?) Miss Fellowes is more than a strident castrating woman who reduces Shannon to feebly demonstrating his manhood by urinating on the luggage; she is a butch lesbian. Her protégée, Charlotte Goodall, flings herself hysterically, masochistically at Shannon "like a teen-age Medea" (p. 294). Both women make celibacy attractive. The Fahrenkopfs may be the most telling of all. No one could be more exuberantly physical and sexual than these caricatures who charge in and out of the drama bulging out of their scant swimming suits, clutching at one another, swilling beer, and booming out marching songs. It is no accident that these gross honeymooners are also part of the most monstrous political machine in Western civilization. The most overtly sexual characters, they are also the most grotesque, dangerous, and genuinely obscene.

Clearly, then, some less explicit elements in *Iguana* make its optimistic conclusion untenable. Considering the subterranean aspects of the play, Shannon's staying with Maxine means he is putting himself in the maw of a devouring monster. Obviously he cannot do so optimistically or happily. In effect, the different levels of the play pull the audience in opposite directions, an uncomfortable feeling created even in Williams' best works. *Cat* is another example. Overtly, the play demonstrates that Brick's extreme idealism, his refusal to grow up or old, is unhealthy and damaging, presaging death rather than life. But the abundant animal imagery and the behavior of the other characters graphically support his attitude toward reality and sex: human beings are mean, greedy, pathetic, cruel, and beastlike, and when they make love they are no different from, or better than, "two cats on a—fence humping" (III, 123). As in *Iguana* we are made to think one way and feel another.

What is usually at the heart of the internal conflict in Williams' works is a disgust with and terrible fear of the sexual act. As I mentioned at the outset, these ideas are not always easy to discern. They are contrary to his general reputation as a sexual libertine, in his life and works; and though his plays are obviously about sex and violence, critics and reviewers usually do not recognize that sex itself, not the brutal world, causes the violence. The fundamental rejection of sexuality is hard to see also because sex usually is made to bear a heavy and confusing burden. A character may behave at various times as if sex is an immensely pleasurable activity, an assertion of life in the face of death, a means of staying young, a degrading or bestial act, a source of guilt, and a means of expiating this guilt. Add to them the feeling that sex is dangerous and obscene, a feeling that is the more insidious because it is not explicit, and the works add up to a welter of confusion about how to regard human sexuality. It is not as if sex is presented as a complex phenomenon; rather, the characters act, at successive moments, as if one particular attitude is true and all the others are nonexistent. The plays themselves reinforce this problem by providing nothing or no one to point out that at these moments the characters are confused, incorrect, or self-contradictory.

Iguana may look like a new kind of play for Williams, but it is not. What makes it more of the same, despite its surface optimism, are the feelings about sex that emerge from the subterranean world of the play. Early in his career Williams captured vividly the nature of these feelings in the short story "Desire and the Black Masseur." It is a grotesque and violent tale of a helpless little man who puts himself in the hands of a huge black man. The masseur beats him repeatedly and cruelly and at the climax of the story, after beating him to death, eats him. Desire, the story suggests, *is* the black masseur, is a gigantic dark force that batters human beings and finally devours them. *The Night of the Iguana* shows that thirteen years after the publication of the story, this fear of sex is still a part of Williams' work and undermines whatever positive values the playwright consciously wishes to attribute to human relations.

The Artist against the Reality in the Plays of Tennessee Williams

GEORGE NIESEN

What can be Created Can be Destroyed.
(William Blake, "The Laocoön")

From Val in *Battle of Angels* (1940) or the Writer in *The Long Goodbye* (1940) to the two players in search of an author, a cast, and an audience in *The Two-Character Play* (1976), Tennessee Williams has indulged his penchant for creating in his plays characters who are artists of one sort or another. Not all his plays feature such characters, but most of the plays include someone in the cast with the qualities if not the title of an artist. In each case the figure is sensitive, creative, and, paradoxically, destructive. He is sensitive to time, to his own feelings, and to others and their feelings. He is generally so sensitive, in fact, that he cannot function well in the real world. He creates, of course. The artist attempts to give some kind of meaning to life and death. He reaches for the unobtainable and often fashions an idealistic fiction to replace a frustrating reality. Finally and surprisingly, the artist is invariably associated with destruction, either his own or that of someone close to him. *In the early plays his sensitivity usually leads to his death. In the later plays he is an "angel of death."*

However, the artist never withdraws from his world in the face of his problems—which may help to explain Williams' popularity. The artist never appears in the ivory tower, but is instead tested in the crucible of the reality of the play—a reality which, with its brutality and cruelty, and despite its strangeness and grotesqueness, is created

81

carefully enough that it is acceptable and believable to the audience. The result is standard dramatic conflict with strong social content. As Nathan A. Scott (*The Broken Center*) puts it, "the self achieves definition only as it pits itself against the hard, recalcitrant stuff of social and political reality" (p. 225). Clearly Williams is telling his audience something about their world and the problems that a sensitive individual faces in dealing with it (cf. both Weales and Skloot).

Williams' ideas are most strikingly stated in *Suddenly Last Summer* (1958) which dramatizes the entire world view of the dead poet. Sebastian's reactions to social and human pressures reveal the playwright's most significant delineation of the artist figure, even though the artist himself never appears. Furthermore the play is a restatement of nearly all Williams has said about art and the artist in his earlier plays. In none of Williams' plays is the designing influence of an artist so strong, so oppressive, in fact, as is Sebastian's in *Suddenly*. The poet or creator who refuses to "correct a human situation" or to "interfere in any way," nevertheless exerts, even when dead, a profound control over the lives of the members of his family.

The artistic influence for Williams, then, in *Suddenly* and in the earlier plays, is destructive rather than creative. Sebastian sees horror beside beauty wherever he turns. The God he sees in the caviar-colored beach and the equally black sky, for example, is the destroyer as well as the creator of the world. The lush hothouse plants suggest "organs of a body, torn out, still glistening with undried blood" (III, 349). His mother and procurer, Violet, loses her beauty to a disfiguring stroke. Sebastian's horrible death may mean life to the starving urchins who devour him. In any case the artist (who is frequently a Christ or other sacrificial figure) cannot relate the horror to the beauty and can do little more than imbue an inevitable death with some semblance of meaning. He does not create life. Rather, he makes death stand for something.

Suddenly also marks a major turning point for Williams, for in the plays following *Suddenly* he assumes a different view of existence, one in which his characters generally opt for survival. Although they are often in some way impotent (as with the destructive nature of creators, impotence is also a paradoxical trait for the supposedly productive character), they manage somehow to come to grips with their world and function well enough in it to remain alive at least. Of course a great, dramatic death, and usually even a pathetic one, is inherently more interesting dramatically than survival, no matter how great the struggle, and Williams' earlier plays have been more successful on stage than the later ones. Furthermore, as Williams turned his thoughts after *Suddenly* to a new appreciation of life, he had to learn a new dramatic mode and has not again reached his former dramatic heights. With *The Two-Character Play*, however, Williams has finally achieved a new intellectual statement which ranks with that of *Suddenly*. *The Two-Character Play* is a cri de coeur, a plea for survival and for a place to be somebody, a play which, despite its dramatic failings, clearly delineates the problems the artist faces in trying to survive in a hostile environment.

Tennessee Williams is telling us all how to survive. He insists that both horror and beauty surround us and that we must learn how to relate to them. He also sees that it is impossible to reconcile them and that the artist, who must create beauty and still face the horror, is forever in an untenable bind. That bind is my subject; and to determine the qualities that define the Williams artist and discover the nature of the reality with which the artist must deal, I will examine the plays of the Williams canon. In addition I will analyze the two phases of Williams' career which *Suddenly Last Summer* and *The Two-Character Play* represent especially well. Both plays focus sharply on the sensitive artist, yet they offer two distinct answers to the question of the artist's relationship to an insensitive society. In the early plays the artist cannot deal with his reality, except by escaping it, usually through death. In the later plays the artist endures the impossible bind. He is never reconciled, certainly, but he survives. In neither case can the artist create in the traditional manner, and in either case he is more or less destructive. Williams' world view is indeed bleak.

Williams' early plays show a wide range of destructive tendencies, from a simple denial of the real and the substitution of fiction—to holocaust. *The Glass Menagerie* (1945) and both Broadway and Hollywood versions (see Sacksteder) of *Cat on a Hot Tin Roof* (1955) represent Williams' successful resolution of his soft line, wherein the protagonist survives and presumably goes on to create something from the ruins of his past. *Battle of Angels* outlines Williams' hard line—wherein the protagonist cannot survive—which has bedeviled Williams ever since. In any case, however, little in the plays is creative or constructive.

The Long Goodbye is an early one act version of *The Glass Menagerie*, in which Joe, a young writer, talks to Silva and watches the moving men empty his flat of its furniture. In flashbacks Joe's sister enters three times and his mother once. Toward the end Joe says, "You're saying goodbye all the time, every minute you live. Because that's what life is, just a long, long goodbye! To one thing after another! Till you get to the last one, Silva, and that's—goodbye to yourself!" (*27 Wagons*, p. 178).

Very near the beginning Joe tells Silva that he is leaving. "All of this here is dead for me. The goldfish is dead. I forgot to feed it. . . . I shouldn't have left the bowl setting right here in the sun. It probably cooked the poor bastard" (p. 163). A short time later Joe and Silva watch the movers carry out the bed: "JOE: Mother died on it. SILVA: Yeah? She went pretty quick for cancer. Most of 'em hang on longer an' suffer a hell of a lot. JOE: She killed herself. I found the empty bottle that morning in a waste-basket. It wasn't the pain, it was the doctor an' hospital bills that she was scared of. She wanted us to have the insurance" (p. 165). Joe calls his sister Myra a whore on her third appearance and she leaves, saying "they'll move every stick a furniture out a this place before they do you!" (p. 177). The father disappeared years before, "tired of living a regular middle-class life" (p. 177). Finally the movers remove the last stick of furniture and a child in the background cries "olly—olly—oxen-free!" (p. 179), which suggests Joe's new freedom now that he has shed his family and his past.

The Glass Menagerie is a memory play, soft in tone, which nevertheless uses both the family and the destructive overtones of *The Long Goodbye*. The individual members of the family are totally different in the long play—more sympathetic certainly—but retain the basic interpersonal relationships and individual drives of their counterparts in the early sketch.

Laura, the fragile figurine of *The Glass Menagerie*, is a much revised Myra, delicate and pitiable. The gentleman caller who provides "the climax of her secret life" (I, 210) also, by announcing his engagement, snuffs out "The holy candles in the altar of Laura's face" (p. 230). Amanda, the mother, is no longer the passive victim of *The Long Goodbye* but a dictatorial force who plans either marriage or a business career for Laura (p. 157) and who insists that Tom not "jeopardize" a secure job he detests (p. 163). The father, much as in the shorter play, "was a telephone man who fell in love with long distances . . . and skipped the light fantastic out of town" (p. 145).

Tom, however, a poet who eventually is fired for writing a poem on the lid of a shoe box, is the artist character who must escape the reality of his existence (cf. King). He finds some solace in the fantasy world of movies but he is still ensnared by the responsibilities which his father abandoned—a dominant, security conscious mother and a weak, dependent sister. Tom has "no single thing" (p. 161) he can call his own. He is not "in love with the Continental Shoemakers" (p. 163). He is afraid of getting himself nailed into a coffin (p. 167), of finding himself trapped by a dismal life.

When the gentleman caller arrives, though, we learn that Tom is "waking up. . . . The signs are interior" (p. 200). He has paid his Union of Merchant Seamen dues with the light bill money. Shortly afterward, of course, the lights go out—in the house, in Laura's face, in Amanda's life. Amanda berates Tom for not knowing of the gentleman caller's engagement. When Tom protests that "The warehouse is where I work, not where I know things about people," Amanda replies, "You don't know things anywhere! You live in a dream; you manufacture illusions!" (p. 235). Tom then "smashes his glass," which causes Laura to scream out, and he goes off to the illusory world of the movies, a world which is his only antidote to the reality of the play. Eventually Tom goes even further than the movies and, like his father before him, abandons his family in his search for self. Amanda is easy enough to leave, but Laura continues to haunt him. Since Tom is not about to return to the stifling world of St. Louis tenements, however, his only escape from Laura is through mindless activity, drink, the movies or strangers, through whatever can blow out her candles (p. 237) and destroy his image of her.

A look back at *The Long Goodbye* clarifies Tom's situation and the destructive nature of his actions. Joe, like Tom, is trapped, though less by responsibility than by an inability to leave. Joe's release comes only with the dissolution of the family and all mementos of it (from the bed the mother died on to the last stick of furniture), only after everything in the home is dead, including the goldfish which he inadvertently destroys. The mother kills herself for the sake of Joe and his dreams. He drives his sister away. Joe is in no way directly responsible for his family's fate, yet his freedom is contingent on its death.

Tom, like Joe, represents a destructive force, though more subtly. Tom's final lines, for example, indicate that he is trying to erase Laura and her candles from his memory. Laura is identified with light—her school yearbook is *The Torch*, "she is like a piece of translucent glass touched by light" (p. 191)—yet an important metaphor in the play is that of snuffing out her candles. If the gentleman caller arrives at the climax of her life, her future looks dark. Tom's departure at the end of the play, when he smashes his glass and causes Laura to scream, recalls his earlier attempted departure when, after calling Amanda an "ugly . . . old—*witch*," he rips off his coat and throws it across the room, shattering some of Laura's glass menagerie. She "cries out as if wounded" (p. 164). Since Laura is closely identified with her menagerie, and since she cries out when glass is broken (her unicorn is only altered, not destroyed, and Jim's clumsiness elicits no scream), I see in Tom's thoughts and actions an attempt (perhaps conscious, perhaps not) to destroy her. On Tom's command, Laura blows out her gentle candles to end the play.

Tom cannot abandon Laura without destroying her, however, for they are kindred spirits. They both "live in a dream" which is for them an omnipresent world. Tom has no such attachment to Amanda and can leave her freely. He destroys some of her hopes and dreams, he shatters her dictates, but she remains, finally, with her "dignity and tragic beauty" (p. 236).

Joe and Tom, in their attempts to become artists and to fulfill themselves, must break away from their environments and families. Like the phoenix, they must create from the ashes of the past they have destroyed.

Presumably Joe and Tom, who escape with psychic wounds and intact bodies, will become artists. Valentine Xavier of *Battle of*

Angels (Williams' early hard line play) and *Orpheus Descending* (1957) fares far less well.

In both plays Val, a young, virile artist, enters the Hell of the small southern town on the note of a Choctaw cry. He becomes involved with two women who are in many respects similar to the mother and the sister in each of the plays discussed above. He ends up in a situation analogous to Tom's and Joe's but far grimmer.

Val is searching for something. He thinks it is love and he teaches "love" to the Cajun girl but, as he says, "afterwards I wasn't sure that was it, but from that time the question wasn't much plainer than the answer. . . . I went to New Orleans in this snakeskin jacket. . . . I learned that I had something to sell besides snakeskins and other wild things' skins I caught on the bayou. I was corrupted! That's the answer" (III, 273).

Lady (Myra in *Battle*) knows that "corruption ain't the answer" (p. 273). In act one she says to Val, "I'm not interested in your perfect functions, in fact you don't interest me no more than the air that you stand in" (p. 266)—air which she must breathe to remain alive. Yet a short time later Lady tries to buy life from Val. "NO, NO, DON'T GO . . . I NEED YOU! ! ! TO LIVE. . . . TO GO ON LIVING! ! !" (p. 305). She offers him a room that will cost him nothing. She threatens to withhold money. "If you try to walk out on me, now, tonight, without notice!— You're going to get just nothing! A great big zero" (p. 331). She offers him money. "Everything in this rotten store is yours, not just your pay, but everything Death's scraped together down here!—but Death has got to die before we can go" (p. 333). Val takes the first bribe and stays at the store, collecting his "commissions" (p. 310) and bringing life and subsequent death to Lady.

After the sheriff tells him to leave town, Val can very nearly resist Lady's offers. When he learns she is pregnant, however, he looks back once, and Jabe, her dying husband (who killed her father), kills her. Orpheus himself must die, of course, and he does at the hands of a lynch mob after Jabe accuses him of murdering Lady.

The Carol of *Orpheus* is quite different from the Cassandra of *Battle*. Cassandra clutches passionately for Val, almost as strongly as Myra. Val is torn between the two women. But Carol is less developed as a character and less central to much of the action. After

Val is killed, Cassandra drives into the river, while Carol only suggests suicide, "so the fugitive kind can always follow their kind" (p. 341). Some of their traits are identical, however. They both have a translucent "fugitive beauty" (p. 236). They are both "lewd vagrants" (p. 252) who want to live but die instead. They remind one of Laura with their "transparence," their fragility and lonesomeness —"The act of lovemaking is almost unbearably painful, and yet, of course, I do bear it, because to be not alone, even for a few moments, is worth the pain and the danger" (p. 282)—and their pathetic sterility: "I'm not built for childbearing" (p. 282).

And Lady is like Amanda in some respects. Both are burdened with metaphorically dead husbands. Both grasp for a type of security embodied in a young male figure. Each reaches for the memory of a romantic past, Amanda in receiving the new gentleman caller and Lady by redecorating the confectionery in the style of her father's wine garden.

Val, like Tom, is an artist who finds himself a slave to his environment and its women. In Williams' more violent plays, though, the definition of the environment is much more profound than in *The Glass Menagerie*. Val cannot simply escape the environment of the play, as Tom does, for he has found in his wanderings that corruption *is* the answer, everywhere. Lady has "sold" herself (p. 285) and she tries to buy Val. Carol has become a "lewd vagrant." Each character is a synthesis of life and death—Lady conceives and then dies because of it, Carol goes to the Cypress Hill cemetery to hear her ancestors say "live," and Val himself becomes the true "angel of death" who brings life and hope to Lady and Carol just before he brings them destruction. Even basic life and death is a corruption, however, and the artist's answer, for which Val has looked so long, is a phoenixlike self-destructive purification by fire. To achieve his escape he too must first be instrumental in the destruction of those to whom he is tied.

Williams' notions of fire, destruction and purification are obvious in the early one act *Auto-Da-Fé* and appear again in *I Rise in Flame, Cried the Phoenix* (1951), where the symbolism of light, heat, gold, fire, the phoenix, and the sun is almost overbearing. D. H. Lawrence is the artist hero who insists "there will always be light— And I am the prophet of it!" (*Dragon Country*, p. 74) and that if he ever finds his god he will "tear the heart out of my body and burn it before him" (p. 62). Here too is a version of the image of the sun killing goldfish. Frieda accuses Lawrence of "sucking the fierce red sun in your body all day and turning it into venom to spew in my face!" (p. 61). Lawrence's "body's a house that's made out of tissue paper and caught on fire" (p. 67). The sun, heat, and fire are clearly destructive and can bring about a renewal only after death, consummation, and the resulting purification. The sun itself, according to Lawrence, dies nightly in copulation with the "harlot of darkness" (p. 74), and the masculine sun becomes as tied to cycles as any feminine symbol.

The Dylan Thomas poem, "Do Not Go Gentle into That Good Night," is a far more appropriate epigraph to *I Rise in Flame* than to *Cat on a Hot Tin Roof*, where it appears. Lawrence does not want to die and rages against his death, yet in taking the phoenix for his symbol he has already accepted death (and presumably resurrection).

The point is that in the Williams play Lawrence is preoccupied with destruction and his own death. His art leads to book bannings and near burnings of canvases. His raging hastens his own death. All his creative impulses, in the world of the play at least, lead to destruction, and once again Williams confirms the artist's untenable position in the world (at least during the artist's own lifetime).

The phoenix is the appropriate symbol for Williams' destructive plays. Tom deprives his family of light and is, in a way, the "harlot of darkness." Val burns, and Lawrence is consumed with fever. Sebastian dies under the blazing white sun. Some sort of resurrection may later occur but in each play Williams is concerned only with the end of past and present.

The heart is the symbol of Williams' plays of denial; and it offers a suitable contrast to the phoenix, even though frequently rent from the body and burned (as Lawrence threatens). The heart represents or creates reality as it ought to be. The heart's function is to turn "chaos into—*order*," as Byron puts it in *Camino Real* (II, 507), and to create a fiction which is more bearable and more sympathetic than the real world which, according to the Writer in *The Lady of Larkspur Lotion* (as for Big Daddy years later in *Cat*), "is a hideous fabrication of lies! Lies! Lies!" (*27 Wagons*, p. 71).

The Lady of Larkspur Lotion (1941) is another early short play which features a writer as character and which prefigures a number of later plays. It is the first in the line of those plays which in one way or another deny reality, and its bleak but less than totally destructive viewpoint points to Williams' later period. "What if there *is* no rubber king in her life!" the Writer says. "There *ought* to be rubber kings in her life! . . . Suppose that I live in this world of pitiful fiction! What satisfaction can it give you . . . to tear it to pieces, to crush it—call it a *lie?*" (27 *Wagons*, pp. 70–1). And thus the Brazilian rubber plantation is on the Mediterranean and in full view of the cliffs of Dover. "Compassion and understanding" take over to destroy the reality of cockroaches, prostitution, "body vermin," and a hard nosed, tightly drawn landlady (Mrs. Wire). The fiction makes life in such surroundings passable for the Lady and the Writer for at least one more night. Yet, the denial of reality is not far removed from destruction. Neither has much hope; for both the Lady and the Writer must deny the real world of rent payments—at who knows what cost—to create an alternate fiction.

Aspects of denial leading to destruction appear in Williams' two most experimental plays, *Camino Real* (1953), with its Lord Byron as artist character, and the early verse play, *The Purification* (1944), which does not include an artist in the cast but which is, in many ways, *Camino Real's* forerunner. The Son and Daughter (Elena) of Casa Blanca in *The Purification*, for example, share the usual qualities of Williams' artists. They are sensitive, passionate, and unable, because of their passion and incestuous relationship, to exist in the usual real world. They attempt to transcend that world through their passion. "Resistless it was,/this coming of birds together/in heaven's center . . ./Plumage—song—the dizzy spirals of flight/all suddenly forced together/in one brief, burning conjunction!" But "Afterwards, shattered,/we found our bodies in grass" (27 *Wagons*, p. 45). The only reality for an unacceptable love affair is purification through death and a psychic or spiritual resurrection. The end of the play, in fact, suggests that it has been an analogue to the celebration of the Mass. "The play is done!" the Judge announces (p. 62). And the incest, the passion, and the religiosity of the play link it to *Camino Real* generally and to Byron in particular.

Byron appears in *Camino Real* only in Block Eight. He tells the story of Shelley's cremation and the snatching of the heart from the "blistering corpse" and "the purifying—blue flame" (II, 506). Byron speaks of the poet's vocation, which "is to influence the heart," which is in turn "A sort of—*instrument!*—that translates *noise* into *music,* chaos into—*order* . . . —*a mysterious order!*" (p. 507). He crosses the Terra Incognita on his way to Athens where "the old pure music" will come to him again. He will "Make a departure!" he says, "From my present self to myself as I used to be!" (p. 503). "*Make voyages!—Attempt them!*—there's nothing else. . . . THIS WAY!" (pp. 508–9).

There are other, mechanical links between the plays. In *The Purification* the brother tells the story of Peeto the pony (pp. 60–61). The survivor in Block Two of *Camino Real* repeats it. The words of the chorus of women in *The Purification,* "rojo de sangre es el sol!" (p. 58), are spoken by La Madrecita in *Camino.* "Rojo está el sol! Rojo está el sol de sangre! . . . Blanca está la luna de miedo!" (p. 451). Red is the sun of blood. White is the moon of fear. Furthermore the tone of Williams' verse play is often reflective of T. S. Eliot's *Murder in the Cathedral,* in which the Archbishop attempts to justify to himself his death while society attempts to justify to itself his murder. In fact, a line from the play appears in *Camino Real.* "Humankind cannot bear very much reality" (p. 580).

Undoubtedly the three plays are linked. The meaning of *The Purification* and *Murder in the Cathedral* is clear enough. The Son joins his sister in death, for "nothing contains" her where she is, in "the wildest and openest places" (p. 59). The Archbishop makes his decision "out of time" to give his life "to the Law of God above the Law of Man." Each character reaches for something beyond the rational and the physical, much as Val in *Battle* wants space around him and wants to stretch his brain out, "right up against the edges of the stars!" (I, 108). Each character wants to substitute an unrealistic fiction for an unbearable reality. Each, facing an inevitable death, wants, at the very least, that final act to be symbolic in some way. Each wants to make his splash against the sky.

The destructive message in *Camino Real* becomes clear. Byron's brief appearance represents a dialogue between body and soul, with the body at once both fascinating and repulsive. Byron ends his lurid story with the statement that "I thought it was a disgusting thing to do, to snatch a man's heart from his body!" (p. 506). Nevertheless what he searches for is not in the clearly corrupt physical realm, a realm which he must transcend. He attempts to return to himself as he used to be—the poet (instead of the versifier) with an uncorrupted vocation, "before it was obscured by vulgar plaudits!" (p. 507). Living and dying is the only true poetic act. He voyages across the great unknown, to the war in Athens where he is killed. His search is not for innocence but for "the old pure music"—the purity which is indeed characteristic of art, which transcends the physical, and which may very well be expressible only in the irreversible act of death. For as Val knows, corruption is really the fact of physical existence.

Basically, purification is the destruction of the physical and an assault on the unknown. Purification is most effectively initiated through ritual death. Of course Kilroy, the great American pragmatist, is incapable of even imagining the suprarational or supraphysical and dies like the survivor, senselessly, without meaning and with the rattle of a dry gourd. His Blakean soul appears, however, enfolded in the humanity of La Madrecita, and after his heart is cut from his body he seizes it and pawns it in a futile and regressive attempt to buy paradise in the person of Esmeralda. As Byron discovered, however, at Shelley's vivisection, the physical heart is corrupt, and it is only after the Gypsy forces him to face the real camino that Kilroy sees the physical world for what it is—"a pile of excrement" (Weales, p. 23, discussing Shannon's view). Idealism, in the person of Quixote, then awakes, Kilroy sees it, and water begins to flow (much as the rains come in *The Purification*) only after the reduction of the world to absolutely basic terms and only after the destruction of all illusions. The play opens with the same basic term when "Sancho mutters the Spanish word for excrement as several pieces of rusty armor fall into the aisle" (p. 433). Only through the course of the play, however, can the characters (and presumably the audience) realize the nature of physical reality.

Thus a baptized, purified Kilroy, embraced by idealism, escapes at last from the camino real to attempt the exploration of the unknown, the Terra Incognita—much as Byron has escaped, much as Jacques and Marguerite escape into the unknown land of love, much as the fugitive kind have flown. Art represents less the destruction than the denial and transcendence of the physical, although the artist must frequently destroy the real world to go beyond it. For Byron, the physical heart may be burned or not; it may be twisted and torn like a loaf of french bread, for it does not matter. What is important to him is the artist's heart, which is a spiritual instrument of order and not a physical organ. What matters is that, as in *Larkspur*, the artist create an acceptable world and reject the real world. Imagination and the ideal are what should exist.

In two important plays preceding *Camino*, *Streetcar Named Desire* (1947) and *Summer and Smoke* (1948), Williams examines the age-old question of the relationship of the physical and real to the ideal and spiritual, and he examines it again much later in *Kingdom of Earth* (1968, 1975). *Kingdom* is very nearly a rerun of *Streetcar*, with Lot analogous to Blanche, Chicken to Stanley, and Myrtle to Stella. Both Myrtle and Stella "choose life." Williams' emphasis on the dichotomy of flesh and spirit in the plays and his refusal to take sides underscore the estrangement of the sensitive person from society. (William Blake is used ironically in *Summer and Smoke*, for no poet was more opposed to the dichotomy of body and soul.) And even though no specific character in either of the earlier plays is an artist, the plays are important since the theme of estrangement recurs often in Williams' work and adds a significant dimension to the role of the artist.

Williams carefully polarizes John and Alma in *Summer and Smoke*, with the only possibility of synthesis embodied in the earthbound angel, eternal and lifeless. John moves away from total sensuality in the course of the play while Alma moves away from complete spirituality. Somewhere near the end of the play the two cross each other's paths with no hope of meeting, and Alma is apparently on the way to becoming another Blanche (see Popkin, p. 47). In *Eccentricities of a Nightingale* (1964), a later and very different version of *Summer and Smoke*, Alma is more clearly a singer and more clearly eccentric (hence the title). She is more nearly an artist figure —sensitive, unable to cope adequately with her environment, passionate, and mildly destructive, at least as far as her own reputation goes. She hazards all for one night of love. She is gentle and pathetic, however, and more akin to Laura Wingfield than to Val or even Tom. She is, after all, a post-*Suddenly* character who does survive.

Blanche, in *Streetcar*, contrasts herself to Stanley. "He acts like an animal! . . . Maybe we are a long way from being made in God's image, but Stella—my sister—there has been *some* progress since then! Such things as art—as poetry and music. . . . In some kinds of people some tenderer feelings have had some little beginning! That we have got to make *grow*! And *cling* to, and hold as our flag! In this dark march toward whatever it is we're approaching. . . . *Don't—don't hang back with the brutes!*" (I, 323). Blanche's remarks reveal her nature. She can't abide the brutality which surrounds her. Even though Stella, the star married to the brute, offers Blanche an example of synthesis, and even though Blanche herself is considerably more free to act than Alma, Blanche is like Alma in succumbing to the sensual at the expense of her ideals and her own wellbeing. In the light of the thrusts of the previous plays, such a resolution suggests two lines of thought.

As Byron and Val state, the submission to the physical (and therefore corrupt) world demands the destruction of the artistic temperament. Thus for Alma and Blanche (who are spiritual characters) a movement toward sensuality represents psychic if not physical destruction. Indeed their attempts to come to terms with the corruption of the physical world end only in corruption. Yet the continued existence of the spiritual person in the physical world is equally impossible. As noted the only solution to the artist's bind is some form of escape from it, often in the form of death. A spiritual beauty and a real horror cannot exist together.

Brick in the original version of *Cat on a Hot Tin Roof* is another early character who will, with a dream, destroy himself and his world rather than submit to its corruption. Brick is an artist, as Gerald Weales notes (p. 19). He is an extremely sensitive person: "One man has one great good true thing in his life. . . . I had friendship with Skipper" (III, 58). Furthermore he wants to transcend the physical, yet is aware of the ravages of time. He wants to "keep on tossing—those long, long!—high, high!—passes that—couldn't be intercepted except by time" (p. 122). Brick is also a destructive power. He tortures Maggie. "Oh, Brick! How long does it have t' go on? This punishment? Haven't I done time enough, haven't I served my term, can't I apply for a—pardon?" (p. 39). And "you asked too goddam much of people that loved you, you—superior creature!—you godlike being!—And so we made love to each other to dream it was you, both of us!" (p. 56). Brick drives Skipper to his death. "Yes—I left out a long distance call which I had from Skipper, in which he made a drunken confession to me and on which I hung up! —last time we spoke to each other in our lives" (p. 124). He pronounces Big Daddy's death sentence. *"How about these birthday congratulations, these many, many happy returns of the day, when ev'rybody but you knows there won't be any!"* (p. 125). When Brick tells Big Daddy to "Leave th' place to Gooper and Mae" (p. 126) he attempts to dispose of his past, his family, and his environment. He in effect sells his birthright.

Brick might insist that he is less interested in destroying his environment and escaping it than in simply transcending it. He drinks to activate a "Switch clicking off in my head, turning the hot light off and the cool night on and . . . all of a sudden there's—peace!" (p. 98). Still, his attempts to transcend the physical have strong self-destructive overtones. "Mendacity is a system that we live in. Liquor is one way out an' death's the other. . . . I'm sorry, Big Daddy. My head don't work any more and it's hard for me to understand how anybody could care if he lived or died or was dying or cared about anything but whether or not there was liquor left in the bottle. . . . Maybe it's being alive that makes them lie, and being almost *not* alive makes me sort of accidentally truthful" (pp. 127–28).

Thus Maggie must lock up Brick's liquor and force him to submit to her. She wins the battle of the physical and indeed wins the physical itself, the plantation which is necessary to support Brick's drinking, but she loses the war. Brick is not concerned with the physical; and at the end (particularly in the original third act) Brick remains as detached as ever. "I don't say anything. I guess there's nothing to say. MARGARET: Oh, you weak people, you weak, beautiful people!—who give up.—What you want is someone to—take hold of you.—Gently, gently, with love! And—I *do* love you Brick, I *do!* BRICK (smiling with charming sadness): Wouldn't it be funny if that was true?" (pp. 165–66). Wouldn't it be funny if anything were true? The frequent repetition of the phrase suggests that very little is true in life aside from death and maybe birth. Perhaps man's only meaningful statement within the mendacious system is in death— a death imbued with some sensibility and meaning.

Sebastian's death as related in *Suddenly Last Summer* is not only extremely symbolic but, in perverse and destructive terms, an artistic triumph. Sebastian's mother, Mrs. Violet Venable, tells Dr. Cukrowicz that "Without me he died last summer, that was his last summer's poem" (III, 354). Too, she says, "nothing was accidental, everything was planned and designed in Sebastian's life and his—(She dabs her forehead with her handkerchief which she had taken from her reticule.)—work!" (p. 351). Her hesitancy to say *work* suggests that had she not paused to think, she might have concluded her statement with the verbal opposite of life—*death*. A few lines later she says "strictly speaking, his *life* was his occupation." Clearly (for Catharine neither disputes nor denies any of her aunt's statements) Sebastian meant his very existence to be meaningful. His death, which is his poem and his last artistic statement, tells a great deal about art and death and the artist's untenable relationship with reality.

Mrs. Venable says that Sebastian "always had a little entourage of the beautiful and the talented and the young!" and that "Both of us were young, and stayed young, Doctor" (p. 359). She would have us believe that Sebastian was chaste, that he was "*Forty*, maybe. We really didn't count birthdays" (p. 361). She is obsessed with youth and grandeur and the necessity of being a cynosure. "Most people's lives—what are they but trails of debris . . . with nothing to clean it all up but, finally, death. . . . My son, Sebastian, and I, . . . we would—carve out each day of our lives like a piece of sculpture. —Yes, we left behind us a trail of days like a gallery of sculpture! But, last summer—I can't forgive him for it, not even now that he's paid for it with his life!—he let in this—*vandal!*" (p. 363). In describing the "vandal" Catharine, Violet in effect describes herself; "they want your blood on the altar steps of their *outraged, outrageous* egos!" (p. 364). Finally, a few sentences later, she admits to having turned into an elderly lady. "We had an agreement between us, a sort of contract or covenant between us which he broke last summer when he broke away from me and took her with him, not me!" (p. 408). Catharine says, "She had a slight stroke in April. It just affected one side, the left side, of her face . . . but it was disfiguring, and after that, Sebastian couldn't use her" (p. 396). Catharine says too, "a—sort of—*umbilical* cord" had broken. "All I know is that suddenly, last summer, he wasn't young any more" (p. 409).

It is nearly impossible to separate Violet and her story from Sebastian's, for, as Catharine says, "I think it started the day he was born in this house" (p. 405). Violet presents herself quite clearly as a woman afraid of mortality, mutability, and death. Her refusal to accept her mortality, however, brands her as the antiartist, in opposition to Sebastian who has seen God only in a cruel, carnivorous universe where violent mutability is the rule. He has seen the need to transcend the corrupt human or physical world, "to go on doing as something in him directed" (p. 419). Violet's violent attempt to stop time, to preserve her youth, to make Sebastian "carve out each day" of his life and record it in a single hand printed volume keeps him alive and functioning and sterile in his brilliant white suit. Sebastian and Violet stand apart from reality, as Violet wishes, in the classic artist's pose. (The violets that break the rocks in *Camino* are clearly not the sterile, inhibiting, decaying Violet Venable.)

However, Sebastian knew from his observations of the raucous, carnivorous birds, from his attention to insectivorous plants, and from his own life, that art is the distillate of past experience and that the process destroys that past. Art is not a synthesis but a pure expression. Death, which cleans up the debris of life, is the ultimate purification and the only monumentally significant action in life.

Tom and Val know that they must cast off and destroy the past before their search for art, truth, and themselves can begin. Val and Byron know that the search cannot take place in the physical realm, but that it must take them into the Terra Incognita, the pure supraphysical region which man normally encounters only through death. Byron and Blanche tell us "not to hang back with the brutes" although the sensual world fascinates them and nearly destroys them.

Sebastian as a young man knew even more—he knew his fate, as Violet indicates. "Poets are always clairvoyant!—And he had rheumatic fever when he was fifteen. . . . 'Violet? Mother? You're going to live longer than me, and then, when I'm gone, it will be yours, in your hands, to do whatever you please with!'—Meaning, of course, his future recognition!—That he *did* want. . . . Well, here is my son's work, Doctor, here's his life going *on!* (She lifts a thin gilt-edged volume from the patio table as if elevating the Host before the altar. . . . The old lady seems to be almost young for a moment)" (p. 353).

Elsewhere Violet says one "long ago summer" Sebastian "promised those sly Buddhist monks that he would give up the world and himself and all his worldly possessions to their mendicant order" (p. 358). Mrs. Venable's strength (sufficient to neglect a dying husband) is overpowering, however, and Sebastian's first attempt to "give himself to mendicants" fails. But Violet's power over Sebastian lies only in her youthfulness and in her ability to procure. Her aneurism destroys her dream of immortality and her power; and once the cord is broken, Sebastian can cast her aside, much as Tom leaves Amanda. Just as Violet's "heart" fails her, just as Shelley's and Kilroy's and Lawrence's hearts have failed them, just as the hearts of the Son and Daughter of Casa Blanca have betrayed them, so Sebastian's heart will betray and help destroy him.

Sebastian's emergence from the false, timeless world of his mother's mind and his resulting new freedom force him to grow older and also permit him to face the inevitability of death and indeed plan for it. He has known all along that he will die before Violet. He knows he has to die to leave her with a significant corpus, his corpse being his last poem. Furthermore, the way in which he dies is important. For the first time in his life he attempts to "correct a human situation" (p. 419)—perhaps his fatal error. He runs up the hill, away from safety, with the burden of a bad heart, to die and be devoured, to leave his blood splattered over the blazing white earth, to leave his mark on the frightening tabula rasa of the universe—an example of Williams' use of red and white. One can compare La Madrecita's red sun of blood and white moon of fear; Lawrence's hemorrhage and his black and white lap robe; Casa Rojo (sic) and Casa Blanca, or more significantly Rosalio (the son) of Casa Blanca in *Purification*; Chance's incipient mutilation and the bright white clothes of the Finley family; Flora Goforth's blood and tissue rose; Mark's canvases in *Tokyo*.

In any case Sebastian consciously seeks death and destruction. He wills and seals his fate with his action. He literally gives himself to mendicants who eat and drink his flesh and blood. Thus, the old lady, with Sebastian's blood on the steps of her altar—ego—elevates the thin volume like "the Host before the altar," and the artist is purified and transcendent.

Sebastian's recognition, which remains in his mother's hands, becomes a part of a ritual cannibalism. As he carved out the days of his life, so the urchins carve out his vital parts, cleaning up the debris of his life. As Christ destroyed the old law, so Sebastian destroys his mother's moral order. The body and the blood are taken, and as Christ permitted himself to be destroyed, subsequently transcending the physical, so does Sebastian. Williams audaciously stresses Sebastian's spiritual presence by eliminating, in the play, any trace of his physical presence. Sebastian's life goes on not as much through his poetry as through the symbolic act of raising the book like a Host, for in structuring his death Sebastian symbolically and literally structures the lives of the members of his family. Like Tom and Val, Sebastian abandons the two women, Violet and Catharine, although his posthumous control over the directions of their lives is the ultimate expression of artistic power—an ironic stance for one who "thought it unfitting to ever take any action about anything whatsoever!" (p. 419).

Suddenly Last Summer is Williams' strongest statement concerning the artist's condition; strong enough, evidently, to cause him to turn away, however slightly, from the examination of totally destructive impulses. *Suddenly* is perhaps his last positive statement on the subject if one considers the self-destructive attempt to transcend the physical as a paradoxically creative effort. In the rest of his plays the artist character is invariably an "angel of death" who, nevertheless, embodies no serious self-destructive tendencies. Each is decadent in the sense that survival and endurance are more immediately important than art (see Callaghan). Each becomes or is rendered impotent in some way. Finally, each is a mysterious, drifting individual who enters the play from somewhere unknown and who departs, alone and lonely, into an equally vague future. The Gypsy in *Camino Real* describes them well when she states that "Humanity is just a work in progress" (p. 543).

Two artists appear in *Sweet Bird of Youth* (1959). Chance is a marginal artist at best, or perhaps simply a failed one, but the Princess Kosmonopolis has been, as Alexandra Del Lago, a famous actress. In the play, however, she is the aging actress, one who fears her own destruction in the passing of her youth. She has attempted a comeback but fled the premiere of her film at the sight of the first closeups of her wrinkled face. During her flight she has picked up Chance Wayne, whom she metaphorically emasculates and who uses her to return to his hometown where he will be physically castrated.

The Princess is a likable character, thanks to her cynical humor—"So . . . I'm being used. Why not? Even a dead race horse is used to make glue" (IV, 49)—and to her genuine sympathy for Chance, yet, as Williams says in a stage direction, "to indicate she is going on to further triumph would be to falsify her future" (p. 122). On the strength of the reports of the success of her film, and perhaps in part because Chance rejects her, she is able to pull herself together enough to end her flight and to return to the real world, to what little remains of her career, and to what will probably be a rather tenuous existence. Her chance encounter with Chance is enough to permit her to be a witness and accessory to his destruction. She is, in a way, his "angel of death," for ultimately her instinct for survival enables her, in her conversation with Sally Powers (an ironic name), to abandon him. Though she later asks Chance to go with her, he insists on staying. Thus both go their ways, alone.

Chance is an actor, obviously assuming various roles throughout the play—son, blackmailer, lover, young romantic with Aunt Nonnie, sophisticate in St. Cloud and at the bar, and finally Fatalist, appealing to the audience for understanding. Chance is not a competent actor, though (he forgot his lines in the high school drama competition), and he is an unsympathetic character. Nonetheless he has some qualities of the artist. He, like Val, is reaching for the sky—for Heavenly, for St. Cloud, for Kosmonopolis (the cosmic city, the New Jerusalem perhaps), for Hollywood. He exhibits self-destructive tendencies and accepts his castration, though it is likely that he is a post-*Suddenly* character who will survive. For though he attempts to hang onto his youth, he says at one point, "to change is to live" (p. 88), and his character indeed changes suddenly at the end of the play (perhaps too suddenly). Yet his attitude is that "Tonight's all that counts" (p. 54), which does not go far in reaching for the sky. Still, for Chance, as for Sebastian, "Something's got to mean something" (p. 121).

Williams' next two plays, *The Night of the Iguana* (1961) and *The Milk Train Doesn't Stop Here Anymore* (1963–64), both explore relationships similar in some ways to the one between Chance and the Princess. Weales notes that in neither *Iguana* nor *Milk Train* is the relationship physical and that "Hannah teaches Shannon to accept life" while "Chris teaches Mrs. Goforth to accept death; it is the same lesson" (p. 32). We can carry the analogy back to *Sweet Bird* (and even ahead to *The Two-Character Play*).

Chance inadvertently helps the Princess accept life: "He's doing the dreadful thing for me, asking the answer for me" (p. 115). And she teaches him to accept his mutilation and leads him to self-recognition: "What else can you be? CHANCE: Nothing . . . but not part of your luggage" (p. 122). The Princess is, in a sense, the Lady of the Lake (Del Lago) who hands Chance his sword of self-recognition with one hand and who takes a sword away with the other when she renders him impotent. The bitter irony of her function is further emphasized by her first name, Alexandra, which means "defender of men." Chance and the Princess do join physically, but the encounter is incomplete and unsatisfactory. She mentions castration, and Chance replies "You did that to me this morning, here on this bed." She in turn acknowledges her own impotence: "Age does the same thing to a woman" (p. 120). "Both are faced with castration," as Williams indicates (p. 122).

Indeed the entire play is one of destruction, castration, and impotence. Boss Finley disenfranchises voters. He is responsible for the Negro's castration and is more at fault than Chance for Heavenly's sterility. Miss Lucy in turn emasculates Boss Finley, out of her frustration with her own lack of place and power, as does the heckler. Aunt Nonnie is powerless to help Chance. Dr. Scudder, an impotent chief of staff who is about to marry the woman he sterilized, can't protect Boss Finley, and so on. Williams' world view is bleak. Still, the Princess and Chance are alive at the end of the play, though alone, powerless, and futureless.

Williams continues to create futureless characters who are "angels of death." In his next play, *Iguana*, the artists are Hannah Jelkes, a painter, and her grandfather, Jonathan Coffin, who is a poet. Both enter the play from nowhere and Hannah, who stands by, at the end, as her grandfather dies, is absolutely isolated: "she looks right and left for someone to call to. There's no one" (IV, 375). She has clearly suborned her art to survival, for she does quick sketches and portraits which she sells to tourists to earn enough to get on to the next hotel. She possesses Faulknerian endurance: "Just by, just by . . . enduring" (p. 353). Hannah, as Weales has seen, is a teacher and creator, but she is impotent as far as her own situation goes. She is a forty-year-old virgin and spinster with two incidences of affection to her credit. Because she has had to care for her grandfather (who is metaphorically her coffin), she has been powerless to lead her own life.

Nonno (no-no, non-non), the grandfather, is a destructive creator in that he effectively prevents Hannah from achieving anything even resembling a normal life. He is her "angel of death" as she is his. His last, dying creative effort, his poem, is destructive in that it consigns Hannah to her fate. "And still the ripe fruit and the branch/ Observe the sky begin to blanch/Without a cry, without a prayer,/ With no betrayal of despair" (p. 372). Hannah must endure, stoically, not as herself but faceless and alone. Maxine says, "What are you? HANNAH: I am his granddaughter. MAXINE: Is that all you are? HAN-NAH: I think it's enough to be" (p. 319). Nonno dies at the end of the play with a burst of creativity, like Val and Sebastian. Nonno is more akin to the later artists, however, since his age (ninety-seven) indicates that he has obviously come to grips with reality enough to survive.

Shannon and Maxine (to say nothing of Gardner and Burton) are dramatically fascinating, but *Iguana* is Hannah's play. Maxine is the "survivor," the realist in the line of Stella and Myrtle. Shannon comes to accept life and his and Maxine's existence. He has come into the play from a very clear past (almost too clear—see the gratuitous Mother and Masturbation First Cause) and remains at the end with a relatively comfortable and predictable future. Hannah, however, is the fair, good angel (in contrast to Maxine), the wisdom of the East—"Miss Thin-Standing-Up-Female-Buddha" (p. 347)— and the moving force of the play. She is one who literally exhausts herself reaching out to others, to Shannon and Nonno particularly. She is spent and futureless, but alive at least at the end of the play, where the focus is clearly on her. She is not the first character to enter the play, but it is only with her entrance that order begins to come out of chaos; for her very presence has a calming influence on Shannon. Her name means "grace," and in the unholy trinity of the play she is the fleshless spirit. She has destroyed herself as both person and human being to save the flotsam of the world— Shannon, Nonno, Maxine, and the underwear salesman at least. She is an artist who has given herself up to the principle of survival.

Christopher Flanders, in *Milk Train*, is Hannah's counterpart. He abstains from a physical relationship with Sissy Goforth. He enters the play from a largely unknown past, except for what gave him the reputation as an "angel of death," and he will evidently retire to the oubliette at the end (V, 105), though he may move on to the elderly spinster in Taormina. He stays where he can when he can, and survives. He comes into money on one or two occasions and as easily gives it away. He too uses his art as a means to survive physically, for it is only at the end of the play, after he has hung his mobile above the dying Mrs. Goforth's bed, that she permits him to have something to eat. And then he permits her to die peacefully.

Sissy Goforth is the first in a series of Williams characters—a series which includes the gnädiges fräulein in the short play which bears her name (1965) and Myrtle in *Kingdom of Earth*. All of them may or may not be termed artists, for they have worked burlesque and the music hall. Mrs. Goforth, in addition, is working on her memoirs (see Weales, p. 19), though she does not complete them. At best they are all marginal artists, however, in that they lack sympathy and sensitivity and their deepest instincts lead them to survival at any cost. Flora Goforth marries for money three times and for love (or sex) the fourth, when it is perhaps too late. She, like Lawrence, rages "against the dying of the light." The gnädiges fräulein, blind and bleeding, fights the cocaloony birds for waste fish thrown from the dock, a trick she learned in the music hall when she had to compete with the seal for affection and thus for psychic survival. Polly and Molly rapaciously steal the fish from her, and Indian Joe in turn takes the fish from them. At the end the gnädiges fräulein simply goes out for more fish when the boat whistle blows. Somehow she survives in a "cocaloony eat cocaloony world," a competitive and cruel world of free enterprise (see Callaghan, p. 57).

Myrtle too survives. She comes with the pale, effeminate Lot, his mother's child, to the family place to function as his "angel of death." The virile, dark Chicken, however, offers her the choice of life with him or death in the flood, and Myrtle, despite her culturally conditioned reservations, chooses life, attempting, at the end of the play, to cook Chicken's supper in what is now her kitchen while Lot is dying in the crystal and velvet parlor. It is as if the angels of decadent art and of earthy vitality have struggled for her soul, though the case is not that clear cut. Chicken is not entirely black— he can almost pass for white, evidently— and Lot is not entirely fair, for he bleaches his hair (however expertly). Still, Chicken is one of the "brutes" (as his name suggests) and clearly a life force. He is associated with food and sex. He throws the cat in the flooded basement, but knows the cat will swim to the woodpile, and at the end of the scene he rescues it. The purifying floods which will destroy Lot's parlor will also, according to Chicken, "make the land richer" (V, 183) and bring it new life. And he hopes Myrtle can provide him a child. Chicken is, at the end, ascendant (presumably with Myrtle), on the roof above the flood, and heir to the property anyway by virtue of a superior constitution. Lot descends to an ironic death by water. As in *Streetcar*, those who survive in the *Kingdom of Earth* are those who are strong and brutal. Myrtle, if she is an artist (she is one of those storytellers who never comes to the point), is clearly one in Williams' later mode. Lot, were he an artist, would be one from the early period. He, like Leona's dead brother in *Confessional* (later to become *Small Craft Warnings*), or like Sebastian, is too good, too pure, too sensitive to survive. And as Jean Renoir suggests in his film *The Grand Illusion*, it is the strong, vigorous, brutal, and rising lower middle class who shall inherit the earth. Or, as Williams has it in *The Two-Character Play*, it is the gross man (Mr. Grossman) who prospers.

The message or the focus of the later plays is clear. It is survival. Myrtle, like the Princess, like Hannah, like Christopher (and Mrs. Goforth in a way), and like all the characters in *Gnädiges Fräulein*, opts for existence, even at the price of the destruction of the beautiful.

In the Bar of a Tokyo Hotel (1969–70) is a strange play, an aberration perhaps, for it is one with the usual Williams characters— Miriam, who is afraid of aging and who will refuse to age, and her husband Mark, the painter whose canvases consume him—but without Williams' usual sure sense of language (see Cohn, p. 129). The preponderance of end-stopped fragments, the non sequiturs, and the pseudoidiomatic English spoken by the Japanese barman (Williams has never been successful with any pidgin dialogue) all make the play and the relationships difficult to follow. *Tokyo Hotel* is also the only post-*Suddenly* play which fits the early pattern, wherein art and artists are totally destructive. It is an anomaly in Williams' career and probably for Williams very much like one of Mark's canvases—intimate, terrifying, uncontrollable, and deadly.

Mark is so literally wrapped up in his work that he cannot tear himself away from it, yet he is totally dependent on his wife, and he presumably dies because, among other reasons, she refuses to stay with him. She, on the other hand, professes independence, but we see her, after his death and her supposed release, with "no plans" and "nowhere to go" (*Dragon Country*, p. 53). She is evidently as dependent on him and his "circle of light," his attempt to wrench beauty from life, as he is on her, and through their interdependence they tend to destroy each other with themselves. Miriam carries a poison pill in her Regency snuff box, and though she insists that "death . . . would have to remove, wrench, tear!—the bracelets off my arms" (p. 37), "she wrenches the bracelets from her arms and flings them to her feet" (p. 53) at the end of the play. Is she death? It is not clear whether or not she poisons her husband literally—though she does metaphorically—but the possibility is there. Does she die as she wrenches off the bracelets? Her sudden conversion from a released, free spirit to one with no plans and no place to go suggests that she has metaphorically died with her husband. The circular bracelets symbolize the "circle of light" outside of which she refuses to step, but which must inevitably fade with time and despite the demise of her husband. The bracelets also suggest the circular, symbiotic, interdependent relationship between Mark and Miriam, a relationship which she has attempted to overlook.

This focus on Miriam demonstrates how widely Mark's destructive influences reach. The emphasis, however, should properly be on Mark, who is at once fighting his canvas and trying, even physically, to achieve a oneness with it. According to Miriam, he shouts at his canvas, "You bitch, it's *you* or *me!*" (p. 38). The feminine epithet suggests the similarity of his relationships to his canvas and his wife.

There is no hope for survival, however, and in this play it is Mark and his world (including Miriam) who succumb. The canvases suck the life out of him.

It is this victory of art over man, however, that separates the play from the early ones and tends to align it with the late plays. Art for Mark becomes a virtual impossibility; and while Sebastian's death is a rather clear statement, Mark's death results from his inability to make a statement. The message of the play, then, is to capitulate. Death and insanity are no longer viable solutions or meaningful statements, and Alexandra Del Lago's acceptance of the corruption, her capitulation to mortality, and her resignation to imperfection enable her to survive and enable semblances of art to exist. There is no other answer, as *The Two-Character Play* so clearly demonstrates.

The Two-Character Play is Williams' most intellectually realistic statement concerning the artist's untenable and isolated position in a modern culture. The inability of Felice and Clare (ironic names, both) to hold an audience or to communicate directly with it (they need an interpreter, V, 334), to keep a company together, to escape from the prison of the theater, or even to make a coherent artistic statement indicates the artist cannot very well communicate his ideas to anyone else. Further, he cannot play his role in society and becomes frustrated. Of course, one solution for him is to make the sort of statement no one can ignore. But Williams has come, after *Suddenly* (and perhaps with it, through Catharine's true story, which is stranger than fiction), to reject insanity and death as means of dealing with reality. In *Out Cry* especially (the 1973 version of what is renamed *The Two-Character Play*) Felice and Clare are struggling desperately against the tide of insanity. In the later version they very clearly reject suicide, for neither can come to kill the other. Their only course of action, then, is to endure their condition. However, they endure not as Hannah, in a stoic, determined, Faulknerian sense, but rather in a neverending, dreary, and pointless Beckettian fashion.

The Beckettian echoes in *The Two-Character Play* are striking. The set itself, the freezing, dimming "state theatre of a state unknown" (p. 313), the "prison, this last theatre" (p. 364), with its solitary slit of a hole in the backstage wall, is right out of *Endgame*.

Felice's description of his own play, "It's possible for a play to have no ending in the usual sense of an ending, in order to make a point about nothing really ending" (p. 360), and his statement, "With no place to return to, we have to go on" (p. 316), apply equally to *Waiting for Godot*. His concern for "the love and the—substitutions, the surrogate attachments, doomed to brief duration" (p. 310) parallels Beckett's instant gleam of light in *Godot* (p. 57b), and Beckett's contempt of his audience (pp. 10a, 10b) is not far removed from Clare's description of it as "enemy forces" (p. 317). Furthermore, Williams virtually lifts one line from *Godot*. "There's nothing to be done" (p. 366; cf. pp. 8a, 14b in *Godot*). In *Out Cry* Clare asks Felice to help her up. "He rises to help her but topples onto the cushions." She says, "Will we ever get up" (p. 63), which brings to mind Beckett's four characters, all sprawled on the floor in act two of *Godot*, unable to get up.

Felice and Clare are like Winnie and Willie, acting out their happy days as they sink into the mire, or like the character in *Act Without Words I*, from whom everything is withdrawn and who remains, at the end, lying on a bare stage looking at his hands. They are like Hamm, whose function is "to play" and to endure his misery. Like Beckett's bums, they have entered the play from an endless road trip; they attempt suicide but fail; and they have nowhere to go at the end. Their function is to pass the time, to entertain each other, to enjoy their "little canters."

Williams, to emphasize the significance of the play and the act of playing, confuses the relationship of illusion to reality. Felice and Clare perform in a play within a play, but their names and their characters' names are the same, and the play is apparently based on reality. The theater is at once their home (p. 315) and their prison. Godotlike outer worlds are associated with both the frame and the play, but Clare and Felice can function in neither outer world. They are "confined" to their roles as actors and artists, and though they play before empty houses, play they must. Thus the audience is incapable of discovering when they are in and out of character.

Williams has been more careful in the 1976 than in the 1973 version to indicate clearly the difference between the frame and the play. In *The Two-Character Play* Clare and Felice more definitely move from frame to play and back. Even so their frequent and obvious improvisation in the play indicates they are not entirely within it. Near the beginning of act three Clare says, "Have you dried up, Felice? . . . I'm afraid I have, too. FELICE: Improvise something till I— CLARE: All right. Sit down. Breathe quietly. Rest a little, Felice, I'll—" (p. 340). Elsewhere, in the frame, she says, "Sometimes you work on a play by inventing situations in life that, that—correspond to those in the play, and you're so skillfull at it that even I'm taken in . . ." (p. 365). Or, as Felice makes explicit in the frame, "the backstage phone is lifeless as the phone in The Two-Character Play was, finally was" (p. 362). Life, as Oscar Wilde said in The Decay of Lying, imitates art. Life, for the artist or actor, is one long play, a continuous creation, "a trail of days like a gallery of sculpture," to use Violet Venable's words, and the egocentric act of creation is all that matters to the artist, as the business with the revolver indicates.

The revolver exists as a prop in the play, where Felice very nervously manages to load it. "Now I remove the blank cartridges and insert the real ones . . ." (p. 356). Shortly afterward, he and Clare come out of the play, into the frame, and resolve to use the gun. But to use it they have to go back into the play where, nonetheless, they fail. The resolve, evidently, is real and the act itself unbearable, unthinkable, even in a play—or perhaps especially in a play, for what seems to keep Clare and Felice alive is the continuous activity of acting. Clare says, "Do we stop where we stopped tonight or do we look for an ending?" Felice, referring to the revolver, replies, "I think that you will find it wherever you hid it, Clare" (p. 367). The world of the play is the only one that exists for them, and the only way to end the play is to end their lives—which they seriously consider but cannot bring themselves to do.

The magic of art or the fictional world of the play which fends off the real world and "too much reality" for Felice and Clare goes back to The Lady of Larkspur Lotion; and the hypothetical insurance receipts in the play part of The Two-Character Play or the nebulous receipts, in the frame, from its production, echo the delinquent revenues from the Brazilian rubber plantation. And even on a very physical level the charade of the play keeps Clare and Felice alive, for to keep from freezing, literally, they have to reenter, at the end, the warm climate of the play within the play. Since the Williams artist is often associated with heat and light, appropriately Felice and Clare are warm only when they function as artists, in character. As real personae they freeze.

Their (and presumably Williams') commitment to art is clear in *Out Cry*. In both versions Felice insists that they perform, and Clare, though reluctant, picks up the gauntlet thrown by a hostile audience. But only in *Out Cry* Felice states, "if we're not artists, we're nothing" (p. 22), and, at the end, "Magic is the habit of our existence" (p. 72). Clare, lost in her illusory world, is oblivious to time, and she indicates that Felice is unaware of anyone around him. "Felice, there was hardly a soul in the company whose name you could remember" (p. 63). The lack of a sharp distinction, in *Out Cry*, between frame and play and between actor and character puts the focus on the play of life and on the creative act that shapes the artist's being. (In *The Two-Character Play*, Clare quite clearly moves in and out of character.)

Clare and Felice survive in *Out Cry*. Clare says, "This isn't the first time I've had to save you from self-destruction which would destroy me, too" (p. 20). They do not use the gun, but neither do they absolutely reject it, and Williams closes the play with "The lights fade, and they accept its fading, as a death, somehow transcended" (p. 72). They go on with their "magic" but it is not clear for how long.

In contrast, the commitment to life (no matter how confining) is explicit in *The Two-Character Play*. Clare picks up the gun, points it, drops it, and ends the play with, "*I can't!* . . . Can you?" (pp. 369–70). Felice wordlessly follows suit. Furthermore Williams has deleted the references, in *Out Cry*, to the old painter, "seated in *rigor mortis* before a totally blank canvas" (p. 11) and to Gwendolyn Forbes' death in a hotel fire (p. 63).

Clare is a much stronger figure in *The Two-Character Play* than in *Out Cry*. She and Felice swear at each other and argue about the script. During intermission they are at each other; "there has obviously been a physical struggle between the stars" (p. 340). Toward the end, in the frame, Felice bloodies his hands trying to claw his way out of the theater (p. 363). Throughout, their energies go more into the struggle of life than into the play or the charade of life.

Still, life is dreary and they must amuse themselves, Beckettian fashion. The play, then, is not life but the substance of life that fills the time and the void, and the artist's function is to play, even without an audience, and to create for no apparent purpose. Such is the modern condition, the reality the artist faces today. The grand gesture is passé and no more productive than mere endurance.

Clearly Felice and Clare are late-period figures, as their survival, albeit a Lady and Tiger one, indicates. They enter the nowhere of the play from nowhere and remain there. They are isolated, drifting characters rendered impotent by the world (or prison) about them. Evidently they have no control over their Company, their bookings, their theater, or even, with their latest disastrous performance, over their audience. In addition they are fearful, and the gun of the abnormality of family insanity is apparently pointed at them, rendering them powerless to leave the house, the stage, or the theater. They are also, in a way, "angels of death." In *The Two-Character Play* they indicate they have witnessed their parents' deaths. In the frame of *Out Cry* they describe the old painter's end and Gwendolyn Forbes' death. Quite possibly they will preside at each other's deaths some time in the future.

Despite their problems, however, they endure for the time of the play. They survive. They make a feeble attempt at creating art. They become, finally, as illusion and reality merge, their own "work in progress."

Clearly, that body of Williams' work which precedes and includes *Suddenly Last Summer* is, paradoxically, far more vital, in its concern with destruction, than the later work, which sacrifices any intense and clear action by an artist character for a somewhat less important ability to survive. Williams foregoes violent and meaningful death for less meaningful endurance. It is as if the "something unspoken" in the play of the same name permits characters to live in an apparent equanimity, while the spoken truth, as in *Suddenly Last Summer* (with which *Something Unspoken* ran off Broadway) tears down contrived worlds for better or, more commonly, worse. Thus the artist, who speaks out, is destructive in a very real sense for Williams (as I have tried to indicate) because his truth destroys the illusions with which man must surround himself in order to survive.

Brick knows that very well, and Eliot has expressed the idea clearly: "Humankind cannot bear very much reality."

If man cannot survive without his illusions, and if the artist discovers that fact and the truth at the same time, he in effect destroys himself along with those whose illusions he destroys.

Unfortunately for Williams, his later artists shatter the illusions of other characters without purifying themselves, without distilling their own experience into a pure statement, without transcending the physical and cleaning up the debris of their own lives. This is not to say that Williams' later artists have not come to grips with themselves. I think they have, and therefore they can live to help others toward a meaningful existence or the meaningful demise which has been so important for Williams' earlier artists. But the artist's slow, sure awakening in the later plays is not as striking dramatically as his blinding realizations, in the early plays, that death is inevitable, that life is the phoenix cycle, and that art is a destructive force.

The artist's job, then, is to salvage something from the ashes of the past and to contribute that something to the ashes of the future. Art becomes the process of turning a very real and unavoidable destruction into a positive statement. It is the mad process which keeps man free. It is the concurrent destruction and creation of man himself and whatever else he can lay his hands on. Ultimately the artist's most profound statement lies in his own destruction and resurrection. "Humanity is just a work in progress."

Williams' Power of the Keys

JOHN MacNICHOLAS

I

God, like other people, has two kinds of hands, one hand
with which to strike and another to soothe and caress with.
("Mama's Old Stucco House," *The Knightly Quest*, p. 121)

DECLINE, NOT SEX, obsesses Tennessee Wil-
liams. "*There is a passion for declivity in this world!*" the Byron of
Camino Real declaims (II, 508), and the same may be observed in
the world of Williams' plays. Their historical macrocosms often present a world nearing collapse. The debacle of World War I frames
the action of *Summer and Smoke* and *The Eccentricities of a Nightingale*, and World War II is prominently insinuated into the temporal backgrounds of *The Glass Menagerie* and *The Night of the
Iguana*. The protagonists of these plays are likewise struggling with
problems which exhaust their personal resources. The question informing the substrata of all Williams' major work is: does personal
disintegration press merely toward insignificant inanition, or can the
soul in painful disrepair regenerate itself? Although Williams presents this question in various manners, its thematic center is the Fall,
the loss of Eden: "sooner or later, at some point in your life, the
thing that you lived for is lost or abandoned," the Princess Kosmonopolis informs Chance Wayne, "and then . . . you die, or find something else" (*Sweet Bird of Youth*, IV, 35). The interval between loss,
or more specifically *recognition* of loss, and subsequent recovery or
its impossibility, is the typical focus of most of Williams' plays. The
initiating action in Nonno's poem occurs immediately following the
zenith of the tree's life—its "second history" and onset of "mist and

113

mould." Two aspects of primal loss seem constant: the obstruction of passion and the erosion of sincerity in either the central character or his society, or both. The deepest despair in Williams' tragic plays arises from the inadequacy of the "something else" to remedy disorder and especially middle-age sorrow. Williams' central characters, then, are usually confronted with the decision of participating in their own destruction or, by exercising an enormous act of will, altering their spiritual environment. Quite simply, he is concerned with damnation and redemption.

The purpose of this essay will be, first, to trace the etiology of damnation in Williams' plays and define the methods which utilize its dramatic potential; and second, to discuss how redemption (a much more difficult subject to dramatize) may arise out of acute despair. The apostolic power of the keys, the binding and loosing of spiritual life, is the dynamic which runs constant throughout the canon.

The thematic force of Williams' vivid minor characters and their physical worlds derives from his perception that society and the individual both are responsible for spiritual life. Binding has the effect of excommunication, though not necessarily in the formal sense of an ecclesiastical ostracism. Rather it is the failure of the body politic to see in its fear of passion a separation from the only divinity which can be certainly known on earth. If a theology were to be constructed from Williams' plays, these tenets would be cardinal: energy is holy; and if a God the Creator exists he is remote from our daily concerns, an abstraction who teases his creatures out of thought. The only deity Williams acknowledges is an untrammeled possession of the self, a Blakean aseity: "Thou art a Man, God is no more [than Man],/Thy own humanity learn to adore" ("Everlasting Gospel"). Williams consistently represents the dynamic of binding in terms of an individual passion, which is usually but not always a highly visible sexuality, opposed by a repressively centristic society. His most unqualified dramatic sympathy falls upon victims of a truncated sexuality: Laura Wingfield, Lucretia Collins ("Portrait of a Madonna"), Blanche DuBois, Heavenly Finley, Alma Winemiller, Myra Torrance, Hannah Jelkes, and Violet and Quentin (*Small Craft Warnings*). A deep fear of an enduring sexual (and hence, in her society, a personal and familial) dispossession animates Margaret's struggle in *Cat on a Hot Tin Roof*.

Williams, like Lawrence and Blake, can conceive of no greater wasteland than that which traps and neuters individual passion. He recognizes that the real evil of prostitution is not its routine social depredations, which are in themselves terrible enough, but the spiritual dispossession which it enforces upon both parties. And so he acutely depicts the anguish arising from having no *self* to retreat into. Such dispossession (or the threat of it) may be seen in the physical and emotional entropy of Bertha in *Hello from Bertha*; in the Old Woman's desperate exploitation of her personal past in *Lord Byron's Love Letter*; in the unsuccessful breach Cornelia Scott attempts to make in Grace's privacy (*Something Unspoken*); in Vacarro's revenge upon Jake (*27 Wagons*); in the humiliating way the Princess orders Chance Wayne to her bed in the first scene of *Sweet Bird of Youth*; in Gutman's description of the ambiance of *Camino Real*, "a bazaar where the human heart is a part of the bargain" (II, 452); in the pathos of the brief interview between Myra Torrance and David Cutrere, which establishes that Myra lost once that passion which Jabe will deprive her of again: "You made whores of us both!" she tells an assenting David (*Orpheus*, III, 285); and in Sebastian Venable's pitiless exploitation of Catharine's sexuality in *Suddenly Last Summer*. The most surprising element of Williams' short story, "Two on a Party," is that Billy and Cora, whose "party" expends human resources faster than they can reasonably be replenished, have found in each other a home, a part of themselves which is private. The mystery of that privacy arrested Williams' imagination, for they are his only prostitutes who tolerate themselves. Social evil, therefore, is most keenly felt when it attempts to kill or trivialize the Orc-like energy of Val Xavier and Carol Cutrere, or Serafina Delle Rose. Blanche is most unsympathetic when she attempts to camouflage her own sexuality by degrading Stanley's, and her spiritual prototype, Amanda, is the most absurd and repressive as she removes Lawrence's novels from Tom's room and badgers him about his nocturnal activities.

A society which attacks passion or a personality which undermines it with insincerity or guilt is thus bound, cut off from vital joy.

Sweet Bird of Youth presents both forces simultaneously. No greater caricature of a meanminded social order exists in Williams' canon than Boss Finley's political machine. However, it is not Finley's wounded pride and pursuit of vengeance, but Chance Wayne's inability to atone for infecting Heavenly with syphilis that guides Wayne to his doom. The play is weakened by the fragmentation of dramatic energy inherent in the protagonist's confusion. He wants the society which is supposedly envious of his sexuality to admire him for being the wealthy young movie star that he is not. He desires from people whom he detests an acceptance of him as "local boy makes good." He wants to reclaim Heavenly, and simultaneously he desires punishment for inflicting his disease upon her. More than anything else, Wayne seeks to maneuver Finley into servicing his extraordinary masochism. The occlusion of motive from effective action here is characteristic of Williams' concept of damnation. Wayne makes his choice; however, it is hardly an informed action. In the final act he continues on his course of self-destruction, oblivious of trenchant commentary coming from the townspeople, who do not care whether he destroys himself, and from his Aunt Nonnie and the Princess, who do care for him. Defining his concept of tragedy, Williams writes: "The great and only possible dignity of man lies in his power deliberately to choose certain moral values by which to live as steadfastly as if he, too, like a character in a play, were immured against the corrupting rush of time" (II, 262). But those characters whose actions Williams seeks to invest with a tragic tone—Blanche, Val Xavier, or Chance Wayne—seem to have very little choice during their moments upon the stage. Their lives have more to do with desperation than with choice.

During the course of a tragedy, the protagonist is at times likely to be desperate—indeed, almost necessarily—but what defines his soul may not consist primarily of desperation. The self-transcendence of a tragic character is manifested at least partially in an almost kingly indifference to cost, loss, and circumstance which hitherto had made him fearful or anguished. If such indifference is predicated upon rigid self-ignorance, as Chance Wayne's is, then the dramatist to that extent forfeits the tragic tone. Aristotle, whose concept of tragedy Williams evidently respects, reserved for highest praise the tragic structure which caused the reversal to proceed immediately out of recognition. The audience is never allowed to witness Chance Wayne's recognition because it never occurs. At the end of *Sweet Bird of Youth*, he is essentially unchanged, the willing slave of a monomaniacal drive to reclaim the past with Heavenly. His character has in effect been ossified by a masochistic guilt whose very origins prevent him from carrying out his wish to be reunited with Heavenly. Even the pretense that this design is feasible obligates Chance to ignore temporal bonds. Therefore he is immunized from self-recognition, whose dramatic power always issues from a delayed and morally informed realignment of past causes and present effects. Even Blanche in the grip of psychosis comes closer than Chance Wayne in understanding the causes of her suffering. (The special nature of Blanche's recognition will be discussed in detail below.)

Not Williams' formal statements about tragedy, but the recurrent metaphors characterizing it, yield the useful insight into his drama. His favorite vehicle to convey the results of thwarted passion is disease; its reiterated expression is: the world is a hospital. His canon is filled with people whose illnesses are directly traceable to emotional causes. Willie's malapropism for the cause of her promiscuous sister's death—"lung affection" (*This Property Is Condemned, 27 Wagons*, p. 201)—precisely condenses Williams' belief that there is no greater destructive potential, even on a physical basis, than displaced eros. One thinks of the "malaria" of Amanda, Blanche, Lucretia Collins, and Alma Winemiller. In Alma especially, the effects of sexual deprivation have surfaced in physical pathology: her "heart disturbances," a pronounced physical emaciation (the stage directions of scene nine of *Summer and Smoke* describe her as though she had suffered a long illness), her stiff fingers and throat spasms, and her climactic acknowledgment of her "affliction of love." Her lover and physician, John Buchanan, compares the location of their furtive tryst to a hospital room. Carol Cutrere has survived pneumonia. Laura Wingfield's emotional pathology appears both in her glass and in her limp. Even her nickname, "Blue Roses," playfully attached to her by Jim O'Connor during their high school years, homonymically derives from her having contracted pleurosis. Myra Torrance lives in a state of "artificial respiration" (*Battle*, I, 75). Syphilis and alcoholism invade several lives in *Sweet Bird of Youth*. Violet Venable, who has had an aneurism, jokes about being kept alive by a drugstore. Her son Sebastian, who suffered from "fever," sexually debased and traumatized Catharine so that a physician who specializes in lobotomy is summoned to cut "disease" (the truth) out of Catharine's brain. Kilroy is taken out of the ring by the medics because he has "heart disease." Personal and societal decline is given an impassioned febrile description in *Auto-Da-Fé*. Elio, a prototype for Tom Wingfield, obsessively associates his slum dwelling in the Vieux Carré of New Orleans with carcinoma: "This is the primary lesion, the—focal infection, the—chancre! In medical language, it spreads by—metastasis! It creeps through the capillaries and into the main blood vessels. From there it is spread all through the surrounding tissue!" (*27 Wagons*, p. 110).

Period of Adjustment, in which the duration of the "period" is of course a lifetime, presents the metaphor in the starkest terms. The romance of George and Isabel Haverstick began in the hospital in which George attempted to recover from "the shakes" and Isabel worked as a nurse. Isabel's sexual fantasy, however, has more to do with a "youngish middle-aged doctor" than with a traumatized war veteran. The imaginary doctor's passion for her is not stinted by the leprosy which she must contract as they bravely perform missionary work side by side in an obscure tropical country. When her physician clasps her, he too becomes infected with contagion. *Period* culminates upon the same metaphor to which Thomas Mann gave definitive treatment in *The Magic Mountain*. She tells George that the world is indeed a hospital, "a big neurological ward," in which she is a student (IV, 244). This sentiment is close to Chance Wayne's description of his compulsive and dangerous return trips to see Heavenly—"like going to a hospital" (IV, 50). Now it is known that Williams himself contracted several painful and severe childhood illnesses and that during his early adult years he worked in a state hospital, but his personal experience alone cannot account for the insistency with which he represents the hospital world upon his stage. Sickness and disease are linked to a binding process, a psychomachia in which the powerfully expressive personality, such as Shannon or Blanche, will resort to visible means of self-destruction when all else fails. The more reticent personality, such as Laura Wingfield or Violet in *Small Craft Warnings*, suffers a less flamboyant but equally certain inner decay.

Every sickness seeks a physician and a victim. Williams' drama identifies these in the gentleman caller and the artist-priest respectively. The archetype for them both is the savior. The gentleman caller's function is less social than medicinal. He is a healer, and his method is to apply to the patient a benevolent rationality consonant with the assumptions of his society. He is paternal though young, kind, personably establishmentarian. He—or the expectations which inevitably gather about him—promises redemption. Tom describes the gentleman caller in openly messianic terms: "he is the long-delayed but always expected something that we live for" (I, 145). The corresponding character in *Streetcar* is Mitch. Although crudely fumbling with words and emotions, he is witheringly sincere. To a lesser extent, the pattern of *Streetcar* approximates the major theme of *Menagerie*. The seemingly plausible redemption of the frail woman by means of an eligible gentleman caller fails. Blanche's curtain line following Mitch's proposal of marriage ("Sometimes—there's God—so quickly!") confirms that she fully expects him to bear the burdens of her soul. Even after Blanche has become psychotic, the gentleman caller appears again in the form of a physician, whose firm kindness subdues her hysteria and supports the play's concluding and dignified stasis. Instead of using threats (trimming fingernails is the matron's idea of de-sexing Blanche as well as disarming her), he instructs the matron to release Blanche, whom he then leads out calmly, arm in arm—the basic gesture of all gentleman callers.

Neither cynical nor sentimental (though Tom Wingfield says otherwise), *Menagerie* and *Streetcar* are toughminded works. Each action recognizes that romantic manna may not reliably be expected to fall to earth, no matter how desperately it may be needed. The emotion aroused by these plays stems in part from Williams' technical mastery of theater, but in much larger measure from the inner structure of their action. *The Glass Menagerie* is not simply a "mood play," as it has been so often called (the term itself is unsatisfactory and vague), gingerly though brilliantly wrought upon anemic substance. Its action is a parody of one of the oldest secular fables of redemption, the sleeping beauty. The princess sleeps because her virtues are shrouded by a "sickness," but she will some day be awakened by the kiss of a prince—the gentleman caller—who correctly perceives those virtues. Jim O'Connor crudely, and not altogether inaccurately, diagnoses Laura's sickness as an inferiority complex; he is intelligent enough to respond to certain of her virtues, which he praises sincerely. He even bestows the magical kiss, which for a moment makes the dream incarnate, even though his stumbling has been revealed long before his engagement to be married is disclosed. O'Connor's fascination with money, marketable knowledge, and administrative power are far removed from mending Laura's compulsive retreat into silent glass. Correspondingly, one hardly surmises in retrospect that Mitch, whose idea of social small talk is to discuss his perspiration problems, will be a suitable man for Blanche, but her loneliness and her accurate understanding that Mitch is neither rapacious like Stanley nor callous like the poker group make the courtship with him at least credible. Blanche's repeated and desperate invocations of Shep Huntleigh, a patently impossible gentleman caller, augment the audience's belief in her romance with Mitch, whose desire and even need for her has been firmly established in scenes three and six. Huntleigh is a fantasy: Mitch is not. The pattern of the chief action in The Glass Menagerie is repeated with variations in Streetcar's subplot; for Blanche's failure to retain Mitch's respect is the prelude to her complete disintegration.

Other gentlemen callers are, however, successful. In the second act of The Rose Tattoo, Serafina Delle Rose is as desperate as Blanche. She has retreated into a darkened and locked house, and she is under attack by her neighbors, her priest, and (she imagines) her daughter. Her fanatical worship of her dead husband, whom she literally enshrines, has been shattered by the strong suspicion that he had been unfaithful. Furthermore, Williams has drawn Serafina's character with a tragic tension. She has denied temporal bonds altogether, having sought in sexual passion with her husband the condition of the angels: "Each time is the first time with him. Time doesn't pass . . ." (II, 280). Her incanted strident wish—"Lady give me a sign"—conveys an urgency in her struggle whose dignity arises partly from the "Lady's" protracted silence. And indeed, her gentleman caller Alvaro appears unexpectedly; a comic gratuitousness characterizes her rescue. No questing designs were laid to make him appear. He is the dramatic cousin of Jim O'Connor and Mitch because he is "normal" and seeks his due in the world; but he differs from them in having no delusions about either Serafina herself or his own desires. So his return to her house in the final act absorbs all the tragic tension generated at the beginning. The resolution of this play dramatizes a fundamental assumption of Williams: nothing kills passion more certainly than insincerity. Serafina's and Alvaro's actions toward each other are consonant with their intentions, even when each is embarrassed to declare them, and so their relationship thrives. Jim O'Connor's kiss ironically validates the sincerity of his praise of Laura while it misrepresents his intentions toward her, and Mitch is humiliated by having believed Blanche's protestations about the reserve of a lady. He then seeks not love, only sexual revenge.

Although both Doctor Cukrowicz and John Buchanan are gentlemen callers, their functions differ considerably. Cukrowicz is an outsider whose benevolent nature is revealed when he subordinates professional fund raising to a discovery of the truth. He is an intelligent but incompletely informed eiron who milks the truth from recalcitrant, self-interested people (Catharine excepted). The structure of *Suddenly Last Summer* was drawn from Cukrowicz's perspective, for his discovery of the causes of *Catharine's* trauma is the audience's as well. His evident lack of sexual involvement with Catharine is required to make him an outsider. Quite the opposite is the relationship between Alma and John Buchanan, for both *Summer and Smoke* and *Eccentricities* (the revision) turn upon the futility of a continuing sexual relationship between them. The nature of John's involvement with Alma was a difficult matter for Williams, as a comparison of the two plays reveals. *Eccentricities* omits the subplot of Rosa Gonzales and her father, thus diminishing Buchanan's role. For in the latter play, he is no longer a hell-raising rake; and though he is restless, it is a very establishmentarian species of unrest. *Eccentricities* is more centrally organized about Alma, whereas *Summer and Smoke* is evenly divided between representing her angst and John's sexual and alcoholic excesses. Why did Williams so drastically recast Buchanan's characterization?

One response is implicit in the analysis above: the change focuses the play upon one character. The dramatist became more concerned with the destruction of Alma than with the redemption of John Buchanan. The sea-change of John Buchanan between *Summer and*

Smoke and *Eccentricities* illustrates the second kind of character mentioned above, for in the former play he is an artist-priest, in the latter a gentleman caller. Their instincts are categorically alien from each other. The artist-priest is Williams' favorite protagonist: confused, tempestuous, impatient, keenly subjective, troubled about deep and deeply felt injustices, fiercely and proudly an exile from society, his commitment is to life conducted exclusively on his own terms ("Shannon obeys only Shannon"). Val Xavier and Cassandra Whiteside are two of the earliest exemplars of this character type. They are artists in the Blakean sense of possessing an abundance of primal energy and imagination. Vee Talbot's characterization is obviously based upon that of D. H. Lawrence in the early play, *I Rise in Flame, Cried the Phoenix*. She is laughed at, considered "peculiar" (the word is used so consistently throughout the canon that it is a standard marker for Williams' outsiders), her painting is technically crude, but she *sees*. And they are priests by virtue of making their catalytic energy available to others in a quasieucharistic manner. They have passion; they know and obey its imperatives, whether mental or physical; they live without surcease in an electrified consciousness; they are intolerant of social and personal entropy; and those who do not kill themselves appear to regain their identities by means of the same supercharged volition which threatened to destroy them. A controlling dynamic characteristic of Williams' dramaturgy, then, is the polarizing energy of the Orc figure: the society which reluctantly feeds from him (or her) and envies him may reject him violently as a wanton Christ. Cassandra Whiteside, for example, proclaims, "Whoever has too much passion, we're going to be burned like witches because we know too much." When Myra asks what she is talking about, Cassandra replies: "Damnation! You see my lips have been touched by prophetic fire" (*Battle*, I, 99). Myra's deflationary retort about Cassandra's drunkenness does little to invalidate the sentiment of her words, which in fact comment upon Myra's own situation. Myra clearly expects her union with Val to save her from the barren bondage to Jabe: "I guess my heart knew that somebody must be coming to take me out of this hell! You did," she exclaims to Val in *Orpheus* (III, 333). The same desire to be saved by his passion runs throughout the last act of the earlier *Battle*; her redemption is imaged in the fig tree, which also presages the futility of her hope. Although Williams supplies a heavy handed symbolic macrocosm to both *Battle* and *Orpheus,* and to Val Xavier, the matter of "crucifixion" has little to do with Christian ideology. It has everything to do with Blake's fallen world of the devourers and the devoured, and his belief that "energy is eternal delight." Chance Wayne universalizes the Blakean division on the basis of pleasure. Those who have found pleasure in love have a sustaining meaning in their lives; those who have found no such pleasure can merely envy and look on (*Sweet Bird,* IV, 50). As Jabe Torrance's actions indicate, their envious voyeurism can have violent consequences. It provides the impetus for most of Williams' "crucifixions."

The latent cannibalism of the Eucharist, and the artist-priest who becomes an unwilling Host, are both treated dyslogistically in *Suddenly Last Summer.* When Violet Venable introduces Doctor Cukrowicz to her son's past, she holds up his book—as if to validate his function as a poet. The stage instructions indicate that she reveres it as if it were the "Host before the altar," and her gesture is punctuated with the clear note of a bird (III, 353). Similarly, as John Buchanan appears before Alma's intellectual circle, its members stare at him "with a curious sort of greediness" (*Summer and Smoke,* II, 172). When Williams revised the play, he reiterated the manner in which Buchanan arouses their envy: "How we all devoured you with our eyes," Alma tells him later, "you were like holy bread being broken among us" (*Eccentricities,* II, 79). Sexuality, which Williams regards as another secular medium for the Eucharist, is represented by an altar-bed in *Sweet Bird of Youth* and *Cat on a Hot Tin Roof.* Maggie is one of Williams' primal women who, like Serafina, want to produce "the glory." "To me," Serafina avers, "the big bed was beautiful like a religion" (II, 342). Violet's connection with "religion" is even more overt in *Small Craft Warnings.* Their drive is ruthless. Maggie decides to lock up Brick's liquor until he satisfies her sexually. Her curtain speech in the Broadway script, though softer than in the original script, does not diminish her role as initiator. Brick needs someone who can "take hold of you—gently, with love, and hand your life back to you" (III, 215). As the curtain closes, the audience can only assume that Maggie's passion establishes at last her position in the family from which she has been an exile and Brick a vegetable.

Williams identifies precisely the danger of narcosis inherent in the release of sexual passion. His characters frequently abuse sex to extinguish momentarily the demands of ego, self-consciousness, even awareness of the past. Knowing too well the terrain of "Dragon Country" and its inhospitable pain, Princess Kosmonopolis frantically seeks a narcotic oblivion. Vodka and hashish are insufficient: "I have only one way to forget these things I don't want to remember and that's through the act of love-making" (IV, 44). A shame similar to Camille's in *Camino Real*—to be an aging voluptuary who must pay rather than receive payment—is ironically one of the things the Princess wishes to forget. Various metaphors of narcosis define the self-destructive edge on which such protagonists live: the "click" which Brick Pollitt constantly drinks toward, the gambling and drinking of John Buchanan, Shannon's weakness for young girls, Chance Wayne's pills, Alma Winemiller's tranquilizer prescription, whose number she described as "the telephone number to God," the brutality of homosexuals whose act of love Quentin compares to the "jabbing of a hypodermic needle to which they're addicted but which is more and more empty of real interest and surprise" (V, 260). All paralytically stalk in vicious circles and yearn not merely for escape. They seek a prelapsarian innocence: "Now get a little sweet music on the radio," the Princess instructs Chance, "and come here to me and make me almost believe that we're a pair of young lovers without any shame" (IV, 44). An impassioned memory of the past can function narcotically, for when evoked it displaces awareness of hostile present circumstances. Retreat from consciousness varies from an undrugged abuse, such as Laura's records and glass collection (the only unthreatening repository of her girlhood), to the extreme of lobotomy which Violet Venable seeks to inflict upon Catharine. Even the mild stroke Violet has had could be considered as a quasilobotomy she has suffered to forget that her advancing age had disqualified her to be Sebastian's companion. What she has suffered, Catharine must suffer in magnified degree. All are elements of the decline which obsesses Williams; they are damning. The abdication of consciousness acquits the moral faculty from making any choice whatsoever. How can expulsion from Eden have consequential guilt if its inhabitants had no consenting part in their damnation? But when the murk of narcosis recedes, the protagonist's guilt—which was never expelled, only obscured—becomes even more insistently painful. Atonement is therefore pursued so feverishly that even when means are available they are unrecognized. Chance's urge to be punished renders him deaf to the Princess' emotionally honest offer of the only kind of relationship he can have. Tom Wingfield runs from city to city, bar to bar, in futile quest to blow out his sister's candles. Shannon, similarly wallowing in masochistic penance, perhaps hears Hannah's penetrating appraisal of his anxiety. Self-crucifixion, whether it is pursued with drugs, spooks, women, or alcohol, turns upon a self-indulgent and hence ineffective penance, which then generates fresh guilt and another round of self-abuse. Only an authentic relocation of emotion can interrupt the process. Such an action must be taken alone; but as *Night of the Iguana* implies, a basic reversal does not seem possible without the benevolent intervention of human contact.

The sadomasochistic circle of guilt and penance accounts for much of the conflict which the artist-priest experiences. The characteristic agon is defined by his search for a release from guilt by pursuing a relationship with two women, one of whom is saintly, the other whorish. But his vacillation between these two is itself a basis for sustained guilt. Thus John Buchanan moves between Alma and Rosa; Shannon between Hannah and Maxine; Chance between Heavenly and Princess; and Kilroy between Esmeralda and La Madrecita. The same dynamic is represented with homosexual overtones in *Cat*, for clearly Brick believes that his relationship with Skipper was somehow elevated above carnal desire (whether he is lying is here beside the point), whereas his connection to Maggie, or more precisely, to Maggie's flesh, disgusts him. Williams has perfectly cathected the dynamic in his characterization of Blanche, who in the course of the play appears as both saint and whore to Mitch. It is Stanley's resentment of her neurotically aggressive pretensions to a fleshless sexuality (a tenet from her cultural past's idealized concept of womanhood) that instigates his vengeful degradation of her.

The names of Williams' saintly women suggest their transcendental view of existence. The Hebrew root of "Hannah" is "grace";

"Blanche" and "La Madrecita" have obvious connotations. Alma seems proud that her name is the Spanish word for "soul." She has looked through telescopes but not microscopes; she has never been subject to youth, just as Hannah's physical appearance should seem independent of time. Heavenly needs no gloss, other than to recall that Chance, with Joycean unselfconsciousness, describes her as Venus on the half-shell. In each of these plays virtually no dramatic interplay occurs between the saintly women and their counterparts. Maxine can barely tolerate the sight of Hannah, and Blanche's mental stability is largely predicated upon repressing the Blanche known at Laurel's Flamingo Hotel. Body and psyche of the saintly women in these plays are thus schizophrenically conjoined, a discord uniquely suited to self-destruction. For obvious reasons, Williams' drama *must* keep the two types from early reconciliation, or the play risks collapse of the tension which animates their mutual exile in which the masculine protagonist stumbles to find breath. Except in *Camino Real*, Williams' dramatization of the saint-whore cathexis does not approach allegory. Yet so firmly divided are the two principles that one cannot entirely avoid the hypothesis that their characterizations are fragments of one idealized psyche. Hannah stands so utterly apart from the flesh, and Maxine is so utterly obtuse to spiritual reality, that they move like antagonistic though complementary hemispheres of one entity which may not exist except hypostatically in the artist's mind. That these personalities respond with reflexive mutual aversion holds, of course, the potential of tragedy. Williams presents their conflict as part of a triangular stalemate: Hannah understands Shannon's unfitting clerical buttons and his neck lacerations inflicted by his crucifix, but she will participate in no active part of his sexuality; Maxine, having no understanding of Shannon's spiritual torment, only a limited toleration, solicits Shannon's sexual compliance (if not obedience).

But as *Night of the Iguana* illustrates, damnation is not simply a question of excess sexuality or faulty apprehension of abstruse spirituality. Williams draws characters who mercilessly seek human contact by actions which alienate them from the people willing or able to give it. Chance spurns his Aunt Nonnie, who risks some peril to continue caring for him; Brick resists Maggie adamantly; Blanche seeks comfort and security from her sister whose husband she attacks; Violet, whom Leona befriended and nursed provisionally back into society, cannot keep her hands off Leona's man (*Small Craft*). Amanda, desperate for Tom's support, drives him further away. The family, an institution whose function is presumably to provide a mutual support system for its members, is nearly always represented in Williams' plays as a destructive trap. The enforced physical and emotional proximity within it magnifies the potential of disruption. The most anguished decision in *The Glass Menagerie*, for example, is not Jim O'Connor's—for he is ignorant of, indeed innocent of, Laura's deepest problems—but Tom's. His departure from home has generated a nearly intolerable and permanent guilt. But if he had remained, his talent and privacy would have been asphyxiated under Amanda's constant siege. Tom drunkenly discovers the emblem of his family life in the stage magician's show: how do you get out of a coffin without removing one nail? His monologues imply that he is a prodigal son who can never be reconciled with his family. Although he has bolted out of the coffin, he still feels its nails.

The prodigal may be apprehended in the roots of Brick Pollitt, John Buchanan, and Chance Wayne. By exploiting the expectation of an ultimate redemption associated with prodigals, Williams heightens the despair of these men when that possibility aborts or falls into a narcotic void. In each instance, they reject family bonds. Even in death the family offers little succor. The woman of *I Can't Imagine Tomorrow* illustrates her pain by recounting the story of an Eskimo woman who asked her family to put her on an ice floe so that she could drift away on the sea to die alone. While Big Daddy is dying, he is lied to by his family and schemed against by his elder son while his favored younger son gazes on, seemingly imperturbable in alcoholic indolence. Williams' original script of *Cat* reveals that his conception of Brick's situation did not allow for any reconciliation at all. In fact, he commented on the intractability of Brick's "moral paralysis," which Kazan wanted altered for the Broadway production: "to show a dramatic progression [in Brick's characterization] would obscure the meaning of that tragedy in him and . . . I don't believe that a conversation [Brick's with his father in act two],

however revelatory, ever effects so immediate a change in the heart
or even conduct of a person in Brick's state of spiritual disrepair"
(III, 168).

In the first scene of *Streetcar*, Blanche's account of the succession
of death in her family at Belle Reve establishes that her compulsion
to wash herself and her fear of emotional apathy are the residue of
a moribund family system which has depleted most of her resources.
Her speech about death in the last scene paradoxically links the
physical corruption resulting from eating an unwashed grape with
the timeless laving of the ocean into which she would be cast. Her
fantasy of personal salvation conferred by the mysterious astringency
of death derives great force from the intensity of image, the pathos
of her manner of departure from Stella's household, and finally
from the perspective in which she sees herself. It has not that fullness
of tragic dimension because her self-evaluation is evidently made in
madness. Self-transcendence is possible when the personality can
stand apart from itself at a little distance and perceive itself whole
and in relation to the past. It is a perspective from which the protagonist surveys his life as a completed action; hence it is necessarily
dramatic. Aristotelian recognition or disclosure brutally enforces
upon the tragic protagonist this special and terrible objectivity: "I
pray you, in your letters,/When you shall these unlucky deeds relate,/Speak of me as I am; nothing extenuate,/Nor set down aught
in malice." Blanche's images of the unwashed grape, the physician's
silver watch, and her burial in a white sack at sea sum up the forces
against which she has waged a losing battle: physical corruption in
a world headed toward death and in which she has found no effective
solace. From her speech emerges the same kind of self-evaluation
which Othello above confesses, but unlike his it comes from a psy-
chotically detached mind. Othello acknowledges full responsibility
for his actions. Lear, for example, bursts into madness rather than
make a similar acknowledgment, but Shakespeare brings Lear to
the same pass, as the aged king confesses to his daughter a true account. Blanche's fantasy does give an imaginatively true account of
her destruction, but she remains—*must* remain—unaware of it. That
Streetcar does not equal the achievement of *Lear* is hardly a depre-
catory judgment. No finer picture of a lost soul appears in Williams'

canon. One must go to O'Neill's study of Mary Tyrone in *Long Day's Journey* to find an equivalent achievement in American drama.

II

He who waits to be righteous before he
enters into the Saviour's kingdom, the Divine Body, will never enter there.
                    Blake (*Jerusalem*, Plate 3)

In a world from which God the Creator has apparently absconded ("His oblivious majesty," as Shannon calls him), the only source of redemption lies within humanity itself. Williams' stage tableaux repeatedly suggest the pietà, for that representation, more than any other in Christian iconography, transfixes the human bond between Christ and his mother. His mutilated adult male body, father-forsaken, recumbent with death, concentrates a defeated suffering humanity into an image which powerfully animates Williams' imagination. Yet he dissociates the pietà theme from original sin. Hereditary evil springs only from the havoc caused within the soul by the uniquely human foreknowledge of physical corruption and death: "there is no way to beat the game of *being* against *nonbeing*" (II, 262). Nor is there aboriginal grace, no matter how constantly an institutionalized Christianity preaches to the contrary. No sign comes upon Serafina's impassioned supplications to the Lady, and the Blessed Mother gives Kilroy nothing but a silence. *Night of the Iguana* suggests nothing numenal to fill in the blank of Hannah's incomplete sentence. God is realized only in the actions of human beings who "play God" by responding mercifully to the suffering around them.

The plays in which Williams specifically addresses himself to redemption are, of course, comedies: *The Rose Tattoo, Camino Real, Period of Adjustment, Night of the Iguana, Kingdom of Earth,* and *Small Craft Warnings.* The tension of these plays inheres in the protagonist's reaching out for surcease from loneliness, not in the remedy itself. Two assumptions characteristic of Williams support the comic tone. As mentioned above, communication which nourishes the soul of another is sacramental. Like Portia's mercy, it is twice blessed. The redemptive quality of human communication is the basis of interaction between Hannah and Shannon, and between Ralph Bates and Isabel Haverstick in the first act of *Period of Adjustment*. And beauty itself, its creation and perception, nurtures the soul; for in the Shelleyan sense which Williams constantly ramifies, beauty is both the stimulus and the response of the religious instinct. Because the beautiful extenuates human communication, it carries the potential of redemption. It also carries liabilities. The dilemma which ensnares many of Williams' protagonists was densely formulated by Richard Rowan, the Jesuitically minded hero of Joyce's play *Exiles*: even if we are led to desire through the sense of beauty, can what we desire be called beautiful? Insofar as it generates life (Blanche says that the opposite of desire is death), Williams' characters answer Rowan's question affirmatively.

The redemptive theme in these comedies may be approached from Williams' concepts of the nature of theater, which in his view generates both beauty and intense communication. His early statement, "The History of a Play (With Parentheses)," appended to the first publication of *Battle of Angels* (*Pharos*, Spring 1945), is actually a spiritual-artistic apologia. Its tone of self-justification and wounded pride does not obscure the announcement of a dedication which, like most Romantic manifestos written since the early nineteenth century, equates artist and priest: theater offers a communion to redeem our society from its spiritual night. Before the opening of *Camino Real*, Williams wrote that his own creed as a playwright derived from Shaw's painter in *The Doctor's Dilemma*: "'I believe in Michelangelo, Velasquez and Rembrandt; in the might of design, the mystery of color, the redemption of all things by beauty everlasting and the message of art that has made these hands blessed. Amen'" (II, 423–24).

Those characters who create and respect beauty are invariably recommended to the audience's approval; conversely, the most sordid actions which Williams stages involve the willful destruction of beauty. Stanley desires to wound the best part of Blanche's soul— he rapes more than her body. Alma's response to the mystery and design of the gothic cathedral is not vague sentiment. The cathedral represents the consummation of unity and harmony which are absent from her own life. The perception of beauty is the most vital impulse of many of Williams' characters: one recalls Laura's glass and Amanda's desperate attempts to make her home attractive; Myra Torrance's thwarted desire to import her lost orchard into the confectionery, and the curtain embroidered with golden birds she places over Val's door; the small means Blanche uses to soften the environment of Stanley's apartment; the delight of Isabel and Dorothea over the negligee each wears to bed at the conclusion of *Adjustment*; Hannah's facility to put the revealing detail in a sketch, and her response to the eyes of those lying in the House of the Dying in Shanghai ("Nothing I've ever seen has seemed as beautiful to me," IV, 356); Leona's remorse over her dead brother, who was a violinist: "I'm proud that I've had something beautiful to remember as long as I live in my lifetime." Without at least one beautiful thing, she sobs, the heart inevitably corrupts: "it's all a deathtime" (V, 247–8). Although Leona's aggressive remorse is a comic self-indulgence, her pain is real and her words sincere. Earning her living as a professional beautician, she is another of Williams' tempestuous artist-priests, for she has put Violet back on her feet and given her beauty treatments without charge.

Although *Camino Real* is Williams' least successful major play, it is also one of his most ambitious efforts. According to the "Foreword" published just before the Broadway premiere, the freedom of flight was the guiding principle of its composition and production stylization. *Camino Real* should present on stage "something wild and unrestricted that [runs] like water in the mountains, or clouds changing shape in a gale, or the continually dissolving and transforming images of a dream" (II, 420). Various methods were employed to stage this difficult vision. For example, a large painted silk phoenix was placed on the window behind the balcony of the Siete Mares Hotel: "this should be softly lighted now and then in the play, since resurrections are so much a part of its meaning" (p. 431). Other images of the bird are used to represent resurrection in this play. This is appropriate enough, for the bird is here, as elsewhere, Williams' dramatic vehicle for the soul: "All of us have a desperate bird in our hearts," Jacques tells Marguerite, "a memory of—some distant mother with—wings" (p. 525). When the autopsy is performed upon Kilroy, La Madrecita exhorts, "Rise, ghost! Go! Go bird!" (p. 580). But redemption is more poignantly dramatized in the struggle of Jacques and Marguerite, the romantic center of *Camino Real*. The jaundiced courtesan informs Jacques, "Caged birds accept each other but flight is what they long for" (p. 501). The Fugitivo, which promised escape by air, proved merely capricious, hence an illusory escape, unearned. Marguerite subsequently prepares to leave Jacques for the charms of a younger man with whom she hopes to forget that she missed the Fugitivo. Seeking the same futile oblivion desired by the Princess Kosmonopolis, she utterly rejects Jacques's belief in tenderness, thus providing the foundation for her return—and the play's comic movement. When the lovers clasp each other at the very end of the play, Quixote, repeating Jacques's metaphor for tenderness, declaims that the violets in the mountains have broken the rocks—even though such flowers have been fed with the droppings of carrion birds. The tone of this metaphor borrows from biblical paradox, such as Christ's assertion that faith like that of a mustard seed can move mountains. Throughout *Camino Real* the playwright's intent has been to demonstrate that the cycle of decline from wholeness and sanity to fragmented desire and barbarism can be symmetrically reversed: carrion deeds may smuggle a contraband of remorse into the human heart. The necessary pain of this reversal must be written onto the lovers' faces as the curtain closes. But the melodramatic reversal of Marguerite's emotions, whose unstaged causes must be inferred, and the platitudinous advice about self-pity which Quixote gives Kilroy are theatrically anemic compared to the ravages of the streetcleaners, omnipresent buzzards, the repeated humiliations suffered by all the principals, the indifference of time enforced by Gutman's enunciations, and the unrelenting claustrophobic atmosphere of the entire action. The pain of lost paradise, imaged in La Madrecita's adjuration to remember Kilroy in "his time of greatness, when he was not faded" (p. 578), is invested with incomparably greater dramatic energy than the renewal signaled by the violets rooting in the mountains.

In formulaic terms, the most successful of Williams' comedies are *The Rose Tattoo, Period of Adjustment,* and *Kingdom of Earth,* for in each of these the thwarted passion convincingly overturns the obstacles to find an appropriate locus. In *Tattoo,* for example, Williams found the image of a flying bird appropriate to portray the recovery of Serafina's passion locked in guilt and remorse. As Alvaro considers what would happen to her if the urn containing her husband's ashes should break, he imagines that he can see her heart released from a prison: then he "whistles like a bird and makes graceful winglike motions with his hands" (II, 372). This scene of their first encounter initiates the reversal of Serafina's steady decline since the beginning of the play. Williams even instructs Alvaro to make his exit by imitating with whistles a bird flying off; and so his gaiety adumbrates the fortunate direction of their relationship. *The Rose Tattoo* defines and resolves in comic terms the difficulties the protagonists have in releasing a mutually interdependent sexuality. *Kingdom of Earth* presents a similar struggle in its most doctrinaire form. Chicken, a hybrid of Stanley Kowalski and Val Xavier, lives by a stark philosophy based upon "personal satisfaction": "With human beings, the ones I known in my life, what counts most is personal satisfaction, and God knows you'll never get that by denying yourself what you want most in the world by straining and struggling for what they call salvation when it's something you're just not cut out for" (p. 105). Both the story (which opens with the same assertion slightly reworded) and the play endow the expletive "God knows" with a broad irony, for the tone of each makes it plain that Williams' God, like Blake's, *does* know that salvation and personal satisfaction are not antithetical but inseparable.

Williams constantly returns to the enduring paradox that his central characters are so often outsiders, yet they seek the warmth of the society which they scorn and become its reciprocal targets of scorn. The artist himself is the prototype for seeking such acceptance from strangers. The tone of Williams' *Pharos* essay on the opening of *Battle* strongly implies that the hostile Boston audience rejected the Eucharist. Commenting fifteen years later upon the relationship of biography and art, Williams defined lyricism as the "outcry of prisoner to prisoner from the cell in solitary where each is confined for the duration of his life" (III, 3). This metaphor recurs in Val's conversation with Myra in the second act of *Battle* and in its rewrite *Orpheus*, and also it appears in Shannon's ironic suggestion that Hannah communicate with him by wall-tapping "like convicts in separate cells" (IV, 366). Confinement within the solitary self allowed Williams, as he phrased it, to talk to the audience "as freely and intimately about what we live and die for as if I knew you better than anyone else whom you know" (III, 7). Hence the artist's self-revelatory compulsion, which Clurman has identified as the basis of Williams' Romanticism.

The "kindness of strangers," which is sought by so many of Williams' protagonists, stimulates a brief but vital osmosis among the "cells of solitary confinement." This emotional seepage, which Williams pointedly distinguishes from physical sex, reaffirms both self-hood and community; it makes possible the mutual tolerance which, in a sense, confirms the *right to live*. The cellular structures of Maxine's hotel, Alma's window which overlooks the intolerable propinquity of John Buchanan's adjacent house, the opposing hotels in *Camino Real*, the small space between the double bed and the couch in Maggie and Brick's bedroom—these mise en scènes illustrate both the need and the difficulties of vital communication among the frightened people whose living space they define. Redemption may be considered as the process of emotional osmosis enabling people to discover and accept the self and its environment. "Accept whatever situation you cannot improve" is the quintessence of Hannah's interaction with Shannon (IV, 363). Throughout *Night of the Iguana* she has constantly had to accept things entirely beyond her power to improve, yet she maintains her dignity. These words stand in direct opposition to Alma Winemiller's bitter dictum: "Ask for all, but be prepared to get nothing!" (II, 241). Alma's personal world, governed by an absolutism worthy of Antigone, must therefore fracture. Hannah's acceptance is an affirmation of life, a desire to survive intact; it is not merely a cynical submission to the world's depredations, as Shannon either mistakenly or willfully misinterprets. Her actions, her entire past, prevents her advice from being a reductive platitude.

Confession promotes Williams' societies because it speaks through cellular barriers, just as the confessional box in the Roman Church is constructed. *Small Craft Warnings*, whose original title was *Confessional*, depicts a group of outcasts who in their nexus of loneliness at Monk's bar provide a temporary home for one another. Williams does not sentimentalize this "family." Doc, Bill, Leona, and Violet treat one another roughly, and by the end of the play the fragile stability which they had been enjoying has all but completely disintegrated. Leona ejects Bill from her trailer and prepares to leave town, Bobby rejects the home Leona offers him, Quentin and Doc— both intensely self-destructive—seem likely to remain permanent outcasts. Their sorrows and despair are presented as forcefully as that which animates Williams' earlier characters, but they do not live by an all-or-nothing absolutism. They confess. Confession is, of course, the first action in the penitential sequence culminating in grace. In Williams' church, confession is the admission of human frailty which, being uttered, *claimed*, becomes a community strength: "the stories, the jokes, the confidences and confessions I've heard that night," Monk reminisces, "it makes me feel not alone" (V, 265–6). Commenting upon his receipt of a tiny legacy, the residue of remembrance from a customer absent for over five years, Monk says simply, "A thing like that is beautiful as music. These things, these people, take the place of a family in my life" (p. 265).

However briefly or inadequately, the other characters in Monk's bar have provided one another a family too. Their family is not so much a death-trap as the other families represented in Williams' canon, for escape is far simpler, but their unanchored fragile society supported by the kindness of strangers is portrayed with extraordinary sympathy. *Small Craft* closes upon an act of kindness. Monk gives Violet a temporary home which, as he realizes, is probably not so temporary. The two complementary metaphors in his curtain monologue, Violet's wornout slippers and the shower he urges her to take, respectively convey endurance in spite of human mortality, and the cleansing renewal of human contact: "I am not going up there till she's took a shower" (p. 286). Pondering his decision about Violet, he opens the doors to welcome the odor and sound of the fresh Pacific air, and then he hears the sound of her shower: "That ain't rain" (p. 287). This curtain line succinctly conveys a redemptive baptismal which is wholly integrated into the play's situational realism.

Hannah Jelkes, who is kind and equally dependent upon gratuitous kindness, defines home as "a thing that two people have between them in which each can . . . well, nest—rest—live in, emotionally speaking" (IV, 356–57). The emotional structure so built is not necessarily guided by concerns of permanence or mating, as her own history proves. And so she rejects the offer of a relationship with

Shannon, for she knows that there is no place in him in which she could rest. Yet she has benefitted from his kindness, which has been shown almost instinctively to her and Nonno, even in their first scene together. He coaxes Maxine to allow them to stay at the hotel, he prevents Nonno from falling, he brings them water to drink and urges Hannah to attend to a scratch she incurred while pushing Nonno up the hill. In the final scene he gives her his golden crucifix to pawn for travelling money. These actions form a network establishing the emotional center of the play. *Iguana* is Williams' most convincing dramatization of authentic redemption, for it is not simplistic in promoting a guiltless unselfconsciousness which characterizes the conclusion of *Kingdom of Earth*. Its resolution is neither farcical nor formulaic as those of *The Rose Tattoo* and *Period of Adjustment*. It states human separation with force and dignity and it refuses to opt for the easy solution which Shannon himself proposes. Like *Small Craft Warnings*, it celebrates the endurance, if not triumph, of lives facing rather large obstacles. For Shannon, Hannah, and Maxine will simply continue, just as Violet's slipper will still be used after the cardboard soles have been worn through, even after it is "past all repair." The rhetorical climax of Nonno's poem summons courage to live in this fallen world. The artist naturally yearns for the inviolability and timelessness of the sphere inhabited by "beings of a golden kind"—as Yeats yearned for Byzantium and Keats mused upon his unravished bride of quietness. But the imagination confers to nobody a sublunary immunity from physical corruption. Courage—which Williams characterizes as the force of spirit required to give life dignity in the onrush of time—supports man's redemptive hope, for it makes civilization possible. Otherwise, kindness, sacrifice, all artistic contemplation, would be brushed aside in a general attempt to outdistance the earth's "obscene corrupting love." That Williams assigns this poem to Nonno emphasizes the point about endurance. Redemption must occur in *this* world, not in the hypothetical next. Nonno is Williams' only character who earns the right to die; the others who die have death inflicted upon them. Considering the size of the self-destructive populace in the canon, it is remarkable that virtually none of them actively contemplates suicide. The dignity of endurance illuminates the characterizations not only of Nonno and Hannah but also of Brinda's mother in "Mama's Old Stucco House" and the generous and stoic grand-mother of "Grand."

Many lapses appear in Williams' portrayal of damnation and redemption. Chance Wayne's frenzy and obtuse refusal to examine his motives deprive his curtain appeal of any real force. One does not think of him and his situation, "This is true"; instead, "How horrific is this spectacle!" Has not the structure of *Suddenly Last Summer* been similarly weakened by pouring Catharine's recollection neatly into the mold of a pièce bien faite? One wonders also how Shannon can be so thoroughly acquainted with sexual abuse yet repelled by Hannah's account of the underwear salesman's fetish. Is he in any better position to haul his life up the hill, even with Maxine's help, if he takes the petty revenge of urinating upon his antagonists' luggage? An indictment of unearned horror and the too facile line which sacrifice tone to an inferior end could be easily lengthened. But Williams' understanding of despair, his urgent belief in community, and his celebration of endurance and human dignity are authentic. These values and the dramatic skill which inscribe them upon the stage confirm Williams' elevated position among dramatists of this century.

Symbol, Myth, and Ritual in *The Glass Menagerie, The Rose Tattoo,* and *Orpheus Descending*

JUDITH J. THOMPSON

IN "FOREWORD" TO *Camino Real,* Tennessee Williams says "symbols are nothing but the natural speech of drama" (II, 421). According to C. G. Jung, a symbol is "a term, a name, or even a picture that may be familiar in daily life, yet that possesses specific connotations in addition to its conventional and obvious meaning. . . . It has a wider 'unconscious' aspect that is never precisely defined or fully explained" (*Man and his Symbols,* pp. 3–4). Williams' belief in the evocative value of symbols closely resembles Jung's theories of the "collective unconscious," that second psychic system of a "collective, universal, and impersonal nature which is identical in all individuals" (*Portable Jung,* p. 60). As Williams notes, "We all have in our conscious and unconscious minds a great vocabulary of images, and I think all human communication is based on these images as are our dreams" (II, 421). Based on familiar religious, mythical, and literary associations, Williams' symbols tap the emotional depths of the collective unconscious with its store of "archetypes," those "mental forms . . . which seem to be aboriginal, innate, and inherited shapes of the human mind" (*Man and his Symbols,* p. 57).

Williams' dramatic use of universally evocative symbols derives from his concept of and concern with the interrelationship of the playwright, the audience, and the play. He characterizes himself as one of those playwrights "permitted only to feel" (II, 423). Creative motivation, he believes, has its source in "the particular and sometimes peculiar concerns of the artist himself" (III, 3). Williams is keenly aware, however, that the unique nature of individual consciousness both defines the ego and serves as a barrier separating the self from the other, to the extent that "We're all of us sentenced to solitary confinement inside our own skins" (III, 3). Thus, in his *Playboy* interview, Williams identifies "loneliness" as his major and recurrent theme (p. 76). Not content simply to dramatize this fundamental condition of human existence, Williams offers his theater as a kind of corrective for it. He attests to "a highly personal, even intimate relationship with people who go to see plays" (III, 5), and conceives of his plays as vehicles through which he works toward an embrace with the audience. Describing his dramatic mode as "personal lyricism," he seeks to elicit from an audience that "outcry of prisoner to prisoner from the cell in solitary where each is confined for the duration of his life" (III, 3): a cri de coeur intended to purge the individual of personal loneliness by his recognition of and participation in the suffering of his fellow isolato.

The fundamental theatrical concern of Williams, then, is to transform his personal emotions, as they are embodied in the particular and sometimes peculiar maladies, neuroses, and illusions of his characters, into recognizably universal feelings. He would rise "above the singular to the plural concern, from personal to general import" (III, 4). Through the communal associations provided by mythical symbols and ritual patterns, Williams attempts to create in his audience an empathetic response to his characterizations of the lonely, the neurotic, the alienated, and persecuted, thereby evoking that shock of recognition by which the audience acknowledges as familiar the characters' psychic conflicts. As Williams describes the experience, "Our hearts are wrung by recognition and pity, so that the dusky shell of the auditorium where we are gathered anonymously together is flooded with an almost liquid warmth of unchecked human sympathies, relieved of self-consciousness, allowed to function . . ." (II, 262). A major function of Williams' symbols, then, is to form an emotional bridge with the audience, to create a drama so emotionally charged with the concrete universals of archetypal images that their realization breaks down the psychological walls of our separate selves, making the particular general, the strange familiar, and even the grotesque recognizable as but another dimension of the human condition.

Two types of symbols, concrete and transcendent, are used by Williams to evoke this communal response. Concrete symbols embody the psychic reality of the characters in substantial sensory forms, which appeal to the emotions through the physical senses, visual and aural. The subjective world of the characters is thus displayed on stage by the constructs or props of the set, by the significant gestures and movements of the actors, by the sounds of music, often the lyrical, staccato, or antiphonal rhythms of speech itself, and by the effects of light and color. They constitute what T. S. Eliot has defined as the "objective correlatives" of states of mind or feeling, that "set of objects, a situation, a chain of events which shall be the formula of that particular emotion; such that when the external facts . . . are given, the emotion is immediately evoked" (pp. 124–5). Thus, the objective correlatives of a character's wounded psyche may reside in the furniture of the stage set: Laura Wingfield's arrested development in the old-fashioned knick-knack case filled with tiny glass animals, Serafina Delle Rose's repressed sexuality in an urn set in front of a small shrine, Alma Winemiller's frigidity in the form of a massive stone angel, or Shannon's infantile regression in a centrally placed canvas hammock. The emotions of nostalgia or memories of lost innocence may be evoked through music or by the uninhibited voices of children at play; the recurrent bleating of the unleashed goat in The Rose Tattoo reminds us of the necessity of fulfilling the physical present, while the "constant, dry, scuffling sound" of a lizard tied under a porch in The Night of the Iguana evokes the frustrations of unfulfilled desires. A character's futile attempt to recapture the past may be embodied in his costume: in Amanda's yellowed dress and her bouquet of jonquils, in Brick Pollitt's bathrobe and crutch, in Serafina's outgrown girdle, or in the defrocked Shannon's clerical collar that will not stay buttoned. Finally, a character's consciousness may be indicated by nuances of lighting, the rose-colored or shuttered light of dusk and very early daybreak embodying his dreams or fixation with the past, while brief moments of radiance may symbolize his confrontation with the present. These techniques, often used simultaneously, create an atmosphere in which the objective correlatives of the psychic wounds of the characters continuously bombard the senses and stimulate an intensely sympathetic response.

The symbols of transcendence are allusive rather than sensory; they are drawn from religious, mythical, and literary sources rather than from the phenomena of objective reality. Most significant, their function is not to anchor the psychic reality of the character in corresponding sensory forms, but to enlarge and expand our consciousness of his subjective world beyond the time and space of the particular dramatic situation of the play. The nature and pattern of these symbols and their significance to *The Glass Menagerie*, *The Rose Tattoo*, and *Orpheus Descending* are the main concerns of this essay.

One of the most significant functions of these symbols is to give a mythic dimension or stature to the characters. Williams has said, "All my *great* characters are larger than life, not realistic" (*Playboy*, p. 80). One purpose for making his characters larger than life is to universalize the particular and the peculiar, to find those analogues or archetypes in myth, legend, or fairy tale that will tap the collective unconscious and give archetypal meaning to personal plight. Williams rarely makes a one-to-one identification of a character with a mythical archetype, however, for his purpose is not narrowly allegorical but allusive. His characters are made larger than life through a method of multiple images (see Jackson, *Broken World*, pp. 83–5). Each is a composite figure drawn from fragments of pagan and Christian prototypes and their diminutive forms in fairy tale and comic strips. By using both romantic and ironic modes in characterization, Williams stresses the illusory nature of the character's mythic or godlike stature. Thus, Rosario in *The Rose Tattoo* is a composite of the Dionysian god, the popular film star Valentino, and the lecherous goat. Maggie in *Cat on a Hot Tin Roof* is both Diana, goddess of the hunt, the moon, and nature, and "a cat in heat." The diverse images surrounding Chance Wayne in *Sweet Bird of Youth* include those of Adonis, the god of fertility (see Hays, pp. 255–258), Jack and the Beanstalk, a Christ figure, and an aging romance knight. Thus, even as Williams symbolizes the illusions, delusions, and romantic aspirations of his characters to transcend their human limitations, he continually invokes their instinctual animal nature and the flesh-and-blood needs which keep them earthbound.

The method by which Williams invests his characters with mythic dimensions is the story or recollection of the past, told usually by the protagonist about himself, at the beginning of each of these three plays. This story is often an elevated or exaggerated memory of an event or a relationship, invested with idyllic, romantic, or religious overtones. It is because of this memory, usually a vision of intense beauty, that the protagonists are often frozen or transfixed in the posture or attitude of looking backward, their emotional growth arrested, and their human dimensions inflated with romantic illusions of a once perfect condition.

Furthermore, the story itself is retold or dramatized in the course of the play. In essence, the dramatic events of the second half of each play are a reenactment of the story told at its beginning. Thus, Amanda's story of the seventeen gentlemen callers is reenacted by Laura and Jim in *The Glass Menagerie*; Serafina's idealized account of her transcendent relationship with her husband Rosario is reenacted by Serafina and Alvaro in *The Rose Tattoo*; the story of idyllic love and fertility in the wine garden between Lady Torrance and David Cutrere is reenacted by Lady with Val Xavier in *Orpheus Descending*. The recurrent structure of a story told, then reenacted in a second version, is in itself an analogue of myth and ritual. The personal story assumes the dimensions of myth, its reenactment a ritual which parallels the events of the myth. However, unlike the ancient myths and rituals of initiation, fertility, and rebirth or resurrection which these stories suggest, the second version of the original story in Williams' plays rarely culminates in the celebration of fulfilled or realized aspirations.

The diminished myth or unsuccessful ritual which is reenacted reveals as ironic the relationship of mythic symbolism to character, theme, and structure in these plays. In short, Williams invests his characters with mythic stature only to divest them of it in the process of the play. The climax of each play, then, rests in an event of demythicization: that moment when the character is divested of his mythic or godlike dimensions, stripped of his illusions and delusions, and forced to recognize his human limitations, his animal instincts, and his inherently antiheroic nature. Furthermore, the symbolic moment of divestment is generally dramatized through the gesture of breaking, rending, or shattering the concrete symbol which has been identified as the objective correlative of the character's psychic reality. Thus, Jim's breaking of Laura's unicorn in *The Glass Menagerie*, Serafina's shattering the urn of Rosario in *The Rose Tattoo*, Mitch's tearing Blanche's paper lantern from the naked light bulb in *A Streetcar Named Desire*, Shannon's freeing the iguana in *The Night of the Iguana*, Maggie's disposal of Brick's crutch and liquor bottles in *Cat on a Hot Tin Roof*, the crash of the suitcase filled with Casanova's mementos and the literal stripping away of Marguerite's clothes in *Camino Real* are all symbolic acts which divest the characters of their mythic dimensions, deflate their romantic illusions, and force them to confront a diminished or impoverished reality. Paradoxically, it is this moment which generally affords the character the opportunity to assume a new, more fully human, stature, in the expression of love, sympathy, or compassion with another. But for those who cannot or will not accept their self-limitations or the compromise of their mythic world, their lost Eden, the result is destruction or withdrawal.

Williams' plays do not simply recall the old mythic images and religious rituals; they transform them in their reenactment. Many of his plays are based on myths of dying gods, but, unlike the original myth, they culminate in neither rebirth nor resurrection. His drama is structured as ritual, but as a ritual of the divestment of illusion, or as a parody of the romantic quest, whose ironic destination is what Northrop Frye calls the tour abolie, archetypal image of "the goal of the quest that isn't there" (p. 239). Thus, Williams constructs from the old myths and rituals new meanings relevant to an age and culture bereft of a commonly shared mythology. Seeking to restore symbolic meaning to the life of modern man, Williams offers a theatrical experience intended to encourage our investing symbolic significance and value in merely human relationships, however limited and compensatory they might seem. In its sympathetic portrayal of our yearnings for transcendence, its realistic depiction of our inherent limitations, and its utter insistence on the necessity of imbuing with religious significance the rare and transient communion of man with his fellow, Williams' drama is a myth for our time.

The Glass Menagerie is one of Williams' most symbolically informed plays. The symbols—concrete, allusive, and evocative—are so structured as to define a world which is at once existentially constrictive and metaphorically expansive. Even as the physical constructs of time and circumstance identify the characters by their human limitations, the metaphors through which their aspirations are expressed enlarge their individual dimensions to those of archetypal stature and elevate their personal plight to universal significance.

The principal symbol in the play is, as the title suggests, the glass menagerie. It is specifically Laura's symbol, the objective correlative of her fragile, other-worldly beauty. Its stylized animal forms image her own immobilized animal or sexual nature, her arrested emotional development, and her inability to cope with the demands of a flesh-and-blood world. Given broader implications, the separate pieces of the glass collection reflect the fixed attitudes of all the members of the Wingfield family as well as their isolation from one another. Presented as crystallized forms in Tom's memory, each character is shown to be psychologically encased in a world of his own. Seeking escape, refuge, or rebirth, each imagines different versions of a transcendent reality, themselves a collection of isolatos condemned to individual fragmentation and mutual misunderstanding. Finally, in its quintessential form, the glass menagerie is symbolic of stasis, that temporal mode central to the play's internal structure. The underlying structure of *The Glass Menagerie* is formed by a tension between the illusion of moving forward and the reality of moving backward, between dream and destiny, the two so perfectly balanced that the effect is the arrest of time. Within this frozen moment, however, resides the significant action of the play: a cyclical motion of repetition and recurrence, the acting out again and again of a single futile pattern.

The dynamic symbol of that recurrent pattern is Amanda's story of the courtship ritual, herein an ironic process of anticipation, momentary fulfilment, and subsequent loss, desolation, and disillusionment. As symbol, the story of Amanda and her seventeen gentlemen callers forms a paradigm of experience which underlies the structure of the entire play. Life is envisioned as a series of losses, beginning with innocent expectations of its infinite possibilities and ending in confrontation with its inherent limitations. It is, indeed, this story told by Amanda at the beginning of the play which is re-enacted in its second half by Laura and Jim. Furthermore, every other event in the play repeats the process. A similar pattern of great expectations and subsequent despair informs the story of Tom, the aspiring poet whose dreams of life as a meaningful voyage end only in aimless drifting. Although Jim's ability to compromise with a diminished reality differentiates him from the other characters, the pattern also informs his story, for he is the high school hero—"The Pirate of Penzance"—who is reduced to a clerk in a warehouse, his romantic libretto exchanged for a paean to capitalistic enterprise. The pattern of anticipation, brief fulfilment, and subsequent loss is capsulized at the very beginning of the play in the message contained in the father's picture postcard: "Hello—Goodbye!" (I, 145), a microcosmic summary of the play's symbolic structure.

A symbolic embodiment of the last of the gentlemen callers, the father is present throughout the play in the image of a larger-than-life-size photograph which lights up whenever Amanda recalls him, thereby reminding the audience of the entire pattern of her story, from its inflated beginnings to its prosaic end. The inevitability of the pattern is reinforced by implied analogies among the three male figures. As the suitor with the winning smile, the father is linked with Jim, the reincarnated gentleman caller, who shares his charm and grin. As the deserting husband, he is linked with Tom, the prodigal son, who shares his escapist impulse. All three embody the romantic concept of war as heroic adventure in their respective roles of World War I doughboy, make-believe pirate, and merchant seaman. Moreover, Jim's romantic stage role as the Pirate of Penzance in Gilbert and Sullivan's comic opera both foreshadows and mocks Tom's dream of playing a similarly romantic role by joining the Merchant Marines. Thus, Jim's stage symbol, the image of "a sailing vessel with Jolly Roger" (pp. 173, 200)—the black flag of the pirate ship—is flashed on the screen whenever Tom dreams of his maritime adventure, a subliminal undermining of Tom's transcendent aspirations. Even in their family name, juxtaposing wing with field, the symbols of transcendence are fused with the constructs of mundane reality, relentlessly suggesting the painful disparity between aspiration and actuality, or between what the characters would be and what they must be.

The tension between the ideal and the real is also exemplified in the religious imagery which ironically links both the members of this fragmented household and the romanticized Jim to the Christian Holy Family. The incongruity of superimposing the images of Christian archetypes of love and sacrifice onto pathetically inadequate representatives painfully emphasizes modern man's loss of that original mythic union between heaven and earth, the divine and the human, spirit and flesh. At the same time, it poignantly reveals a continued yearning for redemption from a world devoid of spiritually transcendent values. Thus, the intensity of Amanda's disappointment with Laura's failure to fulfill her expectations at Rubicam's Business College suggests her analogy to "the picture of Jesus' mother in the museum" (p. 155), the mater dolorosa of Christian art, image of martyred maternity. Laura herself evokes the image of saint, nun, or child of God whose relics, the profane collection of her father's phonograph records, assume the miraculous function of creating a harmonious sanctuary in which her crippled psyche is momentarily healed of the wounds incurred in a discordant reality. The All-American Jim is elevated to a Christ figure or savior, the news of his coming to dinner referred to as an "annunciation" (p. 181), the promise of birth. Tom suggests an ironic inversion of the archetypal Son, a "bastard son of a bastard" (p. 202), a dispossessed heir who "followed . . . in my father's footsteps" (p. 237) by his liberation from and repudiation of inherited responsibilities. The father himself, "a telephone man—who fell in love with long distance" (p. 204), is thus symbolic of the absent and incommunicado God of the modern world (cf. Fritscher, p. 215).

The play's symbols are not derived exclusively from Christian myth, however. Each character is invested with a matrix of multiple images, drawn from sources both sacred and secular, Christian and pagan. Amanda's character and monologues are infused with a nostalgia which taps an emotional memory far beyond her "Gone With the Wind" account of her southern girlhood. In her first monologue of the seventeen gentlemen callers, the very exaggeration of the number of suitors recalls fairy tale and the legends of romance in which the princess is beleaguered by suitors until the perfect knight or prince appears. The pastoral implications of suitors who are "planters and sons of planters" (p. 148) recall both the Edenic garden and ancient myths of gods and goddesses of fertility. Amanda is an Aphrodite called on by multiple analogues of Adonis. Her story always begins the same, on a Sunday morning in Blue Mountain, combining the Christian religious day with overtones of Olympus, the archetypal point of epiphany. It always ends at Moon Lake, evoking the experience of a fall, from chastity or innocence. At Moon Lake, the pastoral scene disintegrates into a graveyard, the uprooted or unweeded garden, Amanda's admirers having "turned up their toes to the daisies" (p. 149) after meeting violent ends. Success or survival depends on transplantation, the exchange of those genteel values of the fertile Delta of Greene County for those of the cold North, where at least one of her former suitors is transformed from beauty and youth to a lone "Wolf of Wall Street" (p. 149), a modern Midas whose touch turns all sustenance to unregenerative gold. The significance of the allusive imagery and fatalistic pattern of Amanda's story extends beyond that of a paradigm for the historical collapse of the Plantation South in civil strife, beyond the corruption of the New World through mercenary exploitation. It evokes the myth of the Fall itself: humankind's expulsion from Eden, the subsequent violence of brother against brother, and the perversion by man's inherently defective nature of all attempts to cultivate "a paradise within."

In anticipation of a new gentleman caller, Amanda recounts a still earlier memory of spring and courtship, set in a kind of Dionysian meadow where the sexual and the spiritual were once reconciled: fever and flowers, the heat of passion and the sympathetic sensuousness of nature. Amanda's description of that momentous spring when she met her husband is perhaps one of the most lyrical passages in Williams' plays. At a breathless pace, Amanda more nearly sings than speaks her story, repeating the word *jonquils* until its sensuous and lyrical syllables assume incantatory power, invoking a flood of memories of rebirth and rejuvenation. Amanda is endowed with the archetypal attributes of May Queen, the spirit of vegetation and fertility crowned with flowers, who, amidst gaiety and dancing, enacts the ritual of spring, the mating rite. Because the boy she meets is also the husband who abandons her to the dark tenement in an impoverished reality, the story of Amanda also recalls the myth of Persephone, goddess of spring whom Pluto snatched from her flower-gathering to his dark underworld. Like Persephone, Amanda has lost her eternal spring and bitterly mourns the transitory nature of youth, love, and beauty. Her experience has taught her that beauty and charm may be enticements of seduction and love itself an instrument of exploitation. Thus, the youthful Amanda who triggers collective images of Aphrodite, May Queen, Persephone, and Princess also reveals the darker side of the feminine archetype, of woman as entrapment and danger. To Laura she speaks as femme fatale: "All pretty girls are a trap" (p. 192). To Tom, she is the Terrible Mother, the womb of the earth become the devouring maw of the underworld, to which the fairy-tale analogue is the "ugly—babbling old—witch" (p. 164), as Tom calls her. The anticipation of a gentleman caller, however, not only permits Amanda to take on the attributes of May Queen again for a brief time but also allows her to assume the benevolent role of fairy godmother, attempting to transform the crippled Laura into a Cinderella, as she urges her to wish on a "little silver slipper of a moon" (p. 189).

The symbolism associated with Laura is composed largely of religious and ascetic images connoting the innocent other-worldiness of the saint, the cloistered nun, and the chaste virgin. In "Production Notes," Williams says that the light upon Laura should have "a peculiar pristine clarity such as light used in early religious portraits of female saints or madonnas" (pp. 133–34). Appropriately, candle-light, the halo of illumination set before shrines, is her milieu. Jim's attentions light "her inwardly with altar candles" (p. 219), the warmth of religious devotion, while her final disappointment is revealed as if "the holy candles on the altar of Laura's face have been snuffed out" (p. 230), the loss of faith. In reinforcement of her saintly aspect, Amanda, Jim, and Tom call her "Sister," the traditional address for a nun, and she calls herself "an old maid" (p. 150), the eternal virgin. Her favorite animal in the glass menagerie is the mythical unicorn, "emblem of chastity and the lover of virgins" (Frye, p. 152). The recurrent music of "The Glass Menagerie," which may be imagined as the distant sound of a calliope on a merry-go-round, evokes all the other images which characterize Laura's inner world: the tiny stationary glass animals, her childlike nature, and her uniqueness—in circus terms called freakishness; in religious terms, miraculous; in temporal terms, anachronistic. Her symbolic name of "Blue Roses" emphasizes her unnatural or extraterrestrial nature, as does her favorite retreat, "the Jewel Box, that big glass house where they raise the tropical flowers" (p. 155), a metaphor for Laura's inner world, herself the rara avis or exotic flower that cannot survive transplantation to the outside world. Finally, Laura's name resembles *laurel*, the name of the flowering tree into which the mythic Daphne was transformed after evading the sexual pursuit of Apollo, thereby refusing the call to sexual maturity (see Campbell, pp. 60–62).

Images of modern existential man dominate Tom's symbolic characterization: the demonic images of fragmentation, suffocation, and alienation. He identifies both the urban tenement and the warehouse as modern analogues of hell, himself sealed in a coffin, an ironic *"czar of the underworld"* (p. 164), his deepest aspirations smoldering in frustration. Driven by the oppressive and repressive circumstances of his life and seduced by the illusory images of the movie screen to believe in a rainbow at the end of the journey, Tom attempts the sea voyage which is not only his personal quest for self-realization, but also represents the attempt of twentieth century man to restore to wholeness the fragmented self, threatened by dehumanization and disintegration. Tom's struggle to integrate the primal instincts of "a lover, a hunter, a fighter" (p. 174) with the creative impulse of the poet suggests the attempt of modern man to heal that deep split between body and soul, the senses and the spirit, which characterizes the modern malaise. Liberated from Hades, however, Tom finds himself an aimless drifter in its modern equivalent, the Wasteland, self-exiled among the ruins of a nihilistic landscape. All the symbols of hope through which the characters have expressed their private visions of transcendence—Amanda's colorful jonquils, Laura's iridescent glass figures, Tom's flickering screen images, and the large glass sphere in the Paradise Dance Hall—are ultimately revealed as fragments of broken dreams, as "bits of a shattered rainbow" (p. 237). Haunted by his abandonment of the others in his futile quest for self, Tom joins the ranks of other guilt-haunted wanderers—Cain, the Wandering Jew, the Flying Dutchman, the Ancient Mariner—representatives of archetypal alienation. Tom becomes the poète maudit, cursed with existential knowledge of the human condition and compelled to retell his story, a modern fable of the failure of love and of man's inability to transcend his solitude in a world devoid of transcendent goals.

Jim O'Connor is at once the most symbolic character in the play and the most realistic. Accordingly, the allusive imagery from which he is constructed is multiple and paradoxical, romantic and ironic. As a reincarnation of the gentleman caller, he evokes both the infinite possibilities suggested by all seventeen suitors and the limited reality defined by the last caller, the father who abandoned wife and family. Thus, Jim represents both that "long-delayed but always expected something that we live for" (p. 145) and, ironically, "a nice, ordinary, young man" (p. 129), both the ideal and the real. "Like some archetype of the universal unconscious" (p. 159), Jim is invested with multiple heroic images. As the reborn gentleman caller, he may be identified with a fertility god, the regenerative planter; his annunciation signals the rebirth or second coming of Christ as the savior; Amanda's wish upon "the little silver slipper of a moon" casts Jim in the role of Prince Charming to Laura's Cinderella and her Sleeping Beauty. He is the singing Pirate who will charm the Lady, and he is Superman (p. 210) who never fails to rescue Lois Lane. All of these symbols of expectation are invested in a character who is the epitome of the All-American boy—extroverted, dynamic, and optimistic—thoroughly acculturated to the popular version of happiness achieved through technological progress, status, and material success.

The enlargement of the characters through allusive imagery in the first part of the play is designed to heighten the emotional intensity of its climactic scene, the meeting between Laura and Jim. The mythicization of the characters combined with the symbolic value invested in the concrete props of the scene—Laura's physical transformation, the suggestion of rain, the circle of candlelight from the miraculously fire-salvaged candelabrum, and the glass of dandelion wine—all elevate the significance of their meeting beyond mere social ceremony to suggest the pagan ritual of fertility or initiation, the Christian rite of Holy Communion, and the romantic ideal of courtship. In this instance, however, symbol is divorced from substance, the mythical distinguished from the actual, and the bubbles of subjective reality in which the characters have insulated themselves are broken. At the same time, the infusion of symbolic meaning into ordinary human experience evokes an emotional response appropriate to an event of momentous import, thereby deepening the significance of the failure of union between Laura and Jim.

The process of demythicization begins with Jim's breaking of the unicorn, medieval emblem of chastity and innocence, which signals the beginning of Laura's healthy sexual and emotional development and the diminishment of her symbolic dimensions as virgin, saint, and child. As the unicorn divested of its horn is now "just like all the other horses" (p. 226), so Laura no longer feels freakish and estranged from vital human experience. Her emergence into Jim's world of dynamic optimism is dramatically expressed by her cavalier reaction to the broken unicorn, her private world of imaginary animals having become less important than the real one of human relationships. Thus, her use of popular slang parallels Jim's own idiomatic diction: "It's no tragedy, Freckles. Glass breaks so easily" (p. 226). While Laura's sexuality is awakened by Jim's natural exuberance, his deeper sensibilities are aroused by her vulnerability and virginal beauty. Thus, for the brief moment of their kiss, the symbolic fusion of experience and innocence, body and soul, sense and spirit, or reality and dream is achieved. Jim's subsequent revelation of his engagement to another girl and the finality of his departure not only abandon Laura to her shattered dreams but also deflate the entire matrix of mythical, romantic, and religious symbols. Mocked by their symbols of transcendence, the characters are identified starkly as "a mother deserted, an unmarried sister who's crippled" and a son who's a "selfish dreamer" (p. 236). The end of all the images and symbols developed in the play is to evoke an overwhelming sense of loss. The failure of Jim to save Laura is also the failure of the fertility god to complete the initiation rite, the failure of Christ's second coming, the failures of Prince Charming, the Pirate, and Superman to rescue the maiden in distress. Because Williams has so extended the symbolic meaning of Jim, the loss becomes one of "infinite desolation" (p. 230). It is the loss of all heroes, the death of all gods. Thus, through a profusion of symbolic references and a recurrent pattern of anticipation, momentary fulfilment, and ultimate despair, the meaning of the play is enlarged. It is not simply the story of one shy crippled girl, a neurotic mother, and a dreamer of a son, not the story of just one more broken family, but an analogue of modern man's alienation from God and isolation from his fellow man.

The Glass Menagerie embodies Williams' vision of the fundamental human situation as one of solitude in a universe indifferent to our fate. By the infusion of symbol, myth, and ritual into a naturalistic drama, Williams evokes a painful awareness of the central paradox of modern existence, that the transcendent imagination remains undiminished in a world empty of transcendent value. Thus, only by the divestment of deceptive illusions and romantic hopes of transcending the human condition is the communication of self with other possible. However, human love itself is shown as inadequate compensation for our epiphanic desires. Fleeting, incomplete, and too easily betrayed, human love too often leads only to mutual recognition of despair.

The play ends, then, in an ironic family portrait. No longer sealed within private visions of transcendence, the members of the Wingfield family are united in their mutual understanding of their inherent isolation. The ironic embrace is achieved aesthetically by simultaneous views of Amanda, Laura, and the departed Tom. In mime, Amanda makes a gesture of compassion toward Laura, as Laura smiles with new understanding at Amanda, and Tom relates his bitter discovery of an unredemptive reality, threatened by holocaust and ruled by forces inimical to innocence, beauty, or spiritual values. Paradoxically, the symbolic tableau itself transcends for a moment the literal meaning of despair, but only for a moment. The play closes in darkness, all three characters confined to the prisons of self once more in a reality unrelieved by dreams of deliverance.

The structural images of *The Rose Tattoo* are more cohesive, though no less complex, than those of *The Glass Menagerie*, for *The Rose Tattoo* is concerned with union and reconciliation rather than disintegration and alienation. Appropriately, the rose tattoo, the central concrete symbol of the play, is itself an emblem of the union of spirit with flesh. The rose, by itself, evokes a flood of images, both secular and spiritual. It is the conventional symbol of human love, female sexuality, and natural beauty. In its spiritual aspect, the rose is the concrete universal of communion (Frye, p. 144). In its literal form, it reflects the shape of the play's internal structure, a circle, the archetype of wholeness or unity. Most significant to this play, which dramatizes the struggle of its protagonist to reconcile the traditions of Catholic morality with the fulfilment of her own sexual nature, the rose is Dante's symbol for Mary, the miraculous vehicle through whom divinity is humanized: "Here is the Rose, wherein the Word of God/Made itself flesh" (*Portable Dante*, p. 488). The other half of the symbol, the tattoo, also suggests both mundane and mystical meanings. Associated with the sailor and other wanderers and adventurers, the tattoo appears to be an indication of both male virility and sentimentality. Religious connotations derive from its approximation to both the stigmata, those sympathetic scars resembling the wounds of the crucified Christ, and the brand of Cain, marks of infamy and disgrace.

Throughout the play, the symbol reflects the unfolding awareness of life's ambiguities in the mind of Serafina. The religious significance imparted to the image of the rose, which is actually etched on the chest of Rosario, reflects Serafina's own need to create a reality suffused with transcendent meanings. The alleged duplication of the rose tattoo on Serafina's breast as an emblem prophetic of conception represents her inflation of the sexual relations between herself and her husband to the religious experience of mystical union. Accordingly, Serafina's description of the sensations accompanying the mysterious appearance of the rose on her breast suggests not only the process of tattooing but also the ecstatic suffering associated with stigmata: "That night I woke up with a burning pain on me, here, on my left breast! A pain like a needle, quick, quick, hot little stitches" (II, 277). However, even as Serafina imbues her experience with miraculous import, elevating her husband to a Christ figure, herself to a devoted saint, and their sexual union to the level of religious ecstasy, her language derives from her mundane role as a lowly seamstress, who creates fabrications from the raw material of experience. Serafina's analogy between the religious experience and her familiar occupation of sewing suggests that stigmata appear not only to the religiously ecstatic but also to the hysterically neurotic. The sensation of stitches as from a needle which pricks Serafina ironically reveals the image of the rose to be psychosomatically self-inflicted.

Throughout the play, the reduplication of the rose tattoo parallels Serafina's struggle to acknowledge that the glory with which she has exalted Rosario and sanctified herself represents only gross invention. The symbol is corrupted to represent infidelity and adultery when found on Estelle, Rosario's mistress. It is compromised for Serafina when reproduced on the chest of Alvaro, Rosario's clownish double. It reappears on the breast of Serafina as an emblem of birth and re-birth only after she has fully accepted all its meanings and has her-self transcended the need for ego inflation.

While fragmented myths reflect the disintegration of a tran-scendent mythos for Western civilization in *The Glass Menagerie*, in *The Rose Tattoo* a pagan nature myth is offered in its entirety as a viable substitute for religious romanticism. The myth of Dionysus, the Greek seasonal demigod of wine, fertility, and passionate inspira-tion informs characterization, structure, and atmosphere. Like the symbolic rose tattoo, the myth represents a fusion of the sensual and the spiritual. Its structural aspect is the cyclical pattern of a god who dies and is reborn. Rosario embodies the play's initial representation of the archetypal Dionysian spirit. As Dionysus was known as the vegetation or "fruitful" god (Frazer, pp. 351–52), so Rosario repre-sents the apotheosis of sexual prowess and fertility, reflected in his job as the driver of a ten-ton truck of bananas. As Dionysus was often represented as a floral god (Frazer, p. 352), so Rosario is for Serafina "my rose of the world" (p. 345). Finally, like Dionysus, Rosario is to Serafina the god of love who suffers a violent death. He is idealized sexually as "the *first* best, the *only* best" (p. 311), and pictured as an eternally youthful god: "I remember my husband with a body like a young boy and hair on his head as thick and black as mine is and skin on him smooth and sweet as a yellow rose petal" (p. 311). Unable to acknowledge an unalloyed sexuality in human nature, however, Serafina attempts to imbue the Dionysian spirit with Christian symbol in her religious elevation of Rosario. Thus, Serafina makes her sexual union with Rosario seem like an ecstatic ritual: "To me the big bed was beautiful like a religion (p. 342). . . . Each night for twelve years. Four thousand-three hundred-and eighty" (p. 312). The idealized Rosario is to Serafina what the romanticized gentleman caller is to Amanda. Both women must mythicize, romanticize, or civilize the expression of natural instincts to fulfill their longings for transcendent experience.

The Dionysian spirit, however, embodies not only the inspired passion of religious ecstasy to which Serafina would restrict it but also sexuality at its most libidinous and indiscriminate. Serafina attempts to confine the orgiastic impulse of the Dionysian spirit to the monogamous relationship of the marriage vow. The raw sexuality of Rosario is revealed through the discovery of his adulterous relationship with Estelle Hohengarten, who describes him as "wild like a Gypsy" (p. 283). Characteristically, Serafina refuses to acknowledge Rosario's betrayal: "I don't know nothing about wild men and wild women" (p. 283). Appropriately, it is the Strega's goat of which Serafina is most afraid, for Dionysus was often believed reincarnated in the form of a goat and worshipped in ritual as "the one of the Black Goatskin" (Frazer, p. 355). As the objective correlative of the Dionysian spirit of unleashed lust, the black goat also symbolizes Serafina's own unconscious desires, her fear of it deriving from the repression of her own sexuality in its instinctual and unelevated form.

At the death of Rosario, Serafina (like Amanda) is transfixed in the posture of looking backward to a state of idealized and illusory perfection. Attempting to immortalize her elevated image of Rosario while denying his true nature, she puts his ashes into a funeral urn and worships them before the shrine of the Madonna. To so Christianize the Dionysian spirit is to asceticize natural passion and attempt to fix its cyclical nature in an image of heavenly ascension. Serafina attempts to deny the Dionysian impulse in herself, to enshrine her own body by refusing to participate in the regenerative process of life. As Alvaro tells her, "You have put your heart in the marble urn with the ashes" (p. 372).

Like The Glass Menagerie, The Rose Tattoo is a story told then reenacted in a diminished version. Serafina's idealized version of her relationship with Rosario is reenacted in a fully human version between herself and Alvaro. Similarly, the wild or illicit relationship of natural passion between Estelle and Rosario is reenacted in an inherently innocent version between Rosario's daughter, "a twig off the old rosebush" (p. 281) and Jack Hunter, the sailor. In each case, the second version of these parallel stories ends more happily than the first. Rosa's defiance of moral conventions points the way to Serafina's own liberation from false idols and to her realization that human love needs no other consecration than its own expression.

The play turns from its tragic potential to its ultimate comic fulfilment with the appearance of Alvaro, an obvious parody of the exalted Rosario: *"My husband's body, with the head of a clown!"* (p. 354). Accordingly, his social status is not that of the figurehead Baron but that of "the grandson of the village idiot" (p. 366). A compromise of Rosario's idealized virility, Alvaro drives only an eight-ton truck of bananas. Whereas implications of mystery surround Rosario—"On top of the truck is bananas! But underneath— something else!" (p. 279)—nothing is mystifying about Alvaro. His identification with the unelevated sexuality of Dionysus is dramatized by his own resemblance to the goat, which he appropriately catches for Serafina. When the drunken Alvaro spies the sleeping Rosa, his cries of "Che bella" are echoed by the antiphonal responses of the goat's bleating "Baaa" outside, a love song to natural beauty inspired by natural passion. Finally, Alvaro's last name, Mangiaca-vallo, which means "Eat-a-horse" (p. 356), is a pun on the ritual custom of endowing a pagan god with a similar epithet in recognition of his animal reincarnation. Thus, Dionysus, who was believed reincarnated in one form as a bull, was known as "eater-of-bulls" (Frazer, p. 356). The name is here demythicized to the popular hyperbole, to be so hungry one could "eat a horse." Obviously, the ritual custom need not be known or consciously grasped to elicit humor. The animal epithet appears instantly ludicrous by contrast to the other names invested with religious and mystical connotations: Rosario Delle Rose—the rosary of the rose; Serafina Delle Rose—the seraph or archangel of the rose; and Rosa Delle Rose—the rose of the rose.

Alvaro, then, is characterized not as half-mortal, half-divine, but as a fully humanized animal, his humanity elevating him from mind-less bestiality even as his animal instincts lead him to offer "Love and affection!—in a world that is lonely—and cold!" (p. 366). Combining masculine strength with feminine tenderness, Alvaro's androgynous nature is presented as so sympathetic, sensitive, and passionate that it makes up for the loss of a god.

The divestment of Serafina's illusions is dramatized in this play too through an act of breakage: Serafina shatters the urn filled with Rosario's ashes and realizes the Madonna icon is only "a poor little doll with the paint peeling off" (p. 396). Her deflated view of both Rosario and herself is a prelude to the liberation of her Dionysian spirit from all the restraints imposed by her adherence to social conventions, moral strictures, and sexual taboos. The moment of disillusionment is followed not only by the necessary confrontation with human limitations but also by an embrace of the diminished reality. The divestment of her mythical dimensions as Madonna releases her repressed sexual spirit, and her illicit act of passion with Alvaro frees her from the social proprieties and sexually constrictive role of Widow, represented throughout the play by an inanimate and faceless dummy. Similarly, the relinquishment of her exalted social status as Baronessa restores her to the community of Sicilian women. Finally, Rosa's exposure of the hypocritical disparity between Serafina's public image and her private desires, between her moral affectations and her sexual needs, not only frees Serafina from social pretense but also leads her to self-integration and self-acceptance. Thus mitigated by Alvaro's love and sanctioned by Rosa's example, the divestment of Serafina's self-generated mythos and mysticism results neither in the existential loneliness of the Wingfield family nor in the psychic withdrawal of Blanche DuBois. Instead, Serafina's embrace of reality leads to the blossoming of natural experience, itself so full and rich that its expression simultaneously fulfills the imagination and the flesh. She is led to understand the capricious sexual vitality of Rosario in the acceptance of her own animal nature and in her realization of life as a process of fulfilling instinctual and all-too-human needs and desires. As fervently as she had previously attempted to arrest time, she is now able to follow Rosa's example and surrender to its flow. As Williams himself remarked in "The Rose Tattoo," Serafina learns that the spirit of Dionysus "can not be confined to memory nor an urn, nor the conventions and proprieties of a plump little seamstress who wanted to fortify her happiness with the respect of the community," but that "the blood of the wild young daughter was better, as a memorial, than ashes kept in a crematory urn" (*Vogue*, p. 96).

The play ends in a crescendo of color, motion, and music. Serafina's embrace of inclusive experience permits the symbols of corruption, mortality, and death to transcend their meanings in the assumption of the regenerative values of reunion and rebirth. The apocalyptic finality of Christian ontology has been exchanged for the regenerative cycle of the Dionysian spirit. The rose tattoo reproduced on Alvaro reappears on the breast of Serafina, once more as a symbol of conception and of her own passionate rebirth, but also as the imprint of flesh against flesh. The rose silk shirt, symbol of Rosario's infidelity, is invested with Serafina's renewed faith in life as it becomes her gift of love to Alvaro. The wind, symbol of life's transience as well as its vitality, assumes major metaphorical significance. Scattering the ashes of Rosario, it releases the impregnating power of the Dionysian spirit and carries the child's red kite, symbol of Serafina's uninhibited freedom. Finally, it is the windlike motion of the Sicilian women that propels the rose-colored shirt "like a streak of flame shooting up a dry hill" (p. 413), uniting Serafina with Alvaro, with the community, and with her own passionate nature. The shirt is a banner joyfully spread in celebration of the dynamic process of life in all its human complexity and a testimony to the intrinsically transcendent function of passionate human communion. In this play, the annual rebirth of the Dionysian spirit is a ritual successfully reenacted in a fully human version.

In *Orpheus Descending*, the symbolic structure of a story told, then reenacted in a diminished version, is multiplied. Not one, but several stories structure the major events of this play. Furthermore, one of the major stories dramatized by the play is not told by a protagonist in the play but has its reference in the title: the Greek myth of Orpheus and Eurydice. The other major story, which is organic to the human drama, is recounted at the beginning of the play by Dolly and Beulah about Lady Torrance, and is later retold by Lady herself before it is reenacted. Unlike the contrast between inflated myths and circumscribed reality developed in *The Glass Menagerie*, or the fusion of myth with experience achieved in *The Rose Tattoo*, in this play the myth of Orpheus emerges as a separate story with its own protagonist. As a result, the myth too often seems superimposed onto the human conflicts integral to the play. Attempts to fuse these two stories create confusion, for each story vies with the other to assume clarity and focus. (see Nelson, pp. 228–231).

The myth of Orpheus and Eurydice not only informs structure and characterization in the play but is itself reenacted in a modern existential version. In the original myth, Orpheus descends into the underworld in an attempt to rescue Eurydice after she has been bitten by a snake and abducted by Pluto. His music so charms the guardians of Hades that Eurydice's return is promised him on the condition that he not look back at her as she follows him out of the underworld. But Orpheus disobeys and by looking back loses Eurydice to the underworld forever.

Val Xavier has the mythical attributes of Orpheus, while Lady Torrance is his Eurydice; and Jabe Torrance, Lady's dying husband, is Pluto's equivalent. Like Orpheus, Val is a wandering minstrel, his guitar correlative to the Orphic lyre, although his charm resides more in his inherent sexuality than in his music. Nevertheless, his ideal is to attain the Orphic qualities of asceticism, peace, and civilized behavior. The underworld of the provincial southern town into which this Orpheus descends combines the demonic atmosphere of the Christian Hell with a savage and brutal pagan upper world inhabited by the Dionysian Maenads, those female embodiments of passion gone mad who tore the mythic Orpheus to pieces. In this subterranean world, Val finds not only a Eurydice in Lady Torrance but also a Cassandra in Carol Cutrere and a Christian fanatic in Vee Talbot. All three are sexually repressed or frustrated women who either tacitly or verbally implore Val to "Take me out of this hell!" (III, 333). Val fails, as Orpheus did. But Williams' attempt to parallel Val's failure to rescue Lady with the Orphic act of looking back lends confusion to the conclusion of the play. Val tells Lady that he is leaving but that he loves her and indicates that she is to follow him: "I'll wait for you out of this country" (p. 331). However, a series of frenzied indecisions prevent Lady from following Val out of her underworld. Her refusal to leave derives from complications in her own story—in particular, her discovery of her husband's part in the destruction of her father, which motivates her to intentions of revenge: "Death has got to die before we can go" (p. 333). At Lady's insistence, then, Val returns to the underworld and by so looking back loses Lady forever to the play's Pluto, her husband who kills her. Val's act not only causes Lady's destruction but also leads to his own violent analogue of Orphic dismemberment: immolation by blowtorch, administered by the male counterparts to the Maenads, the savage and mad "Dawgs" of this infernal southern town.

In the Orphic myth, the rebirth of the demigod is symbolized by the Muses' salvaging of his severed head, which continues, even after his death, to sing, testifying to the irrepressibility of the transcendent spirit. Not Val's head but his snakeskin jacket is saved (by the Conjure Man) and passed on to Carol Cutrere, the town's promiscuous pariah. As a symbol, the snakeskin evokes multiple associations. Mythically, it brings to mind the snake whose bite kills Eurydice. It also suggests the serpentine guise of Satan whose seduction of Eve brings about the loss of Eden and the fall from innocence. Its stunning appearance evokes the ambivalence with which fallen man regards his sexual nature: his simultaneous attraction to it and repulsion from it. Finally, although the shedding of the snakeskin in nature also seems to connote transformation, in fact its divestment simply heralds the growth of another similar covering. While all of these allusions identify Val (himself called "Snakeskin") as an embodiment of man's inherently fallen nature, his affinity to the mythical bird of Paradise, which spends its life in empyrean purity, reveals his Orphic yearnings to transcend his corporeal and earthbound condition. His story of the bird who never lands on earth is commemorated by Coleridge in "The Eolian Harp," which compares the ethereal music of the harp to "Melodies . . . Footless and wild, like birds of Paradise,/Nor pause, nor perch, hovering on untam'd wing!" (11. 23–5). The failure of Val's efforts to reconcile spirit and flesh—to become, as it were, a winged serpent, mediator between heaven and earth—reveals only how tightly wrapped around him is the snakeskin, concrete symbol of his own earthly nature of tainted sexuality. It is Val who says, "We're all of us sentenced to solitary confinement inside our own skins, for life!" (p. 271). Attempting to mitigate Lady's loneliness, Val becomes a victim of his own intrinsic sexuality and of the world's inherent corruption. Unlike the head of Orpheus, then, the snakeskin jacket does not symbolize the rebirth of man's transcendent spirit or spiritual nature. Its reappearance after Val's death represents only a futile and unregenerative martyrdom, the sacrificial death of its wearer a testimony to man's inability to rise above his own flawed nature, to escape his own skin. Assumed by Carol Cutrere, embittered liberal reformer, the snakeskin is the emblem of "the fugitive kind" (p. 341), idealistic purveyors of love, freedom, and brotherhood, who would deliver humankind from lives filled with frustration, alienation, and oppression, but who are continually persecuted by the forces of hatred, bigotry, and violence, or betrayed by their own carnal needs.

In the course of the play, the symbols elevating Val proliferate, their religious connotations tempered by reminders of his innately profane nature. Valentine Xavier, his very name suggestive of love and salvation, assumes the composite dimensions of a jaded Dionysus, a world-weary Orpheus, and an ironic Christ. Attempting to redeem himself from his Dionysian past, Val not only repudiates his former life of corrupt sensuality but also attempts to deny his inherent sexuality. He becomes the Orphic figure who yearns for a life of ascetic purity. The ballad of "Heavenly Grass" which Val plays refers to a Williams' poem (*In the Winter of Cities*, p. 101) whose lyrics not only express a desire for transcendence from earthly life but also suggest nostalgia for a Wordsworthian preexistence from which humankind is painfully exiled at birth:

> My feet took a walk in heavenly grass.
> All day while the sky shone clear as glass.
> My feet took a walk in heavenly grass,
>
> . . . .
>
> Then my feet come down to walk on earth,
> And my mother cried when she give me birth.
> Now my feet walk far and my feet walk fast,
> But they still got an itch for heavenly grass.

Finally, Val is envisioned through Vee Talbot's eyes as the Christ figure who embodies her desire for both sexual and spiritual fulfilment, sent to redeem her from the corruption and violent reprisals she has witnessed in this world. Interestingly enough, this triadic image of Val and its evolution in his personal history have a basis in the historical progression of the Greco-Roman and Christian religions. According to Joseph L. Henderson in "Ancient Myths and Modern Man," as the rites of Dionysus became too wildly orgiastic, they "lost their emotive religious power. There emerged an almost oriental longing for liberation from their exclusive preoccupation with the purely natural symbols of life and love. . . . These [more ascetic souls] came to experience their religious ecstasies inwardly, in the worship of Orpheus" (*Man and his Symbols*, p. 135). Just as the religion of Dionysus gave way to that of Orpheus, so too "the early Christian church saw in Orpheus the prototype of Christ." Thus, the Dionysian process of seasonal rebirth and the Christian hope of a final and ultimate resurrection "somehow fuse in the figure of Orpheus, the god who remembers Dionysus but looks forward to Christ" (*Man and his Symbols*, p. 140).

Like Orpheus, both Dionysus and Christ make a descent into the underworld: Dionysus to save his mother Semele and Christ to liberate the preChristian faithful. Christian doctrine places the time of Christ's descent into Hell on Holy Saturday, the day which falls between his Crucifixion on Good Friday and his Resurrection on Easter Sunday. Appropriately, the destruction of Val takes place on "the Saturday before Easter" (p. 306). But Val descends into death's underworld and remains there. No resurrection occurs. In a poem entitled "Orpheus Descending" Williams attests to the unredemptive condition of twentieth century man and to the futility of Val's transcendent vision:

> And you must learn, even you, what we have learned,
> the passion there is for declivity in this world,
> the impulse to fall that follows a rising fountain.
>
> Now Orpheus, crawl, O shamefaced fugitive, crawl
> back under the crumbling broken wall of yourself,
> for you are not stars, sky-set in the shape of a lyre,
> but the dust of those who have been dismembered by Furies!
>
> (*In the Winter of Cities*, p. 28)

The conflict dramatized both within Val and between him and the native inhabitants of the small southern town represents the psychic and societal battle between the anarchic energy of the Dionysian spirit and the Orphic impulse to civilize, reform, and redirect that energy toward compassionate and humane ends. In this play, the forces of darkness win.

The second major story told and reenacted in the play is a human drama whose protagonist is Lady Torrance. Its theme is the youth-ful love affair between Lady and David Cutrere, recalled as an idyl-lic moment of passionate fulfilment in the wine garden built by Lady's immigrant father in the orchard on Moon Lake, Williams' recurrent analogue for the fallen world. In the midst of this fallen world, Papa Romero attempts to create an earthly paradise; its "grapevines and fruit trees" (p. 231), its white latticed arbors and couples making love evoke the combined image of Adam and Eve's Edenic bower and the Dionysian wine grove. Both the inspirational and savage aspects of the Dionysian spirit inform this story. The ecstatic passion of David and Lady bears fruit in Lady's conceiving, while the savage side of the Dionysian spirit is embodied in the Mystic Crew, who burn up the wine garden because Papa Romero "sold liquor to niggers" (p. 232). Thus, Papa Romero represents one of "the fugitive kind," who is burned alive by those envious of his attempt to realize an Edenic unity. The result is both a moral and a psychic Wasteland: Lady has an abortion, David is bought by a rich society girl, and, in despair, Lady sells herself to Jabe Torrance, unaware that he is one of the men who burned the wine garden, her father, and her dreams.

Lady Torrance, like Amanda and Serafina, is one of Williams' transfixed or frozen characters; her emotional life is arrested by the memory of her youthful love with David Cutrere and the idyllic vision of the wine garden, her lost Eden. She dreams of recreating the wine garden in the confectionery of her store, but "looking backward" is to be her destruction as well as Val's. Val's arrival not only concurs with her reconstruction of the wine garden but also brings about the reenactment of her entire story, from its passionate beginning to its tragic end. The love affair between Lady and David in the orchard is reenacted between herself and Val in the store be-hind a faded Oriental curtain with the design of "a gold tree with scarlet fruit and fantastic birds" (p. 227), the mere façade of the former earthly paradise. Their passion also leads to fertility and con-ception, but ends in the permanent sterility of their deaths. Although professing love to Lady, Val indicates that he, like David Cutrere, is leaving with "a rich society girl." The girl is, ironically, David's sister, Carol. At the discovery of Lady's pregnancy, Jabe fulfills his role as Pluto, once again imprisoning the play's Eurydice, this time forever, by murdering Lady as she attempts to protect Val. As a final parallel to the original story, Val, like Papa Romero, is burned alive.

In this version of the story, the attempt to restore fertility and love to the underworld is undermined not only by the savagery and brutality of mob action but also by an individual betrayal of love. Lady Torrance, in her loneliness and despair, exploits Val as a means to her own rejuvenation and rebirth, even as her heart remains with David and his with her. She seduces the passive and idealistic Val in the surrogate orchard, thereby corrupting his Orphic attempts to rise above his sexual appetites. She betrays the love he professes for her by dismissing him after he has rendered his sexual service of impregnating her: "You gotta go now. . . . You've done what you came here to do. . . . You've given me life, you can go!" (p. 337). The mythic dimensions of Val as Orpheus, Dionysus, and Christ the Redeemer are reduced to the status of "Male at Stud" (p. 258). It is this story of loneliness, passion, betrayal, and revenge which is organic to the play, but which is obscured and confused by a welter of frenzied actions, multiple allusions, and symbolic attempts to integrate it with the Orphic myth, the Dionysian duality, and an ironic Christ.

The frenzied see-saw of anticipation and loss, of expectation and disappointment, of hope and ultimate despair which characterizes the action is exacerbated in the final act by the introduction of two other stories, both told by Lady Torrance and quickly reenacted. Lady's story of the barren fig tree in her father's garden which miraculously bears fruit and which she adorns with Christmas ornaments as a symbol of her own rebirth invests Lady with the Christian symbolism already surrounding Val. Her story is a kind of apocryphal conclusion to the New Testament parable of the fig tree, wherein the possibility of rebirth is tentative at best. In the gospel, the story is told of the landowner who, consulted about the fate of a barren fig tree, orders it cut down. But his gardener counsels him otherwise: "Let it alone, sir, this year also, till I dig about it and put on manure. And if it bears fruit next year, well and good; but if not, you can cut it down" (Luke 13: 6–9). However, in another version of the parable, the barren fig tree receives no second chance, but instead is given Christ's curse: "In the morning . . . he was hungry. And seeing a fig tree . . . he went to it, and found nothing on it but leaves only. And he said to it, 'May no fruit ever come from you again!' And the fig tree withered at once" (Matthew 21: 18–22). Lady, identified with the fig tree, is first blessed with a second chance for fertility then cursed with total and everlasting sterility.

The other story is also introduced in the last act and is reenacted almost immediately. It is, perhaps, the real story of the play; its theme is the divestment of illusion, the futility of rejuvenation, and the finality of death. The story is told by Lady about a monkey sold to her father by a man who claimed it was young, "but he was a liar, it was a very old monkey, it was on its last legs, ha, ha, ha!" (p. 325). The monkey was dressed up in a "green velvet suit and a little red cap that it tipped and a tambourine that it passed around for money" (p. 325), as the organ grinder played and the monkey danced in the sun. The image of the monkey and the organ grinder reminds us of Lady Torrance herself and her father in the wine garden, where "The Wop and his daughter would sing and play Dago songs" (p. 232). But, as Lady says, "One day, the monkey danced too much in the sun and it was a very old monkey and it dropped dead. . . . My Papa, he turned to the people, he made them a bow and he said, 'The show is over, the monkey is dead.' Ha, ha!" (p. 325). Like the monkey, Lady is an aging woman who attempts to revitalize her youthful passion and restore her fertility. She too attempts rejuvenation by going to the beauty parlor and getting all dressed up on the night of her opening of the recreated wine garden. But it is all artifice, only the illusion of restoration: an "Electric moon, cutout silver-paper stars and artificial vines" (p. 324). She too attempts to "dance in the sun," to infuse life and vitality into her sterile existence. But her final frenzied and grotesque dance in celebration of her fertility and freedom becomes a danse macabre as Jabe descends the stairs and kills her. Thus, Lady's last words, echoing the grim punch line of her father's story, are an admission of ultimate despair, confirming the futility of dreams, the sterility of life, and the finality of death without redemption: "The show is over. The monkey is dead" (p. 339).

Beneath the mythic stories of Orpheus, Dionysus, and Christ, and beyond the human story of loneliness, love, and betrayal lies Williams' darkest tale of humankind's fundamental nature: the story of a monkey and a stud. It is the vision of man as an animal, bought and sold, a slave to his own base instincts and abused by those more brutal than he. As Benjamin Nelson has remarked, "In *Orpheus Descending*, there is the strong sense of disgust with reality. Whatever is human, whatever is of the earth, is prey to corruption" (p. 238). Neither the aesthetic reconciliation which concludes the naturalistic drama in *The Glass Menagerie* nor the essential faith in human instincts expressed in *The Rose Tattoo* redeems Williams' vision in *Orpheus* of the inevitable corruption inherent in human nature. Human sexuality, which Williams has elsewhere suggested is man's only salvation from psychic and metaphysical loneliness, is herein revealed as his original sin. Val and Lady are martyred victims of their own inescapable fallen natures.

In an attempt to reenact several stories in this play rather than just one, Williams sacrifices the clarity achieved by the evocation of a single emotion. The play seems to be an attempt to fuse a tragic vision, an epic consciousness, and an existential or absurdist attitude. The result is not the "*arrest of time* . . . that gives to certain plays their feeling of depth and significance," but an approximation of the "continual rush of time, so violent that it appears to be screaming, that deprives our actual lives of so much dignity and meaning" (II, 259). Furthermore, in this play, Williams does not so much tap the collective unconscious or trigger emotional memory as he tests our knowledge of myth, Christian doctrine, and biblical parable. Because many of his symbols or symbolic references are not evocative but intellectual and often obscure, they can be apprehended only as puzzling or extraneous. Analysis of the profusion of symbols and allusions indicates not that Williams thought too little about his nihilistic theme but that during seventeen years of revising *Battle of Angels*, the play's original version, perhaps he thought too much. Despite its intellectual symbolism and its multiplicity of stories, the central statement of the play emerges clearly from its frenzied action and perhaps justifies its histrionics: it is the single dark vision of life as "a tale/Told by an idiot, full of sound and fury,/Signifying nothing."

The Glass Menagerie, *The Rose Tattoo*, and *Orpheus Descending* are ostensibly completely different dramatic expressions of life and human nature, evoking respectively a tragic sense of life, a comic celebration of human nature, and a violent dramatization of the brutality and savagery that divest life of dignity and meaning. All three, however, have at their core the same fundamental structure of recurrence, of a story first told then reenacted. All three dramatize the plight of a protagonist who is transfixed by an idyllic memory that must be acted out again to liberate her from her illusions. All three dramatize a ritual of divestment, of old myths and of old gods, and attempt to invest new, human, and sometimes shocking meaning into those rites de passage which have become conventional and lost their emotive power: the rites of initiation, of marriage, and of sacrificial atonement.

In his "Foreword" to *Camino Real*, Williams describes that play in terms which may be applied to all his plays and characters as a drama that is "nothing more nor less than my conception of the time and world that I live in, and its people are mostly archetypes of certain basic attitudes and qualities with those mutations that would occur if they had continued along the road to this hypothetical terminal point in it" (II, 419). Williams' genre, then, may be described as that of ironic myth, defined by Northrop Frye as "a parody of romance: the application of romantic mythical forms to a more realistic content which fits them in unexpected ways" (p. 223). The characters in all of his plays are but the "shadow-images" (Jackson, p. 74) of mythical, legendary, and archetypal heroes who once provided exempla of humankind's potential for courage, honor, gentility, and love, but who have since been diminished and demythicized by time, history, and circumstance (see Jackson, pp. 68–74).

That central myth of which the characters are divested in Williams' plays is one that is fundamental to the human psyche. It is the myth of an original wholeness to humankind and of a unified cosmos without dichotomies of heaven and earth, God and man, spirit and flesh. According to Jungian psychology, we emerge from the womb with this inflated sense of totality or at-one-ness with the universe: "This is the original state of unconscious wholeness and perfection which is responsible for the nostalgia we all have toward our origins, both personal and historical" (Edinger, p. 7). This oceanic sense is experienced by the infant or young child before his realization of himself as an individuated ego, differentiated from the world about him. It survives in the collective memory in various forms: in Christian theology, it gives rise to that depiction of harmony and unity between man, nature, and God before man's fall from that Edenic

Paradise; in mythology, it appears in the Platonic belief in an immortal preexistent state of wholeness which man tries throughout his entire earthly existence to regain; its romantic literary expression culminates, perhaps, in Wordsworth's "Ode: Intimations of Immortality," in which the poet-persona nostalgically laments his loss of an intuitive spiritual communion with a deified nature even as he philosophically accepts the compensations offered by an embodied mortal existence: "Though nothing can bring back the hour/Of splendor in the grass, of glory in the flower;/We will grieve not, rather find/Strength in what remains behind" (X, 177–180). Just as Jung insists upon the relinquishing of the inflated infantile ego in the process of healthy self-individuation, so Williams divests his transfixed characters of their dreams of regaining that idyllic state by confrontation with the existential reality of the human condition, marked by its impermanence, its incompleteness, and its intrinsic alienation. In "Desire and the Black Masseur" (*One Arm and Other Stories*), Williams articulates the attitude implicit in his dramatizations of the mythopoeic mind in confrontation with an amoral and naturalistic universe: "For the sins of the world are really only its partialities, its incompletions. . . . The nature of man is full of . . . makeshift arrangements, devised by himself to cover his incompletion. . . . The use of imagination, resorting to dreams or the loftier purpose of art, is a mask he devises to cover his incompletion. . . . Then there is still another compensation. This one is found in the principle of atonement, the surrender of self to violent treatment by others with the idea of thereby cleansing one's self of his guilt" (p. 85).

It is this struggle to reconcile the romantic and the existential views of life that informs all of Williams' work: the conflict between his empirical knowledge of humankind's isolation and alienation from a unified cosmos and his romantic empathy for humankind's yearning for transcendence and for reconciliation with self, other, and a God. Those characters haunted or transfixed by a vision of transcendental wholeness or by a desire for reconcilation between their spiritual aspirations and their sexual needs include not only the Wingfields, Serafina Delle Rose, Lady Torrance and Val Xavier. In *A Streetcar Named Desire* it is Blanche DuBois who attempts to personify the belle reve of an idealized Old South of chivalric love and gentility in order to deny its decadent reality and her own human needs, weaknesses, and guilt. The story Blanche tells is of the idyllic love she held for her husband, destroyed by her discovery and repulsion of his homosexuality, resulting in his suicide. In its reenactment, it is Blanche whose desperate grasp for Mitch's love is thwarted by Stanley's exposure of her own sexual promiscuity, driving her to psychic suicide. In *Cat on a Hot Tin Roof*, the idyllic memory of Platonic love between Brick Pollitt and Skipper immobilizes Brick in alcoholic impotence, preventing a healthy heterosexual relationship between himself and Maggie. In this case, it is the re-telling of the story and its revaluation by Big Daddy that forces Brick to confront his own betrayal of Skipper's love and so purge himself of both his illusions and his guilt. In *Sweet Bird of Youth*, it is the remembered vision of virginal love between Chance Wayne and Heavenly Finley which Chance returns to reclaim, only to discover that he had himself desecrated that dream on his previous return and this time is himself divested of the means ever to realize it. In *Summer and Smoke*, the chaste and idealistic Alma Winemiller exchanges her romantic view of life for the naturalistic one held by John Buchanan just as he ironically embraces her spirituality. Thus, the story Alma tells of Mrs. Ewell, the merry widow of Glorious Hill who waits at the train station to seduce the traveling salesmen, *foretells* her own fate. In *The Night of the Iguana*, both Hannah Jelkes' example and her narration of her personal history free the defrocked Shannon from his illusions of transcending his inherent sexuality and enable him to accept its value as a compensation from an existential loneliness. Finally, in *Camino Real*, the romantic characters—Jacques Casanova, Marguerite Gautier (Camille), Lord Byron, Kilroy, and Don Quixote—must be divested of their fictive and inflated self-images in order to embrace in mutual compassion and sympathy and to continue their quest for love in a diminished reality. The demonic obsession of Sebastian Venable in *Suddenly Last Summer* to be reunited with the "savage face" of God revealed to him by the cannibalistic relationship between the carnivorous birds and the newly-hatched turtles on the Galapagos Islands is, in a sense, only the other side of the romantic vision of Edenic reunion which afflicts Williams' other protagonists. Both the romantic vision of self-transcendence and the demonic vision of self-annihilation by surrender to primal violence represent futile attempts to attain atonement (at-one-ment) or ultimate reconciliation with a universal order. The fundamental story of cannibalism is retold and reenacted multiple times. Melville's dark vision of life on the Galapagos Islands is first retold through Sebastian's witnessing there an elementary voracity in nature subsequently realized through his own dismemberment by the starving natives of Cabeza de Lobo. Even as Catharine narrates these events, she is herself threatened by their reenactment, as the victim of Violet Venable who would force her to undergo a prefrontal lobotomy in an effort to discredit Catharine's realization that Sebastian's horrible vision of an instinctively ruthless nature is but "a true story of our time and the world we live in" (III, 382).

Williams offers no solutions for metaphysical loneliness, except for that rare and transient embrace with our fellow man. His is a carpe diem philosophy elevated to a belief in the inherent potential of man to be God to his fellow, to reach not epiphany but empathy through compassion and understanding. Williams has declared his artistic ethos in similar terms: "Every artist has a basic premise pervading his whole life, . . . and that premise can provide the impulse to everything he creates. For me the dominating premise has been the need for understanding and tenderness and fortitude among individuals trapped by circumstance" (Barnett, Life, p. 116). As compensation for the loss of a transcendent myth and of a primordial unity, Williams offers a theater of atonement, whereby the purgation of self-pity and existential loneliness is made possible: by the recognition of our own transgressions in those of his protagonists, by our compassionate assumption of their sufferings and guilt, and by forgiveness of our mutual deficiencies and inherent limitations. His symbolic representations of violent emotions and tortured psyches are intended to fulfill for us, as for himself, a communal cathartic function, "a release from the sense of meaninglessness and death" (IV, 7). Through the dramatization of modern man's existential angst as ritual, evoking archetypal and mythic images, Williams attempts to create a theatrical experience of such emotional intensity that we his audience will be compelled to "see it feelingly," and so become participants in his own artistic quest to invest a "broken world" (Jackson) with viable meaning.

Williams' Comedy

CHARLES B. BROOKS

SEVERAL OF THE most significant serious play-wrights of the modern era have possessed fine comic gifts which enhance their plays, including Chekhov, O'Casey, Giraudoux, Anouilh, Beckett, and Pinter. Tennessee Williams belongs in this group. Although his vision of the world is not primarily comic, comedy contributes to his success.

A few of his plays he labels comedies: *You Touched Me!* is "A Romantic Comedy," *27 Wagons Full of Cotton* is "A Mississippi Delta Comedy," and *Period of Adjustment* is "A Serious Comedy." The term "serious comedy," like "slapstick tragedy" (for *The Mutilated* and *The Gnädiges Fräulein* in New York in 1966), indicates how intimately his comic vision is woven into his serious outlook.

It is not chiefly a matter of verbal wit or gags, although there are some of these: a character wonders about the whereabouts of a girl who was stood up at her wedding, and another remarks, "Some people say she went crazy an' some people say she went to Cincinnati to study voice" (*Battle of Angels*, I, 40); when Tom tells his mother the gentleman caller's name is James Delancy O'Connor, Amanda exclaims, "Irish on *both* sides! *Gracious!* And doesn't drink?" (*The Glass Menagerie*, I, 185); when, to Stanley's complaint that Blanche is taking too long in the bathroom, she tells him to "Possess your soul in patience!" his answer is "It's not my soul, it's my kidneys I'm worried about!" (A *Streetcar Named Desire*, I, 363–64); in *Period of Adjustment* Isabel's comment on her husband's car is that "It ought to be retired with an old-age pension" (IV, 133), and Ralph complains that, because of her buck teeth, kissing his wife "was like kissing a rock pile" (p. 145); in *The Night of the Iguana*, when Shannon tells Maxine he has been guiding a tour of eleven old maids, she calls them "a football squad" and he comes back with "Yeah, and I'm the football" (IV, 258); in *In the Bar of a Tokyo Hotel*, when Leonard describes the oddities of some of the painters who exhibit in his gallery and mentions that one paints with his penis, Miriam queries, "Erect or soft?" (*Dragon Country*, pp. 40–41).

There are several slapstick gags in *The Gnädiges Fräulein*. As Indian Joe and the Cocaloony bird are sparring and exchanging sounds of "awk" and "ugh," Polly says, "Reminds me of the Lincoln-Douglas debates" (*Dragon Country*, p. 239). When Joe announces, "I feel like a bull," Polly goes "MOOOO! MOOOOO!" and follows him into the house (pp. 250–51).

One exchange in that play goes like this:

POLLY: HOW.
INDIAN JOE: POW.
MOLLY: WOW. (He jerks the screen door open and enters the interior.)
POLLY: Strong character! (p. 240).

This is something more than mere gagging—it caricatures cliché Indian-dialogue, "how" and "pow wow," along with the slang exclamation "wow," just as Joe is a take-off on cliché attitudes towards Indians. Much of Williams' verbal humor has such appropriateness. In *Battle of Angels* after Val, having unexpectedly been promised a job, stammers, "God, I—! Lady, you—!" Myra's comeback points up the vanity which is his weakness, at the same time showing a certain self-awareness of her own weakness—"God you an' lady me, huh. I think you are kind of exaggerating a little in both cases" (I, 33). In *Cat on a Hot Tin Roof*, Maggie suddenly turns on the hi-fi, loud, and Big Daddy, anxious to be the center of attention, shouts to turn it off; just as she complies, Big Mama runs in, and he tells Maggie to turn it back on. Though ostensibly a joke, his words reveal the dislike of her that he expresses clearly later on, and it harmonizes with the portrait of Big Mama as silly and possessive and disliked or ignored by her children and in-laws in spite of the outward fuss they make over her, a portrait that contributes to the play's exposure of the hollowness of many American attitudes. Later Gooper and Mae get in a good dig at Brick—Gooper having asked whether he made his famous run in the Sugar Bowl or the Rose Bowl, Mae shouts that it was the punch bowl—but it's as much another exposure of their malice, closely tied to their jealousy and greed, as it is of Brick's alcoholism. Similarly in *Sweet Bird of Youth* Boss Finley exposes his deep southern prejudice while being consciously and cleverly sarcastic when he suggests that the question of whether a criminal degenerate is sane or insane should be taken to the Supreme Court: "They'll tell you a handsome young criminal degenerate like Chance Wayne is the mental and moral equal of any white man in the country" (IV, 60–61). Shannon's dig in *The Night of the Iguana* at Judith Fellowes is cruel and prejudiced ("Hey, Jake, did you know they had Lesbians in Texas—without the dikes the plains of Texas would be engulfed by the Gulf" [IV, 334]) but at least partly deserved because she has acted so self-righteously and obnoxiously.

Many of the verbal witticisms are thus appropriate to characterization or theme. Wit, however, is not Williams' chief comic technique. More verbal humor is in the styles of speech that so fit characters who unconsciously reveal their follies or weaknesses—Amanda's affected reminiscing about seventeen gentleman callers and her futile attempts on the telephone to praise a trashy magazine serial (*The Glass Menagerie*); Stanley's stilted syntax and frequent repetition, showing brutishness and insensitivity rather than the shrewdness and virility he prides himself on, as he probes Blanche's past and her handling of the estate ("I got an acquaintance" is a characteristic statement of his—a version of the comic stereotype "I got a friend—") (*A Streetcar Named Desire*); Gypsy's New York turns of expression as she gleefully fleeces anyone she can (*Camino Real*); the deliberately vulgar, backwoodsy, bragging speech, full of racial slurs, of Big Daddy (*Cat on a Hot Tin Roof*) and Boss Finley (*Sweet Bird of Youth*); the assertive, accusing, threatening language of Judith Fellowes with her repetitiousness of "It says in the brochure" (*The*

Night of the Iguana). Individuality of speech contributes to the exposure of shortcomings in these characterizations.

As with verbal gags, comic incidents enliven many of the plays without being plentiful, and they relate to character or theme rather than being gratuitous. Tom's love of the vicarious thrills he gets from movies is underscored when he returns, drunk, after the violent quarrel with his mother and while searching for his key brings out "a shower of movie ticket stubs" (*The Glass Menagerie*, I, 166). A funny scene in *You Touched Me!* in which the prudish Emmie and the Reverend are moving toward an agreement to contract a platonic marriage while the maid is trying to keep the drunken Captain quiet in the next room reaches a climax in which at the key moment the Captain bursts forth in pursuit of the maid and the Reverend beats a hasty retreat. In *A Streetcar Named Desire*, Blanche silences Stanley's demand to know how she lost the plantation by pouring out before him an envelope full of papers; when Blanche plays a radio in spite of Stanley's protest, he stalks into the room, snatches it up, and tosses it out a window; and when asked to help clear the table after dinner, he throws dishes to the floor. In *Small Craft Warnings*, after Monk has assured Doc the toilet in the men's room has been repaired and Doc has gone in, he returns, in the midst of a violent altercation, with wet pants cuffs and the rueful announcement that the toilet still overflows.

The most fanciful of the plays, *Camino Real* and *The Gnädiges Fräulein*, are also the ones fullest of activity. *Camino Real* generates comic energy with the running about that occurs, especially the frantic shoving, smuggling, bribing, arresting, inspecting baggage, shouting, and whistling accompanying the departure of the plane El Fugitivo and the "serio-comic, grotesque lyric" Fiesta (II, 533). *The Gnädiges Fräulein* has the Fräulein periodically rushing off to meet an incoming fishing boat so she can fight the birds for cast-off fish; Molly and Polly rocking in their chairs for sexual thrills; Indian Joe going in and out; and the cocaloony bird. The presence of this bird as well as the other fanciful activity is similar to what happens in O'Casey's *Cock-a-Doodle-Dandy*; but O'Casey's cock is a joyful bird while the cocaloony is a mean degenerate of a once self-reliant creature. The comic energy of the wild action competes for effect with the pathos of the Fräulein's situation and the suggestiveness of the rest of the setting, this southernmost point of the United States (or "Disunited Mistakes" [*Dragon Country*, p. 219]) being as degenerate as the cocaloony bird. Similarly, the town portrayed in *Camino Real* is the end of the road; Casanova, the great lover, becomes King of Cuckolds, and Kilroy pawns his golden gloves and loses his heart of gold as big as the head of a baby.

Occasional energetic action occurs in other plays, notably *Cat on a Hot Tin Roof*, where the no-neck monsters are romping about; *The Night of the Iguana*, where Shannon struggles to keep the women from escaping in the bus; and *The Rose Tattoo*, where Serafina periodically struggles with neighbors, a goat that gets into the yard, and her daughter Rosa. A violent serio-comic altercation between Leona and a night watchman takes place off-stage in *Small Craft Warnings* while various conversations are going on in the bar, including Doc's sad story of the deaths of the woman and newborn child he has just illegally treated.

A more important aspect of Williams' comedy than the verbal and the active is characterization. Among his great array of vividly depicted characters are a number of caricatures of American types. The Sheriff, his deputy Pee Wee, and their friends in *Battle of Angels* are thoroughly prejudiced, tough-acting, insensitive southern lawmen—"Pack 'em all off togethuh," one of the men says, "Jews, and radicals, and niggers! Ship 'em all back to *Rooshuh!*" (I, 69). A related, more developed portrait is Boss Finley of *Sweet Bird of Youth*, the redneck who came down barefoot from the clay hills as a boy and with his God-given mission to shield sacred white blood from pollution has built a powerful political empire. He is vulgar, brutal, vain of his power, ruthless in applying it, a demagogue playing on the bigotry of others, a hypocrite who mouths morality but keeps an expensive mistress. He brags of having taken his wife a $15,000 clip so she would think she wasn't going to die yet and is oblivous of his daughter's sarcasm when she points out that, since he got his money back, it cost him nothing to be so generous and thoughtful. Boss Finley and the Sheriff are satiric exposures of a type of southern politician.

Dolly, Beulah, and the Temple sisters in *Battle of Angels* and *Orpheus Descending* are satiric portraits of prying, narrowminded, self-centered, gossipy, hypocritically moral, middle-aged southern women. In *Battle of Angels*, these four along with the Sheriff and Pee Wee and a group of giggling high school girls are present enough throughout to provide a social backdrop, a sort of chorus of towns-people, who contrast with the flawed, tormented, doomed, but more admirably passionate and individual Sandra, Myra, and Val. This aspect of the play is not so present in *Orpheus Descending*, where the Sheriff, Pee Wee, and the Temple sisters are less developed. Dolly and Beulah are the same shallow busybodies, but they don't seem to be meant to suggest society in general. Meanwhile Vee (the Sheriff's wife) is presented in a more clearly comic light as a quite different type—a religious hypocrite who has visions and lusts. The sharpest criticism, in *Orpheus Descending*, of society as an enemy to individual aspiration comes in the first scene, when Vee scolds Beulah and Dolly for their drinking parties and Sunday card gath-erings; Beulah and Dolly retort by attacking her as a gossipmonger, killjoy, and hypocrite; and then, when they have left, the Temple sisters attack them for being common.

Similar to Beulah and Dolly are Bessie and Flora of *The Rose Tattoo* and the one-act *A Perfect Analysis Given by a Parrot*. Wil-liams introduces them in *The Rose Tattoo* as middle-aged clowns. They look down on the "Wop" Serafina, but they are shallow, mean, and interested only in having what they consider to be fun with the Legionnaires on convention. As Lady's depth and dignity are en-hanced by contrast with Beulah and Dolly in *Orpheus Descending*, so Serafina's are by contrast with Bessie and Flora. Reappearing in *A Perfect Analysis Given by a Parrot*, they are attending a conven-tion in St. Louis of the Sons of Mars. While drinking at a bar, they bicker and criticize each other until a couple of Sons of Mars show up, leap-frog over each other to the table, and sing "Mademoiselle from Armentieres" (a song the Legionnaires also sing in *The Rose Tattoo*). This play is a comic exposure of two shallow women and a satiric attack on some conventional American attitudes; the girls think the Sons of Mars are hilarious for doing such things as dropping waterbags out of hotel windows—but also call them a serious orga-nization without which the country would be in a terrible fix. Wil-liams makes fun of the juvenile idea of fun which so many Americans have.

All of these characters and most of Williams' other satiric caricatures are quite southern in their speech, but except for Boss Finley and the Sheriff and Pee Wee, they represent types with prejudices and characteristics common to all of America, not just the South. There is the smooth-talking novelty salesman who crowds Alvaro off the highway in *The Rose Tattoo,* calls him foul names, and in their brief fight takes advantage of his integrity to deliver a dirty blow. In *Period of Adjustment* there are the McGillicuddys, self-centered, vulgar, materialistic, domineering, who sweep through the house in the third act grabbing everything their daughter might possibly have a claim to. George protects the silver tableware from them by sitting on it, getting stuck by the forks in a bit of comic action. They represent a wealthy American couple that has made money in business. They are bossy and self-satisfied, and McGillicuddy takes pleasure in sarcastically calling Ralph "war hero." But their whole system of values is monetary, their possessiveness has practically ruined their daughter psychologically, and they show little respect for each other. The scene in which they appear is rowdy, fast-moving, and vigorous, and through them Williams ridicules the materialistic upper middle class American family. Similarly he ridicules suburban living by setting the play in a house in a development called High Point built over a cavern into which the houses are steadily slipping, a house so similar to all its neighbors that Isabel can't find her way back when she goes for a walk.

Another possessive and snobblish mother is Mrs. Buchanan in *The Eccentricities of a Nightingale,* who does all she can to keep her son from becoming involved with the minister's daughter she is sure is not worthy of him. She is unaware that her son laughs at her pretentions.

A marital relationship similar to that of the McGillicuddys exists between Big Daddy and Big Mama in *Cat on a Hot Tin Roof.* Big Daddy makes no secret to Brick that he can't stand the woman he has lived with all these years. Big Mama is the chief caricature in this play, making a considerable display of affection for her husband and children, but always cutting a silly figure and inspiring contempt in them in spite of their pretense of respect. Child worship is ridiculed by the presentation of the cooing mother, who is actually greedy, selfish, and spiteful, and her five screaming monsters whom she considers darling no matter how they annoy other people. In addition there is the sibling jealousy of Gooper. During this family reunion in celebration of the patriarch's birthday, we have a devastating display of jealousy, cattiness, social climbing, false worship of virility, and hollow marital relationships based on lust or greed.

A minor character in *Cat on a Hot Tin Roof* is the Reverend Tooker, who has a penchant for saying the wrong thing and whose chief interest is in the memorial gift for Big Daddy which the family may present to the church—the foolish clergyman, a typical comic character.

In *A Streetcar Named Desire* there are Steve and Eunice, who are constantly fighting, sometimes quite violently, but have an essentially healthy attachment to each other. After one battle Eunice runs to get the police—and instead stops at a bar for a drink. Going after her, Steve, in a conventional comic moment, peeks timidly around the corner to make sure she is not in sight before boldly chasing her. Steve and Eunice are a reflection in comic caricature of Stanley and Stella.

In *The Night of the Iguana* an effective caricature is Judith Fellowes, the tough masculine leader of the busload of women teachers. She hounds Shannon to stick exactly to the itinerary in the printed brochure. But it is made clear that her hostility to him is principally the result of jealousy because he has seduced the young music pupil she would like for herself. The presentation of Judith and of the busload of women teachers ridicules American tourists. They complain about anything that slightly deviates from the promises of the brochure, no matter what good reason the guide has for the deviation, yet they have taken the cheapest possible tour. A great tour it sounds —Miss Fellowes organizes community sings on the bus, and after supper the math instructor carefully checks the bill. The climax of Shannon's struggle with the ladies occurs after he has been fired. He runs down the hill and urinates on the ladies' luggage, an incident narrated rather than shown but a fitting comic sendoff for this obnoxious busload of tourists.

There is also the German family, the puffed up tank manufacturer who always has a portable radio at his ear playing news broadcasts of Nazi victories or speeches by Hitler, his fat wife, their simple-minded daughter, and her new Wagnerian-tenor bridegroom. From time to time these Germans march haughtily by on their way to or from the beach. They have no doubt that they are a superior race destined to conquer the world. And they insensitively snub the tender, artistic Hannah and her poet grandfather.

There are some fuller comic characterizations. Gypsy in *Camino Real* is a tough, cynical gal who is never at a loss in her quest for money; her forceful style of operation lifts her from the ranks of a stereotype. Mitch in *A Streetcar Named Desire* is a little like Archie, the obtuse, self-satisfied husband of 27 *Wagons Full of Cotton* who so deserves his cuckolding. Mitch rationalizes his weight problem; he has vanity and lack of self-awareness. He is taken in completely by Blanche's coquetry. Knowing that he can't understand French, she makes fun of him by asking in French if he wants to go to bed with her. When, having been told the truth about Blanche, he demands that she make love to him, she makes a fool of him by yelling "Fire," sending him on precipitous flight. But Mitch is pathetic as well as comic. His greatest mistake is not that he is blind to Blanche's blandishments, but that he fails to realize that in spite of her past and her trickery she could rescue him from loneliness. It is a bleak and loveless future he flees to.

Mitch is a bridge between the essentially comic caricatures of Steve and Eunice on the one hand and the portrait of Blanche on the other. Blanche's pretentiousness is constantly exposed by Stanley; she is frequently made to look foolish. But she has outgrown self-delusion. She is aware of her failings, creating her illusions deliberately in a desperate struggle to salvage something of her life. She finally invites sympathy and pathos rather than laughter. Similarly she exposes Stanley's crudeness on many occasions, but he too is presented sympathetically because there is joyous passion in his relationship with Stella.

Alvaro Mangiacavallo in *The Rose Tattoo* frequently manages to look foolish, beginning with his defeat by the vulgar salesman. He has a comical name, is the grandson of a village idiot, has a household of useless relatives to support. Hearing of Serafina's husband's rose tattoo, he has a rose tattooed on his own chest. After a "grotesquely violent and comic chase" (II, 386), he is stopped by Serafina's threat to slam his box of chocolates in his face, and he drops to the floor, sobbing that everything he does turns to this kind of failure. On the morning after his night with Serafina, he clumsily awakens Rosa, revealing to her the truth about her mother. But he is basically honest and loving; his clownishness becomes part of his charm. Serafina has illusions about her former husband; she is laughed at by the neighbors who know the truth; she cuts a ridiculous figure wandering about her house sloppily in a slip, keeping her husband's ashes in an urn to be worshiped, trying to deny her daughter the passion that she herself has found so important. But she is so vigorous, so emotionally alive that she is triumphant rather than foolish. The people who try to ridicule or hurt her are so shallow by comparison to her that she is the victorious one.

In *The Glass Menagerie*, Jim is the most clearly comic character. He is outgoing, anxious to please—when Amanda tells a rather bad joke (when the lights went out, Moses was in the dark), he is quick to laugh (I, 207); when the lights fail, he indicates that he prefers candlelight; he plunges into conversation with anyone, and it is this quality that enables him to draw Laura out of her usually debilitating shyness. But this is part of his egotistic self-confidence. It is himself he is full of. He is taking public speaking in night school, sure he can learn how to influence people. He brags of his psychological insight and proceeds to demonstrate it by saying what is perfectly obvious about Laura. While he is supposedly trying to stir self-confidence in her, he is mainly talking about himself—noticing how big the candlelight makes his shadow, glancing at himself in the mirror. His high school girl friend was a "kraut-head" who invented rumors about his wanting to marry her. He is a gum-chewing optimist who becomes starry-eyed as he dreams of the great future he will have when television gets going—"*Knowledge*—Zzzzzp! *Money*—Zzzzzzp! —*Power!*" His vanity is nearly limitless, but he claims to have had an inferiority complex, and "I guess you think I think a lot of myself!" (p. 222) is a vast understatement. In spite of his vanity and optimism, he is merely a shipping clerk in a warehouse.

Tom is foolish on a number of occasions—in his obsession with the movies, in his illusion that he is a great poet (writing poems on shoeboxes), in his bumbling of the attempt to find a gentleman caller for Laura, in his belief that flight (joining the merchant marine) is a solution to his problem. His explanation of how he became drunk at the movies—volunteering to drink the whisky which the stage magician made out of water—is amusing. But Tom also has flashes of awareness (perhaps developed later in his life) when he explains America's infatuation with movies, liquor, dance halls, and other forms of escapism. He is partly comic, but as a dreamer trapped in a life he hates he develops sympathy.

In spite of her ridiculous inability to cope, Laura is too pathetic and too genuinely tender and sensitive to be comic. Amanda, though, is a rich comic creation, full of folly and yet strong enough to inspire admiration. She seems ridiculous whenever she reminisces about what a beautiful, delicate girl she was, wooed by the most eligible men, especially when she tries to re-create the role for Jim's benefit, draping her sturdy figure with a frilly dress and adopting coquettish airs. Tom makes fun of her with his story of going to opium dens after she has expressed doubt that he spends all his time in the movies. Angry with Tom, and yet having to continue to direct the household, she rather childishly speaks to him only indirectly through Laura; then when he finally apologizes, she becomes sentimental and oversolicitous—but is soon nagging as she always did. When Tom announces that he has invited a visitor, her mind races forward, marrying Laura off before she has even met the visitor. But Amanda does manage to keep the family going; and unselfconscious and mistaken though she may be, she gives the impression of being indestructible no matter how dreadful her situation. Amanda deserves admiration as well as laughter.

One other group of comic characters needs to be mentioned, Alma's "intellectual" group in *Summer and Smoke* and *The Eccentricities of a Nightingale*—the pseudo-poet Vernon, awkward Rosemary, bossy and gossipy Mrs. Bassett, and effeminate Roger. The most humorous scene in *Summer and Smoke* is the club meeting. They bicker about hearing a verse play or a paper on Blake, Mrs. Bassett shows her ignorance of Blake, and they frequently make catty remarks to each other. The individuals and their club are quite foolish. This scene is expanded in *The Eccentricities of a Nightingale*, and Mrs. Buchanan cuttingly describes the group as the "freaks" of the town, people who don't fit in with others, who imagine they have talents, and who band together to bolster each other's illusion that he is unwanted because he is superior. Further humor is provided in these two plays by the imbecilic Mrs. Winemiller, with her love of ice cream cones and her penchant for speaking out at the wrong time, especially revealing truths about her husband and her daughter that they want to hide. Mrs. Winemiller is not herself funny but pathetic, except that at times she gets a malicious pleasure out of embarrassing the other two; there is method in her madness. But her exposures of the pretenses of the others makes her a vehicle for comedy. She is also a reminder that the club members are not altogether to be laughed at; they are "freaks," misfits, people who don't quite fit in and are struggling as best they are able against loneliness and isolation. Mrs. Buchanan's description is vicious, and the possessive Mrs. Buchanan is hardly one whose opinions are to be admired.

Mrs. Winemiller's insanity and the freakish club members help to place Alma, a woman with considerable potential talent, intelligence, and passion but without adequate outlet for them. With her affectations she would be as ridiculous as the other club members if she were not presented with a richer context that suggests what has made her that way and arouses sympathy for her plight. *The Eccentricities of a Nightingale* gives the name for Alma and the others —they are eccentric, different, and therefore usually doomed to disappointment. It is the eccentricities of people that Williams is most concerned with, and he invites understanding of and sympathy with these people to such an extent that the comic and the pathetic vie in the audience's reaction. "Tender irony," he says in "Notes After the Second Invited Audience," is the keynote to the success of *Small Craft Warnings* (V, 289), where the helpless Violet and the tough Leona, the drunken Doc, the vain Bill, the homosexual Quentin are psychologically sick in their different ways and, throughout, more to be pitied than laughed at. In *Kingdom of Earth* a character comments, "I think everything's funny. In this world. I even think it's funny I'm going to die" (V, 167). Here "funny" is much closer to "strange" than to "laughable." When the oddities of people are pretty much beyond their control and drive or expose them to failure, they become tragic or pathetic. The recluse brother and sister of the play-within-a-play in *The Two-Character Play* are frequently ridiculous as they unsuccessfully try to talk themselves into doing something to escape their plight. When the insurance company refused to pay on their father's policy on the "legal technicality" that it was forfeited in case of suicide, they appealed in the interests of humanity, fully expecting to be taken seriously. In the earlier version of this play, *Out Cry*, Williams suggested about one action that it should "have a touch of pathos but not be ludicrous" (p. 51). The line between the pathetic and the ludicrous is thin, as it is in many of his plays.

"The freaks of the cosmic circus are men" ("Carrousel Tune," *In the Winter of Cities*, p. 91)—sometimes to be laughed at, sometimes to be despised, but perhaps most often to be pitied, and sometimes even to be admired.

Characterization is the strongest comic element of Williams' plays. Some of them also have a message that might be called a new romanticism. As in traditional romantic comedy young lovers overcome obstacles and finally enjoy the fruition of their mutual attachment, so Williams sometimes shows sexual satisfaction as a triumph over the miseries or ignominies or lonelinesses of life. I call this "new" romanticism because it is related to the glorification of sexual intercourse that has become prominent in our culture in the last couple of decades. *You Touched Me!* has a conventional ending as Matilda flees with Hadrian. *The Rose Tattoo* ends with Rosa running off with her boy and Serafina waiting for the return of her new lover, both affairs apparently to end in marriage but inspired by strong sexual longing. *Cat on a Hot Tin Roof* ends triumphantly for Maggie when she finally gets Brick to return to her bed. In *A Streetcar Named Desire*, Stella may live a life of hard work in a grim slum, but she is sexually content. Alma in *Summer and Smoke* and even more clearly in *The Eccentricities of a Nightingale* is released from disabling frustrations when she submits to (or achieves) sexual intercourse. *Period of Adjustment* ends with some hope that the two marriages will work out; "The world is a big hospital," Isabel tells George, "and I am a nurse in it" (IV, 244), expressing the idea that sexual satisfaction is a possible solution for an otherwise sick existence.

In *Kingdom of Earth* the earthy Chicken triumphs over his effete half-brother Lot when he seduces Myrtle, at the same time giving her some chance of a future more satisfying than her unfortunate past. Toward the end of the play Chicken expresses this romantic philosophy in a long speech. Nothing in life—property, success— compares with "what's able to happen between a man and a woman." A thoroughly, mutually satisfying sexual relationship compensates even for great poverty (V, 211), and Chicken is thinking physically, not spiritually. There is the new romanticism in a nutshell. *Small Craft Warnings*, after its presentation of the various frustrations and sorrows of the characters, ends on a wistful note as Monk hears Violet bathing and goes upstairs to join her in bed.

Not all the plays present sexuality in this romantic light, as not all the plays are comic. A fruitless search for sexual fulfilment is part of the torment Sandra feels in *Battle of Angels* and her counterpart Carol feels in *Orpheus Descending*. Val in both plays is finally brought to his destruction by the sexual desires he arouses in women, while he himself, proclaiming that he searches for a relationship more fulfilling than the merely physical, tries to flee from any lasting involvement. Chance Wayne in *Sweet Bird of Youth* is similar; he lives by serving rich older women, but he has brought disaster to his true love (partly the fault of her father) and finally expiates that crime by refusing to flee though he will be castrated. In *Suddenly Last Summer*, Sebastian's unusual sexual proclivities eventually devour him. In *Camino Real*, the great lover Casanova is crowned King of Cuckolds and can only escape the ignominy of living in the Ritz Men Only by courting the aging Marguerite (Camille), who in turn has been reduced to paying for men's favors; Kilroy wants to be true to his beloved wife but is chosen to lift the veil of Esmeralda (the booby prize, as Gypsy puts it) and, because of his weak heart, is brought by this action to the dissection table; sexual drives, in this play, are partly what makes living a disaster.

The plot of *The Night of the Iguana* is the opposite of sexual union as a romantic triumph. His sexual drives have contributed to Larry Shannon's downfall, and the play shows his desperate struggle to escape becoming merely Maxine Faulk's lover. He tries to remain independent but fails when he loses his busload of women tourists. His degradation accompanies the death of the ninety-seven-year-old poet just after the poet completes the final poem he has been working on for a long time, a poem about the decay and death of an orange tree, a golden and green kind of being not meant for earth's obscene, corrupting love. Meanwhile the encounter of Hannah and Shannon, though sexless, is a love experience. They manage to comfort each other during this day between the months of suffering that have preceded it and those that will follow.

Love and sex thus vary in their effects. They can contribute to the tragedy or poignancy of life, or they can be joyful experiences. When presented as the latter, they are one of the comic aspects, along with verbal humor, amusing incidents, satire, and characterization, that give Williams' plays such variety.

In his serious fiction, Williams seldom introduces comic moments. An exception is a humorous argument, in the otherwise bleak *The Roman Spring of Mrs. Stone*, between the vain dandy Paolo and his greedy sponsor the Contessa, ending when she hits him in a spot which will put him out of business for the night. Williams has written a few satiric stories. "The Yellow Bird," on which *Summer and Smoke* is loosely based, presents a satiric portrait of a long-winded preacher and his daughter's finally triumphant rebellion. "The Inventory at Fontana Bella" ridicules the hangers-on surrounding an ancient wealthy Principessa. It includes a grotesquely delightful moment when the Principessa wakes up in her deserted palace, thinks she is being dressed, wanders naked to the terrace, and squats on an imaginary pot to relieve herself. "Miss Coynte of Greene" exaggerates nymphomania to the point of being parody. It, too, contains a moment of effective comic surprise and delight, the first rebellion of Miss Coynte. Williams has sympathetically described her plight as the poor relative who has to care for a nasty, demanding, incontinent old lady. One day when the old lady demands a bowl of sherbet, Miss Coynte shocks her to death with a filthy reply.

After that moment, "Miss Coynte of Greene" turns into fantasy. So does the last part of "The Yellow Bird," after Alma goes to New Orleans. "The Coming of Something to the Widow Holly" is a comic fantasy about some impossible roomers in a French Quarter house; two old ladies, constantly battling, tear off the fixtures to throw at each other. The Widow finally triumphs with the help of a metaphysician named Christopher D. Cosmos. In his fiction, fantasy is Williams' chief way of being comic.

Similarly Williams' longest satiric work, *The Knightly Quest*, ends with the hero and his friends escaping in a space ship. Before that Williams has painted some devastating portraits of greed, ambition, lust, and prejudice, chiefly of Braden Pierce, owner of The Project, the ultimate in industrial development, well on the way to taking over the world and destroying all individuality, spirit, and natural beauty. Braden's chief drive is to eliminate color—to get rid of the yellows, blacks, and reds, to make the world white, uniform, mechanical. The churches, represented by a Catholic priest and a Methodist minister, are shown to be thoroughly in the service of this representative of the Establishment. Children are represented by a bratty girl whose mother, after one look at her, bought a diaphragm. In one comic scene Braden is engaged in sexual gymnastics with his wife while in the room below his brother takes advantage of the embarrassment of his mother and her friends to fleece them at bridge. Braden's brother Gewinner, the protagonist, represents the romantic spirit, the essentially gentle, generous, sensitive, beauty-loving knight in eternal struggle against the vulgar, deceitful, selfish materialists. In this particular fantasy, as in Camino Real, the romantic is finally triumphant, though one is not supposed to feel too hopeful that it can be that way in actual life. The triumph is achieved by flight from the world.

Nevertheless, Don Quixote is still abroad, according to Tennessee Williams. The knightly quest has not yet ceased; the nightly one is sometimes rewarding. Despair may be the dominant tone in Williams as in most modern literature, but comic delight sometimes leavens it and livens the works.

Triangles of Transaction
in Tennessee Williams

LEONARD CASPER

W<small>RITING IN</small> "Poetry and Drama" (1951) of the writer's dilemma in trying to decide whether to emphasize the music of poetic drama or its stagecraft, T. S. Eliot counseled seeing each as intensifier of the other. Just such a postmodern solution-by-nonexclusion seems natural to the temperament of Tennessee Williams, for whom theatrics and dramatics are intentional allies, not antagonists; for whom dialogue and progressive action cycle through planes both realistic and figurative; and for whom, philosophically, nothing is repellent but *un-kindness*, denial of human resemblance. Such openness makes the playwright subject, on one hand, to charges of slothful overwriting and even self-indulgent amorality; but, on the other, to respectful reconsideration as a precursor of the New Uncertainty.

Williams has often been declared a Romantic because of his reliance on the symbolic imagination, for the heightened speech and gesture of his plays as well as the visionary dimensioning of so many characters. But if Romanticism implies unqualified faith in heroic individualism, or equates personal will with irreversible destiny, or gives equal weight to all claims of mystic insight: then Williams is as antiromantic as he is antinaturalistic. His plays have consistently admitted the darkness of human conditioning. Only then do they—sometimes—make the postmodern "leap of doubt," in a negation of

189

nihilism. Skepticism turns on itself, after realization that where there is doubt, there is possibility. Postmodern uncertainty sees beyond apparent entropy or absurdity, into paradox regained, preferring even the terror of insoluble mystery to that of an utter void.

In Williams' characters, resilience is earned and cautionary; rather than predetermined and illustrative only. Person after person tends to be self-enclosed, without being permitted self-satisfaction. Their only hope of justifying their existence to themselves is through "intimacy with strangers," in a trial community. Honoring southern values (as well, perhaps, as longing to compensate for personal deficiencies declared in his *Memoirs*, 1975), Williams proclaims the strength of diverse weaknesses unified, while acknowledging how often the effort ends in divisiveness. The struggle for personal emergence, through convergence with others equally imperfect, multiplies grotesque effects. Yet Williams implicitly argues (as Flannery O'Connor does explicitly, in her introduction to *A Memoir of Mary Ann*, 1961) that grotesque appearances may prove only that "in us the good is something under construction."

The circulatory, matchmaking quality of Williams' imagination has already received extensive recognition: in comments, for example, on the dense image-cluster of omnivorousness in *Suddenly Last Summer*—Venus flytrap, birds of prey off the Encantadas, narcissistic incest, homosexuality, cannibalism, prospective lobotomy, and the like; or the harmonics of character names in *The Night of the Iguana*—Shannon, Hannah, Nonno; or the symmetry of reverse roles in *Summer and Smoke*, body and spirit never quite intersecting. In addition, there often has been a *special geometry constructed of triangles*; not necessarily visible in the staging but, however subliminal, organic to the shape of the play's complications.

Sometimes they function as triangles of opposition, where the two base angles exert such counterforce against one another that they threaten to collapse the apex hovering above and between them. *Suddenly Last Summer*, for example, although presented in four scenes, has a two-part dramatic division. Dr. Cukrowicz is required to judge between contrasting versions of the lifestyle and death of Sebastian: that of his mother, Mrs. Venable, and that of his cousin Catharine. The arguments by the "plaintiff" and by the "defense"

are presented in a controlled sequence seemingly as justly propor-
tioned as the placement of counterweights on a balance arm. Yet,
perhaps because Dr. Cukrowicz has had his own integrity suborned
by Mrs. Venable in advance, he refuses the lobotomy which will
silence the ring of truth in Catharine's voice, when he decides, "I
think we ought at least to consider the possibility that the girl's
story could be true . . ." (III, 423). The triangle is dissolved by the
joining of two angles against the other. (The "possibility" seen by
Dr. Cukrowicz thus becomes a dramatic probability, distinct from
such postmodern enigmas as the multiplex of motives one can assign
Sebastian's participation in his own death.)

An equally spectacular triangle of opposition underframes the
eleven scenes of A Streetcar Named Desire. Stella is the apex figure
being pulled down, and apart, by her sister Blanche and her husband
Stanley, usually described as diametrically opposed figures: either
the fragile dreamer versus the natural brute; or, conversely, the
dangerous fantasist versus the defensive realist. However, the fact
that Stella finds it impossible to decide between Blanche's and Stanley's demands may be a clue to more than her preoccupation with
pregnancy or any escapist entrancement in her personal history. It
may well be that the play's greatest irony lies in the mutual mirror-
ing of Blanche and Stanley; its greatest delusion in the effort each
makes to smash that mirror and its reflected truth. Blanche's capacity for compassion is demonstrated by persistent remembrance
of how her rejection of her homosexual husband incited him to suicide. Yet the very erosion of identity and self-esteem which had
made her so dependent on him for definition has reached such extremes, by now, that Blanche is more than ever sensitive to her own
needs only. She mistakes Stanley's aggressiveness for strength, rather
than perceives it to be a defense mechanism much like her own
dreams of importance. Each figure lunges against the other as projection of the inner self with which neither can cope directly. Stella
cannot hold the triangle together because both Blanche and Stanley,
while making familial claims, resist the fullness of a family sense.
The release of tensions with Blanche's removal at the end is deliberately deceptive. Williams knows that the newborn child is Stanley's
next rival and that the triangle of opposition will merely have its
corners recast.

Where a playform is basically one of confrontation, the expected effect is polarization; and the outcome, annihilation of one antagonist by the other. However, Williams' triangles of opposition, at their best, resist reliance on customary "either-or" differences and incline instead towards "both-and" inclusiveness: for example, by letting the identity of assumed opponents converge, as in *Streetcar.* Where the cause of confrontation is not finally exposed as just such lack of comprehension, he has sometimes reacted with guilty restlessness and an urge to reconsider. Only dissatisfaction of this sort can explain the *radical, if gradual, conversion* of *27 Wagons Full of Cotton* into *Kingdom of Earth*, over a period of twenty years.

The earlier play has the spareness of motives and movement proper to a folk classic. Flora Meighan is the helpless victim of Silva Vicarro's revenge against her husband Jake's violence. Jake has burned out the Syndicate Plantation's gin mill, in order that some share of the business will return to him. Flora virtually admits as much, under cross-examination from Silva, the Plantation supervisor. She is a pliant earth-mother figure, not used to human wiles. Silva proceeds to cuckold Jake, in primitive satisfaction of justice: "tit for tat," a travesty of the "good neighbor policy" (*Baby Doll*, pp. 169; 159–60, 187). Jake is too beguiled by the prospect of regularly ginning Plantation cotton to notice his wife's abuse. The play depends on broad, coarse humor (the witless outwitted; the deflowering of Flora), rather than on any deep sympathy with her ravishment by the two men, or on perception of a possible rapport between her and Silva as victims of Jake's self-involvement.

Somewhat more concern, and even admiration, are provided Aunt Rose in *The Long Stay Cut Short, or: The Unsatisfactory Supper.* She evolves rapidly from the pathetic old relative about to be discarded by Archie Lee Bowman and his wife Baby Doll to a figure of durable strength beyond their comprehension or control. True, she "resembles a delicate white-headed monkey" (p. 194); she forgets to light a fire under their greens; the Bowmans are afraid she will break a hip and become a permanent burden to them (she is eighty-five years old). Still she is the only one to stand sturdily against the twister threatening at the end of the play. Nevertheless, in its disposition of the three characters, *The Unsatisfactory Sup-*

per is even more simplified than *27 Wagons Full of Cotton.*
Aunt Rose is caught in the crosscut of Bowman meanness, as the
stage directions strongly suggest: "The evenly cadenced lines of the
dialogue between BABY DOLL and ARCHIE LEE may be given a singsong
reading" and "passages may be divided as strophe and antistrophe"
(p. 192) according to Baby Doll's movements across the porch. The
cleavage is severe and is maintained.

Writing the screenplay for *Baby Doll,* ten years later, Williams
was able to preserve the ribaldry of these originals and at the same
time complicate the characters and their intertwining. Archie Lee
(Meighan now) is as obtuse as ever, but more brutal because of
frustrated lust. He cannot touch his wife until tomorrow, her twentieth birthday. Baby Doll herself has changed significantly: she is
younger, prettier, virginal—twice the prize that Flora was—and "Suddenly grown up" (p. 122). Neither passive nor pathetic, she back-
talks Archie Lee, invites seduction after a playful romp with Silva
(now Vacarro), rocks him gently in her crib, and allies herself with
him against her husband. She considers her marriage contract an-
nulled by Archie Lee's failure to retain their five rooms of furniture.
(Some of these strengths seem to have been borrowed from her
Aunt Rose Comfort, whose role is reduced to helpless victim of
Archie Lee.) Silva, whatever his early impulse towards vindictiveness,
is softened by Baby Doll's innocence. Their frolic is supposed to
resemble the games "of two shy children trying to strike up a friendship" (p. 106). They defend Aunt Rose together, Silva offering her
a place as cook in his household. As the screenplay ends, these three
begin to form a new triangle—of sensitives outside the gross world
of Archie Lee. Silva speaks for all of them (the fugitive kind), when
he asks rhetorically, "Does anyone know where to go, or what to do?"
(p. 139). Several times he has referred to himself defensively as a
"foreign wop"; and in the eye of the blind, Baby Doll and her aunt
are also grotesques. Ultimately their difference from others is both
their bond and their good fortune.

Many of these character insights along with their supportive devices reappear, ripened by a dozen years, in *Kingdom of Earth (The
Seven Descents of Myrtle).* Again, a woman (Myrtle) is manipu-
lated by two men (half-brothers Chicken and Lot) in their struggle

against each other. Again, stage business depends on natural disaster (where there was whirlwind or conflagration before, now there are a hurricane and a flood); on a literal/figurative ascent (to the Meighan attic, where Baby Doll's sense of life is heightened; to the Ravenstock rooftree, where Myrtle hopes to rise above the killing flood); as well as on a document dictated to the woman (Baby Doll's affidavit incriminating her husband; Myrtle's agreement not to inherit Ravenstock when Lot dies). There is even a resemblance between Aunt Rose's failure to heat her greens; and Myrtle's, to peel her potatoes before frying them: a comic index, in each case, to the degree of serious distraction and inner disturbance. But the familiar devices are given added dimension through a re-conception of character. At first it seems as if Williams has playfully reversed the earlier Meighan-Vicarro types. Chicken, identifiable with the vulgarity of Archie Lee, is now also the dark outcast (his mother presumably was negroid; and he is illegitimate). Lot, his younger half-brother, is as civilized as Silva—but impotent and fatally consumptive; he is outwitted and outmaneuvered by Chicken. However, what seems like casual reshuffling of types turns out to be acute recognition of human complexity.

Chicken emerges as a figure of more than carnivorous vitality. Though some evidence has been retracted in the 1975 revisions, Williams seems yet to maintain an open mind about his character's worth. If Chicken is so minuscule a Big Daddy or so crude a Laurentian totem as to be questionable and confusing, still he is never so clearly disclaimed as is Gooper or Meighan. His brutishness is the mask he must wear as the unwanted. Beneath his seeming indifference is a passion for generativeness, completion of some putative potential in himself through another, and extension of that self through identification with what he calls "the kingdom of earth" (V, 211). His language, naturally limited, still parallels rather than parodies Quentin's poetic elaboration of that same kingdom in *Small Craft Warnings* (V, 261). For both, being alive is feeling the fullness of that being. What is fearsome to Quentin (and presumably to Chicken) is not some final annihilation of self circumvented by dreams of an afterlife, but nonbeing now, loss of the capacity to wonder, weightless incompletion.

Myrtle also may be less roundly humanized than Leona in *Small*

Craft Warnings. Still her instincts, though expressed typically in terms of survival, seem to have sources in this same rapport with creation, the dynamics of surprise, the gift of growth. In each of the seven scenes she descends from the bedroom above where Lot is dying to the earthiness of Chicken; and those sanative encounters make possible the final ascension, to the roof top where rescue into a new life may occur. She has nursed Lot unselfishly, even after realizing that he has wed her only to keep the family property from passing on to his half-brother. She is dismayed only by the revelation that he is dying. (In the 1968 version she already had mothered five children but lost them through adoption.) Where can she hang her heart? It is not enough to be the last of the "Hot Shots from Mobile"; she must give life and receive it in return.

Nevertheless, however much more complicated Chicken and Myrtle are than Silva and Baby Doll, the format of *Kingdom of Earth* would not be critically different from that of *Baby Doll* unless the figure of Lot were adjusted too. *27 Wagons Full of Cotton, The Unsatisfactory Supper,* and *Baby Doll* all present variations of two characters ranged against one. Basically, *Kingdom of Earth* also pits Lot and Myrtle against Chicken, then Chicken and Myrtle against Lot. But its inclination to be generous tolerates, and even pities, Lot's identification with his dead mother (a woman of elegant dreams long inhibited by her "hawg" husband). His transvestiture, "both bizarre and beautiful" (pp. 211–12), is described with respect as a transfiguration. There is even something of Aunt Rose Comfort's courage in the way he hangs on to Charlotte's garden hat "as if a wind might blow it away" (p. 212). In the original, Chicken himself conveyed Lot's lifeless body "almost tenderly" (p. 108) to the sofa in his mother's parlor. Perhaps it is only death which, circumventing some symbolic ménage à trois, converts it into a pathetic game of odd-man-out. Essentially each of the three has been seeking self-possession—a sign of acceptance, a sense of home—in the Ravenstock property; and surely Myrtle speaks for them all, at their best, when she assures Lot early in the play that not all desperate people think only of themselves. However, Lot does die; and just as the Silva-Baby Doll-Aunt Rose triad is left incomplete, at the end of the screenplay, so in *Kingdom of Earth* Williams stops short of the metamorphosis of counterforces into counterparts.

In addition to such prototypes of conflict, in which third parties represent either witnesses-in-judgment or the prizes contested, some of Williams' most subtle psychological plays have depended on *triangles not of uncompromising opposition but of compassionate apposition.* Chronologically, this other pattern (appealing to the playwright's impulse towards conciliation rather than closure) is evident as early as *The Glass Menagerie.* At the level of action, Tom and his mother Amanda battle over crippled Laura with all the intense resentment natural to their own roles as poets manqué or displaced persons, among the tenements of St. Louis. Yet their seeming incompatibility is only a surface tension. Even after Tom has "escaped" to the merchant marine and seen the world, his mind like a homing device returns to celebrate his earlier and only life. What the three Wingfields had in common, more important than alienation from their surroundings, was a permanent affection for one another.

It is ironic that their private diversions—Amanda's memorialization of a courtly past; Laura's fixation in her transparent present; Tom's growing obsession with flight to some future "other"—should ever divide them. For these images of belonging are variations on the same larger dream, of individual worth within some familiar/familial array. Loneliness is a birth defect; love and loyalty, its ritual compensations (called imagination, the impulse to transcend the self, in "Desire and the Black Masseur" where alternatives include those more desperate ones of violence and justification through atonement). As memory play, *The Glass Menagerie* offers simultaneously a sense of coffinlike confinement and the comfort of togetherness, of like clinging to like with "dignity and tragic beauty" (I, 236), as Williams describes Amanda's final gesture towards her daughter. Self may be preserved by flight, but never fulfilled. We cannot know how Tom's runaway father feels about his family; but Tom himself is forever inseparable from them. It is only the distances which are imaginary.

In *Cat on a Hot Tin Roof* the three-cornered opposition also proves to be an appearance only. Skipper is as much an offstage presence, if not quite so awesome in his ambiguity, as Sebastian in *Suddenly Last Summer.* Nevertheless, the triangle which Skipper completes recedes drastically in importance, as a parallelogram of forces develops in its stead. Maggie's insecurity, masked as jealousy, requires that she interpret her husband Brick's closeness to Skipper as latent homosexuality. Skipper's impotency with her, during a subsequent trial of his maleness, leaves that possibility still open. Brick's identical fear prevents him from reassuring Skipper and thus forestalling his friend's suicide. The first two acts of the play are filled with the violence needed to pry loose, from Brick, admission of those bone-deep doubts which have caused a series of deaths: Skipper's, the union of Brick and Maggie, and Big Daddy's dream of family continuity as personal transcendence. It is finally Maggie's ability to identify with Big Daddy's mystique of the land as life-force which frees her from the endless turnabout of the Skipper-ridden triangle. When she asserts falsely that she is pregnant, she rejects the past conceived as completion and entrapment, but acknowledges the past as continuum and everpresent promise. Hers is a "true lie," an act of the will to believe, a commitment which may in fact occasion a child but which, in the interim, has at least regenerated Brick's faith in himself and Big Daddy's hope for an heir to his dreams. The third act bonds together two couples, capable of these imaginative leaps into a created future: Maggie and Brick, Big Daddy and Big Mama; contrasted with the breeders of objects, the dull dog-brains: Gooper, Mae, and their brood. Mortality and all other human weaknesses are overwhelmed in that communal enlargement.

The geometry of the true family, planting rows of possibility in its common ground, is officially rare in Williams. Indeed, the theme of the brother's keeper is more often travestied, in figures of buyers and sellers of their own flesh, such as Catharine Holly's relatives, as well as Mrs. Venable or Gooper (and even, intermittently, Amanda Wingfield). Yet the model remains constantly in the corner of Tennessee Williams' eye, if only to measure the deficiency or failure of persons directly in front of him. The achieved parallelogram of *Cat on a Hot Tin Roof* (a double triangle, with Brick-Big Daddy as the common hypotenuse) becomes at least an idealized extension of a whole second order of human systems, conciliatory rather than competitive. Typically, their membership depends more on the "kindness of strangers" than on blood ties or joint real estate; so that they must represent a vision of possibility larger than even the extended family or regional customs of hospitality.

In *Orpheus Descending*, for example, the principal role of Carol Cutrere seems to be that of the hovering witness. A once-committed, considerate person driven to society's periphery by its indifference, her purpose is restored when she sees Val Xavier restore life to Lady, in the innermost circle of death's realm. Lady's husband Jabe once burned down her father's winery, destroying him along with it; then bought Lady, who thought marriage to death appropriate after David Cutrere deserted her and she aborted their child. But the old joy-in-life still stirs in her. She plans a confectionery adjacent to Jabe's drygoods store, and she is encouraged in her feelings by the arrival of Valentine Xavier, dreamer of a legless bird which would die if it ever alighted. Yet, although Val is an orphic figure in so many ways (he carries a guitar autographed by Leadbelly, Bessie Smith, and other passional singers, and wears a snakeskin jacket), Val has wasted his youth and is now in search of seclusion. He is himself rescued from this deadly stasis, as surely as he rescues Lady, by impregnating her. Together they assert a life-affirmation which Jabe's murderous vengeance against them and their unborn child cannot mute. Lady and Val exist in a creative tension, as mutually supportive as Blanche and Stanley in *Streetcar* are destructive. They survive in the rebirth of Carol, whose transformation from spiritual voyeur to renewed voyager is reinforced by her apposition, in turn, with the Conjure Man (whose wild Choctaw cry professes freedom) and Vee, the dull-witted sheriff's visionary wife. In *Suddenly Last Summer* the decisive testimony must come from the intensity of Catharine's vision authenticating itself, while she remains disoriented medium only: a great burden, in antiheroic times. In *Orpheus Descending* any one of the bearers of "the dream," considered singly, might reasonably be ridiculed; but their choric voice can only be disputed, not denied.

In *Sweet Bird of Youth* the two-act division helps establish the polarization between a triangle of apposition (Chance, Princess, Heavenly) and one of opposition (Boss Finley, Tom Jr., Heavenly); between the kindness of strangers and mutilation by kinsmen. Heavenly is the common apex, a figure torn between life-and-death forces.

Initially, Chance and Princess (Alexandra Del Lago) savage one another, in futile misdirected anger against the ravishments of time which both have suffered. Their saving grace is their shame; and the first act ends with an alliance struck, between former scapegoats, to rescue Heavenly from servitude to her father. Erotic escapism and sexual extortion are transformed into a love-kiss of true concern. Although Chance's needs are the more immediate and Princess therefore has the more magnanimous role, she seems to speak for the good will in both when she says, "Believe me, not everybody wants to hurt everybody" (IV, 52).

This early transformation and its declaration are necessary because the second act, with its violent ending, is principally under the control of forces that travesty the claim of one human being on another, and Williams will not risk their confounding the whole-play's nearly classic expression of tragic faith. Similarly, because Princess, Chance, and Boss Finley are all "dreamers," Williams has either to treat them all alike or offer some measure for differentiating the imaginative dreamer from the imaginary. The degree of their capacity for outreach comes to stand for that measure. Occasionally in Boss Finley appears a flicker of genuine feeling for Heavenly. But essentially he is self-infatuated, invoking divine authority for his own ends; and if God can be bent to Boss Finley's will, why not his own children? His messianic frenzies, therefore, are clearly a self-delusion. He is neither generator nor sharer of life (as Big Daddy is) but an inverted kind of Cronos perversely trying to extend his life by devouring his future. By contrast, Chance manages to mature beyond the pathetic role of pure victim assigned him by his earlier words: "all my vices were caught from other people" (p. 37). When he realizes how he infected his lover and robbed her of the power of self-renewal through children, he condemns himself and welcomes castration by Boss Finley's troopers as punishment proper. At the end, he establishes the measure of the play one final time: by foregoing self-pity or justification by contrast; and by soliciting, from whatever strangers constitute the "innocent" bystanders, only recognition of their collective identity, their kind-ness, their part in human imperfection.

The curtain speech does not explicate the play so much as the play offers a reading between lines which otherwise seem quietly despairing, acquiescent to the triumph of time as attrition and certainly to the Cronos figure of Finley. Here the role of Heavenly, for all her remoteness and cryptic silences, becomes more crucially integrative in its play than is Carol Cutrere's in *Orpheus Descending*. At first it may seem as if she has come to symbolize the rot, the void, in all post-paradise experience. Yet just as she once offered her virginity as consolation prize to Chance, and seems to have sent him from St. Cloud originally in order to protect him from her father's fury (although her words are angry, she waves goodbye from a mist of rainbows); so also, having defied Boss Finley by refusing to be an accessory to his politicized Youth movement, nevertheless she appears with him so that Chance will not end up on a garbage scow in the Gulf. In spite of her self-description as "Dry, cold, empty" (p. 71), clearly she is none of these. Her capacity to love has survived the loss of both her virginity and her fertility. That her judgment of Chance and Boss Finley has been remarkably accurate, always, is established by the testimony of Aunt Nonnie and Miss Lucy, proxies in her absence (and parts of an ancillary triangle). To perceive her affirmative role, then, is to consider the possibility that a "comeback" can occur; that the Easter culmination for the action is not sardonic; that by confessing his fault and by accepting his penance, Chance warrants absolution—a superior innocence, after the fall: and if this is a persuasive argument at all for Williams to make, then since innocence and youth have been equated throughout, and regeneration is now conceivable, time as inevitable deterioration does not triumph after all.

Princess returns in the second act; and though she and Chance speak morosely of mutual castration, she serves as other self and companion as far as she can go. But Heavenly, in her own quietly generous way, travels even farther with Chance, farther than he ever knows. Williams clearly is declaring (as Brick did, of Maggie), "This girl has life in her body" (III, 212).

In *The Night of the Iguana*, the triangle of transaction has the peculiarity of seeming to shift its apex figure subtly during the play. On the level of sheer sound compatibility, Shannon and Hannah (reinforced by Nonno, who blesses the world's attunement) unquestionably are mated; and the play divisions confirm this harmony. Act one ends with Shannon (the defrocked minister who just pre-

viously has exclaimed on his own behalf: "Don't! Break! *Human!*
Pride!" IV, 276) successfully pleading with Maxine, his old friend
and protectress, to shelter both the 97-years-young poet, Jonathan
Coffin, and his granddaughter/fellow pilgrim and artist, Hannah
Jelkes. In act two, having chided Shannon for deserting his congregation, regardless of their differences, and having tried to protect
him from Maxine's persistent offers of alcohol, Hannah assures him
that "people have wanted to help you, the little they can" (p. 324),
despite his self-engrossment. In turn, he "shepherds" (p. 325) Nonno
to the back of the verandah, as the tropical rainfall starts. And in the
final act, the central event involves Hannah's rescue of Shannon
from his sense of worthlessness, by tying him in a hammock all
during his darkest night. One might think that such convergences
would create a momentum which could be satisfied only by the (at
least symbolic) marriage of Shannon and Hannah at the end, especially since Nonno has died and she may therefore suffer "blue
devils" of her own again.

However, Nonno's poem, climaxing a long lifetime of thoughtful
experience, describes life as cycling through realms of fruiting, falling,
decomposition, and refertilization. Hannah's prayer is for stasis and
quiet, which she confuses with peace. Her whole life she has been
conditioned to a heightened, but largely withheld, sensitivity. She
longs for a simplicity too abstract for this world (although it is not
to be equated with the Nazis' singlemindedness, excessive to the
point of being antihuman, if only because, as her kabuki robe signi-
fies, Hannah's inclination toward minimal embodiment makes her
physically incapable of doing harm).

It is Maxine—her name marred by that grating interference with
vowels and liquid consonants—who comes closer to the image offered, of life in all its prolific contradictions. Her knowledge of her
own ambivalence ("I know the difference between loving someone
and just sleeping with someone," p. 329), her mixed feelings about
her dead husband Fred, even her distance from the special spiritual
problems of Shannon: these ambiguities resemble the iguana's con-
cealment of delicate meat under hideous armor; the dungheap to
which Shannon takes tourists, so they can see how even offal supports
life, the life of scavengers; and indeed, Nonno's own words about
the transfiguration of death.

Shannon saw God not as a "senile delinquent" (p. 303), but as thunder and lightning, because he yearned to be punished for his fornication and heresy. Since both of these sins, however, seem to have originated in the loneliness of masturbation, poor substitute for a mother's close attendance, his defiance of God is a spiteful provocation, a circuitous prayer that incries be answered and suffering be purposeful. His foreseeable years with Maxine will be equally tempestuous, confused, but above all passionate: affirmative not of etherealization, but of life as a variegated process of human endurance, unsure evolution, and obscure discovery.

The most effective plays of apposition seem to generate a field between two major, matched characters, which animates a third, in turn. When that basic balance is upset, as in *The Milk Train Doesn't Stop Here Anymore*, the ingathering design seems more superimposed than organic. Sissy Goforth is without peer in the play, Chris Flanders serving at best as custodian of the deathwatch. He helps gentle her departure; but it is her rage, her refusal to be less than she was or ever to cease, which keeps the play alive and counterpoints the rhythmic boom-doom! of the waves below. By insisting, with her last breath, "Be here, when I wake up" (V, 118), she offers Chris a chance to be an angel attendant on resurrection, not just the Angel of Death. He has already initiated that ritual of hope himself, having placed the rings "Under her pillow like a Pharaoh's breakfast waiting for the Pharaoh to wake up hungry" (p. 120). Still he reports afterwards to her secretary Blackie that there's no sign of her fierce vitality anywhere, anymore. (Such behavior goes far towards disestablishing him as mystic, and undercutting the prospect of his being a crypto-Christopher, unwitting bearer of Christ.) His agnosticism may well represent Williams' yea-saying undergoing self-restraint (the sea "says 'Boom' and that's what it means. No translation . . ." (p. 120); the voice of God, as in *Sweet Bird of Youth*, is silent, and man must look to the kingdom of the earth). But the effect is a distinct dampening of dramatic spirits.

Blackie, a compassionate and intelligent woman, would be companion enough for Sissy Goforth, did the latter not require at least the facsimile of greater intimacy with life in the flesh. Her memoirs are an effort to restore what seemed only momentary, especially the wondrous presence of her last husband Alex. The one attraction that

Chris has for her, despite all his deficiencies, is his resemblance to Alex: both are poets garbed in lederhosen. But Chris, even in his own eyes, is more apparitional than real. He watches over the dying, hoping to relieve his terror at the present, not prospective, experience of his own nonbeing. The calm he contributes is difficult to distinguish from coldness. Ethereal as Hannah is in *The Night of the Iguana*, she manages to project her presence; by contrast, Chris is an abstract figure. What ought to be rich ambiguity in his conduct becomes diffuseness. His mobile, "The Earth Is a Wheel in a Great Big Gambling Casino," means to be reminiscent of Pascal's famous wager: we have nothing to lose by a leap of faith. But it cannot be Pascalian if its operation is passive rather than self-propelled. Where Sissy is life-enacting, Chris is merely life-asserting—as are the kabuki attendants who realize their superfluity even as they proclaim, at the end, that the muted bugle is blowing reveille for Sissy, not taps.

As a result of the great disproportion between Sissy and her two companions, the triad of solidarity becomes more token than fact. The real death deplored in this play is loneliness, reinforced only by Sissy's literal dying. But if we live in each other or not at all, can a solitary voice be sufficient sign of life triumphant? The metaphysical dimensions of that seeming contradiction are enormous; the dramatic dimensions, perhaps insuperable.

In an earlier model for this play, *I Rise in Flame, Cried the Phoenix*, Williams' intention is far less uncertain. It too concentrates on the last living fraction of a person (D. H. Lawrence) dying of tuberculosis (Sissy has lung cancer), on a sea cliff overlooking the Mediterranean (the Riviera, as against the Divina Costiera), with the banner of a phoenix at his back (Sissy's heraldic device is the griffin: half lion, half eagle). Lawrence, like Sissy, is determined to outstare the sun. With him are his Valkyrian wife Frieda (though her role as the Angel of Death remains latent) and their virginal friend Bertha. Yet despite the closeness which their conversations show they share, for Lawrence woman is the dark night that would permanently sheathe his maleness. He intends to be whole again, and to be whole is to be solitary, self-sustaining. "I want to do it alone" (*Dragon Country*, p. 75), he says of his death. He collapses as the sun sets, having prophesied his own rearising. Even with its overtones of confused love and hate, essentially *I Rise in Flame, Cried the Phoe-*

nix is about the pride and pleasure of being one person, alone and intact. Strategies of both opposition and apposition are presented but kept minimal, even negligible. Lawrence is a blazing fire that throws two transparent shadows. Even the consolation of transcendence offered him at the moment of death, although it connects him with the cosmos, is empowered by his own imperious imagination. The play is a monument to Lorenzo the Magnificent.

In the Laurentian drama, profound ambivalence is not present; nor would it be appropriate. In *The Milk Train Doesn't Stop Here Anymore*, it is present; but its propriety is unclear. Is the dominant sound of this play a shattering outcry, one voice protesting the inevitability of aloneness? Does its eloquence lie in the tenacity with which Sissy holds past life present in her emotions, without the natural confidence of Lawrence (who *is* the life force) and therefore his articulate control? Does the play inscribe a visionary shape of apposition as a ceremony of self-ascendancy, while still conceding the very real loneliness of dying (and of living)? Or is it, plainly, a defective shape: a one-legged woman clutching two sawed-off crutches? Does it fail those transactional conventions which Williams himself has helped evolve; or are such conventions simply not adequate to the admission he proposed to express?

In his *Memoirs*, Williams indicates that his work since *The Night of the Iguana* has become more experimental—whether in stagecraft or fable, he does not specify. *Milk Train* may indeed be as exploratory a piece as he reports Boston critic Elliot Norton once conjectured. Perhaps its asymmetry is deliberate; its simultaneous yea-nays more postmodern, more antiromantic than usual. In the same autobiography Williams intimates that the final version of *Milk Train* remains to be written; consequently, final judgment may have to be suspended. Or can there ever be a final word about the nonfinality of knowledge?

Revision, which can prevent hardening of a speculative mode into self-imitation, has often been part of the history of a Williams play (or story). In addition, Williams has avoided relying exclusively on triangulation for his Q. E. D.'s. (What is the geometry, for example, of *Camino Real*; or of *Small Craft Warnings*; or of *Out Cry*?) Still the extensive use, intended or not, of triangles of transaction may be enough to sour certain critical tastes. It can be interpreted as a sign of excessive reinforcement, caused by the playwright's lack of confidence or loss of artistic control. Particularly is this a likely response to appositional *assistance* (since *resistance* may be assumed requisite to dramatic conflict). Or one might conclude from the preoccupation with design that, for all his seeming compassion, Williams is essentially an abstractionist whose geometric orders are no more man-centered than, say, the data-processing fiction of a Robbe-Grillet.

Nevertheless, the greatest likelihood lies in such third-party configurations being, for Williams, visual/subliminal metaphors of compensation for human fallibility (probationary proofs, . · .) but especially for human incompletion (earthly trinities). Each person has fullest access to himself through others. That would be impossible, were there not some common human condition, some kind-ness. In that realization of coinheritance is the beginning of coinherence. And to the extent that coinherence is achieved and sustained, there is justification for affirming purpose to life, in spite of individual defect or apparent defeat. The triangles may simply represent the cellular structure of a proper community: composed of diverse elements (apposition), but without divisiveness (opposition). In that prospectus, all men are intermediaries to one another's missions; as they are media for engaging their interim mysteries.

Tennessee Williams
at the Delta Brilliant

ALBERT E. KALSON

I

N A MOMENT of ecstatic happiness in *Battle of Angels*, Myra exclaims to Val, "Greta Garbo is at the Delta Brilliant" (I, 79). In the third act of his first full-length play, Tennessee Williams alludes to the movies to suggest the possibility of the merging of illusion and reality, of celluloid world and harsh existence. In *The Eccentricities of a Nightingale* John takes Alma to the Delta Brilliant to see a Mary Pickford film as prelude to a night of love. Life as Hollywood dream, however, fades quickly for Myra and Alma—one is murdered by her husband, and the other loses her lover. For other Williams characters, however, what is playing at the Delta Brilliant emphasizes the gulf between unattainable dream and empty life. Sitting in the white section of the Delta Brilliant, Chicken in *Kingdom of Earth* is aroused by the actresses on the screen but shunned by the women around him because of his Negro blood (p. 101). Willie, the young girl in *This Property Is Condemned*, has been to the Delta Brilliant to see Garbo die beautifully of consumption with "Violins playing. And loads and loads of white flowers" (*27 Wagons*, p. 202). Tuberculosis was not so pretty, however, when her sister Alva, who looked like a movie star and was "The Main Attraction" for the local railroad men, died of the same wasting disease.

207

For many Williams characters, Hollywood is what life never is—but ought to be. Kilroy in *Camino Real* remembers his wife as "a platinum blonde the same as Jean Harlow," but it is the film star, not the wife, about whom he dreams: "Wouldn't it be wonderful if you could sprinkle them ashes over the ground like seeds, and out of each would spring another Jean Harlow? And when spring comes you could just walk out and pick them off the bush!" (II, 551). He is about to pay dearly for the lesser charms of Esmeralda, the Gypsy's daughter, who spends her time between customers reading *Screen Secrets*, and dreaming, as Kilroy suggests, of seeing herself in Paramount Pictures (p. 558).

For other Williams characters, to make it in the movies is life's ultimate goal, and one must at least dress the part while waiting. Sometime-stripper Myrtle of *Kingdom of Earth*, whose "appearance suggests an imitation of a Hollywood glamor girl which doesn't succeed as a good imitation" (V, 127), tells Chicken, "like every girl in show business, and many out of it, too, Hollywood was my dream" (p. 149). If the dream will never come true for Myrtle, she can still attempt to provide Lot's farmhouse parlor with a gaudy splendor: she will wash the crystal pendants "and make them shine like the chandelier in *Loew's State* on Main Street in Memphis!" (p. 134). In *Sweet Bird of Youth*, Chance Wayne resorts to blackmail in an attempt to break into films. In his younger days as barman of the Royal Palms Hotel, he had copied his uniform "from an outfit Vic Mature wore in a Foreign Legion picture, and I looked better in it than he did," he says (IV, 78). In the surreal *Gnädiges Fräulein*, blond Indian Joe is dressed like a Hollywood Indian, for, as the author reveals in his production notes, "he doesn't have to be anything but an erotic fantasy in appearance" (*Dragon Country*, p. 218).

A few Williams characters even attempt to turn erotic fantasy into reality under the cover of darkness in motion picture palaces. After being bored by Roger's blurred magic lantern stills in *Eccentricities*, Alma is stimulated by the moving pictures at the Delta Brilliant to the point where she dares to apply pressure to John's knee. She tells him later that she had once rushed out of the theater when she had felt the pressure of a stranger's knee. She now wonders if she would have sprung from her seat had the stranger even faintly resembled John, "a dangerous speculation for a minister's daughter!" (II, 93). In *The Night of the Iguana* Hannah tells Shannon about one of the few encounters in her life that she considers a love experience: at sixteen, she was at the Saturday matinee at the Nantucket movie theater when a young man pushed his knee against hers; she had screamed, and he had been arrested for molesting a minor. Later, she got him off by telling the police she was just overexcited by the Clara Bow picture (IV, 361). In the short stories "Hard Candy" and "The Mysteries of the Joy Rio," two men ignore the images on the screen as they seek sexual gratification in the dark recesses of the balcony of the Joy Rio. For both, the search ends in death.

Filmgoing for the rest of Williams' characters is less dangerous. In fact for most, the movies offer a refuge, a temporary haven, a place of protection if not always a place to dream. Laura in *The Glass Menagerie* takes shelter there from the rigors of secretarial school. Stella in *Streetcar* uses the movies to keep Blanche from Stanley's squalid poker night; and to cheer up her despairing friend Trinket, Celeste in *The Mutilated* suggests "an afternoon at the movies with a large size Hershey" (*Dragon Country*, p. 126).

For at least one Williams character who does not aspire to stardom, the movies provide an idealized goal. Isabel Haverstick in *Period of Adjustment* has become a nurse, she tells Ralph Bates, because she thought she had a vocation. She saw herself "as a Florence Nightingale. . . . Establishin' clinics in the—upper Amazon country . . . working side by side with a . . . doctor . . . administering to the plague victims in the jungle, exposing myself to contagion." Blemishes would appear on her hands and progress to the wrists and forearms. Discovering she has contracted the plague, "the *youngish middle-aged* doctor" would seize her in his arms—thus exposing himself. "And love is stronger than death," Isabel continues. "You get the picture?" "Yep, I've seen the picture," Ralph responds as they both laugh (IV, 152–54). Inspired by the likes of Garbo in *The Painted Veil*, Bette Davis in *Jezebel* and Greer Garson in *Madame Curie*, Nurse Isabel has actually had no great demands exacted from her, has made no romantic sacrifice. Instead she has become involved with a neurotic young man suffering with the shakes, and she has married him.

In a conversation with Ralph later in the play, Isabel's husband George prepares the way for one of Williams' most telling statements concerning the necessary function of the movies in American life. By 1960, the time of *Period of Adjustment*, technological progress has made it possible for man to pursue his dreams at home. He no longer needs to go out to the Delta Brilliant; he merely flicks a switch:

> GEORGE: Turn on your TV any late afternoon or early evenin' and what do you get—beside the commercials, I mean? A goddam Western, on film. Y'know what I see, outside the camera range? A big painted sign that says: "Haverstick-Bates Ranch." . . . "The Last Stand of the Texas Longhorn, a Dignified Beast! We breed cattle for TV Westerns." We breed us some buffalo, too. The buffalo is also a dignified beast, almost extinct, only thirty thousand head of the buffalo left in this land. . . . Hell, we could double that number befo' we—
> RALPH: Hang up our boots an' saddles under the—dignified sky of West Texas?
> GEORGE (with feeling): There *is* dignity in that sky! There's dignity in the agrarian, the pastoral—way of—existence! A dignity too long lost out of the—American dream—(IV, 197).

As luck—and Williams—would have it, they turn the set on in time to watch a cowboy comfort his sweetheart and start a cattle stampede:

> GEORGE: Will you look at that? A Western on Christmas Eve, even! It's a goddam NATIONAL OBSESSIONAL.
> RALPH: Yep, a national homesickness in the American heart for the old wild frontiers with the yelping redskins and the covered wagons on fire . . . (IV, 205).

There are no worlds to be conquered, no frontiers to be tamed. Romance and adventure have gone out of American life. Yet twentieth-century man still yearns for something more daring than the life of factory hand, bank teller, or sales clerk. But only vicarious experience—the film experience—can assuage the pain of the uneventful present for the two veterans of the Korean conflict.

For Tom Wingfield in *The Glass Menagerie*, the movies become the impetus for his desertion of the drab hell of home and factory for the more stimulating hell of a world at war. Written near the end of World War II, sixteen years before *Period of Adjustment*, *Menagerie* provides a portrait of the budding artist for which Williams himself served as model. Tom typifies a generation stultified by the Depression, anticipating the coming war as a means of escape into a world of adventure. "I'm going to the *movies!*" is his plaintive leitmotif, his repeated response to every crisis at home. When his mother accuses him of lying—after all no normal young man goes nightly to the movies—Tom turns on her: "I'm going to opium dens! . . . I'm a hired assassin, I carry a tommy gun in a violin case! . . . They call me Killer, Killer Wingfield, I'm leading a double-life, a simple, honest warehouse worker by day, by night a dynamic *czar* of the *underworld, Mother*. I go to gambling casinos. . . . sometimes I put on green whiskers. On those occasions they call me—*El Diablo!* . . . My enemies plan to dynamite this place. They're going to blow us all sky-high some night! . . . You'll go up, up on a broomstick, over Blue Mountain with seventeen gentlemen callers! You ugly—babbling old—*witch . . .*" (I, 164).

His vehement response is an obvious giveaway, for only the movies could have provided the shy young warehouse hand with such a fantasized impression of underworld life. Tom seems to have been to a double bill of *Scarface* and *The Wizard of Oz!* When he comes home a little drunk one night and fishes in his pockets for his key, the "shower of movie ticket stubs" that appears unmistakably reveals that Tom has not been lying to Amanda. Nor does he lie to Laura when he explains why he is so late: "There was a very long program. There was a Garbo picture and a Mickey Mouse and a travelogue and a newsreel and a preview of coming attractions. And there was an organ solo and a collection for the Milk Fund—simultaneously—which ended up in a terrible fight between a fat lady and an usher!" (pp. 166–67).

Every moviegoer of the thirties and forties has shared Tom's experience. And every moviegoer has at one time or another shared his eventual exasperation for falling under the spell of an illusionary world on film. "I'm tired of the movies," he tells his friend Jim. As "the incandescent marquees and signs of the first-run movie houses light his face from across the alley," Tom continues his anguished outburst: "All of those glamorous people—having adventures—hogging it all, gobbling the whole thing up! You know what happens?

People go to the *movies* instead of *moving!* Hollywood characters are supposed to have all the adventures for everybody in America, while everybody in America sits in a dark room and watches them have them! Yes, until there's a war. That's when adventure becomes available to the masses! . . . It's our turn now, to go to the South Sea Island . . . to be exotic, far-off! But I'm not patient. I don't want to wait till then. I'm tired of the *movies* and I am *about* to *move!*" (pp. 200–201).

At the end of *Menagerie*, however, Williams reveals that even as a merchant seaman far from his St. Louis home, Tom still must rely on the movies as a means of escape. At home he dreamt of adventure; out in the world he is haunted by the memory of the sister he deserted. The memory brings too much pain; it must be obliterated, and there is a way: "I reach for a cigarette, I cross the street, I run into the movies . . ." (p. 237).

II

Like Tom Wingfield, Tennessee Williams is an inveterate moviegoer—and for the same reasons. The young Williams found the movies his only escape from the reality of an unhappy home until he took further solace in writing. While still a teenager, he wrote a review of the silent film version of *Stella Dallas* which won him ten dollars in a contest sponsored by the Loew's State Theatre in St. Louis. Movies were at times so intensely exciting for him that he recalls an attack of heart palpitations on his way home from one— *The Scarlet Pimpernel*.

His first work for the motion pictures was as an usher in a Broadway movie house when he was down on his luck in New York in 1943. By then he had suffered the closing of his first play in Boston, *Battle of Angels*, and written a fantasy containing a flashback dream sequence, *Stairs to the Roof*, for both stage and screen, which he could not sell. For a time the job as usher seemed the closest he would get to the film industry, until his remarkable agent Audrey Wood landed him a six-month contract as scriptwriter at Metro-Goldwyn-Mayer. He went to Hollywood, but stayed with MGM for only a month. First assigned to adapt *The Sun Is My Undoing* to the screen, he was transferred briefly to a Lana Turner vehicle, *Marriage Is a Private Affair*, only to part company with his employers after a difference of opinion concerning a script for child star Margaret O'Brien. Shortly afterwards he sent MGM a script entitled *The Gentleman Caller*, which he claimed would "run twice as long as *Gone With the Wind*." When the script was rejected, he revised it as a play. *The Gentleman Caller* became *The Glass Menagerie*, and Williams' career as a successful dramatist was launched. Since then he has returned to Hollywood from time to time, as sole author of the films *Baby Doll* (1956), an amalgamation of some shorter works, and *Boom!* (1968), based on *The Milk Train Doesn't Stop Here Anymore*, and as collaborator on the film versions of several of his plays—*The Glass Menagerie* (1950), *A Streetcar Named Desire* (1951), *The Rose Tattoo* (1955), *Suddenly Last Summer* (1959), and *The Fugitive Kind* (1960).

In the light of Williams' varied film career, that some of his plays contain transfigured moments from Hollywood movies is hardly surprising. Although Maria Ley-Piscator claims in *The Piscator Experiment* that *Menagerie* owes a debt to her husband's epic theater, surely the screen device and captions for that play are to some extent the writer's homage to the silent screen which nurtured him in his younger days.[1] Piscator and Brecht might well have applauded such a caption as "The Crust of Humility" (I, 155), but they would not have tolerated the sentiment of "The accent of a coming foot" (p. 191), "A pretty trap" (p. 192), "This is my sister: Celebrate her with strings!" (p. 193), "Terror!" "The Opening of a Door!" (p. 196), "A souvenir" (p. 228) and "And so goodbye . . ." (p. 236). D. W. Griffith, on the other hand, might have written them himself!

Films of the sound era influenced him too. The effect toward which Williams and his collaborator Donald Windham are striving at the entrance of the hero in *You Touched Me!*, produced on Broadway after *Menagerie* although written before it, is a calculated gamble which probably cannot be brought off on stage: "There is the sound of a train pulling in and the clanging of iron bells. After a little while, the front door is pushed open and HADRIAN enters quietly. At this moment the sun emerges. The smoke from the engine which is directly across the road puffs into the open door about his figure and the mist has a yellowish glow" (p. 12). There is no further reference to the train which pulls up remarkably close to the residence in which the play is set; it exists to provide that one puff of smoke.

A face materializing through the billowing smoke of an arriving train had worked wondrously on screen when the face was Garbo's at her first appearance in *Anna Karenina* (1935). It proved an unforgettable moment—at least for Williams and Windham.

That Williams' first play, *Battle of Angels*, is set within a flashback frame, a convention traditional to the screen but alien to the stage, further emphasizes the influence of the movies on Williams' techniques. *Battle of Angels* offers more convincing proof that certain films have imbedded themselves somewhere in the Williams subconscious: Jabe's climactic first entrance late in the play is described in terms which bring to mind the most chilling moments of the horror films of the thirties: "The door slams open on the landing. At this instant a flickering match light appears on the stairs and spills down them and across the floor. Heavy dragging footsteps and hoarse breathing are heard." "Christ in Heaven, what's that?" Myra whispers as the suspenseful build-up to Jabe's entrance continues: "The ghastly, phantomlike effect of this entrance is dramatically underlined. JABE's shadow precedes him down the stairs and his approach has the slow, clumping fatality of the traditional spook's. He is a living symbol of death. . . . He wears a purple bathrobe which hangs shroudlike about his figure and his face is a virtual death mask. Just as he appears in full view of the stairwell, the match which he holds under his face flickers out and disappears from view, swallowed in darkness like a vanished apparition." Myra's unloved husband is as frightening as Frankenstein's monster, as sinister as Count Dracula:

> MYRA (horrified, incredulous) : Jabe.
> JABE (hoarsely) : Yes, it's me! (He strikes another match and this time his face wears a grotesque, grinning expression.) (I, 111).

Realizing that the lurid horror-film effect was overdone, Williams gives Jabe in the play's revision, *Orpheus Descending*, a brief scene in the first act, and considerably tones down his second entrance.

Whereas *You Touched Me!* and *Battle of Angels* indicate isolated borrowings from films, at least one play reveals genuine indebtedness to Hollywood. Describing the setting of *Camino Real*, the 1953 revision of a shorter play of the early forties first published in *American Blues* in 1948, the dramatist writes in the prologue: "[The plaza] belongs to a tropical seaport that bears a confusing, but somehow harmonious, resemblance to such widely scattered ports as Tangiers, Havana, Vera Cruz, Casablanca, Shanghai, New Orleans" (II, 431). The fourth-named city, Casablanca, provides more than an ambiance for Williams' play. The general atmosphere, several of the characters, even a major incident in *Camino Real* have been filtered through Williams' perhaps unconscious memory of Warner Brothers' 1943 Academy-Award-winning film *Casablanca*, directed by Michael Curtiz from a script by Julius J. and Philip G. Epstein and Howard Koch.

The film *Casablanca* concerns Ingrid Bergman's desperate attempt to secure a flight for herself and her screen husband Paul Henreid from Casablanca, a no-man's-land where the permanent residents are outnumbered by the transients stranded by World War II. All are eager to obtain exit visas to continue by plane to Lisbon, point of embarkation for the United States and freedom. Flight is the film's motif, and flight was the motivating word for Williams and director Elia Kazan as they prepared the Broadway production of *Camino Real*. Williams states in his foreword, "We have kept saying the word 'flight' to each other as if the play were merely an abstraction of the impulse to fly" (II, 420).

World War II Casablanca becomes in *Camino Real* a de Chirico landscape, a universal Everywhere for each frustrated human being who has lost direction, hope and love, facing the fact that time is running out while he frequents, in the play as well as the film, hotels, bars, pawn shops and gambling dens. The scene in the play most reminiscent of the film is Block Nine, one added to the revised version, in which Marguerite Gautier hears a noise in the sky and learns that the Fugitivo, an unscheduled plane, is landing and will soon take off again. (*Casablanca* opens with all eyes watching a descending plane which each character hopes soon to board.) Marguerite tries every means to get on the flight, but her francs are unacceptable, and her lover Jacques Casanova will not surrender her identity papers to her. He himself must remain, waiting for the remittance checks which will never arrive. He does not want to lose the little warmth which Marguerite's love has provided him. The scene indeed inverts the most famous, most widely imitated scene of any Hollywood 'forties film: in *Casablanca*'s final scene Bogart as Rick pretends to be leaving on the plane with Bergman, but demonstrates at the last moment that he has retained what all of Williams' characters have lost—a sense of honor. In a quixotic gesture, he gives up his two letters of transit to Bergman and Henreid (unlike Marguerite, Bergman would have given up her place to secure passage for Henreid) and walks off into the night with Claude Rains in search of a better world where honorable men can lead honorable lives. In *Camino Real*, Marguerite would leave the man she supposedly loves, is frustrated in the attempt, and finally remains only to be unfaithful to him.

Despite the inverted Fugitivo scene, *Camino Real* ends as *Casablanca* does. Don Quixote, who has lost his Sancho Panza early in the play, finds a new companion in Kilroy, a down-and-out fighter, and goes off with him into Terra Incognita, a desert wasteland. Before joining forces with Rains, the prefect of police, Rick-Bogart had restlessly roamed the world with his own Sancho Panza, Sam, the black piano player who sings a song whose title suggests the themes of mutability and mortality which run through Williams' *Camino Real* and much of his later work—"As Time Goes By." ("Time goes by so fast," says Big Mama in *Cat on a Hot Tin Roof*, III, 157). Rick has arranged for Sam to remain in Casablanca in the employ of Signor Ferrari, who runs a seedy bar which is actually the front for the black market. The role is played by Warner Brothers' archetypal fat man, Sidney Greenstreet, who also finds his way into *Camino Real* as Gutman, sinister proprietor of the Siete Mares Hotel. It is surely no coincidence that Greenstreet's most famous screen characterization was that of Kasper Gutman, archvillain of *The Maltese Falcon* (1941), a film of desperate characters seeking the cure to their frustrations in a supposedly priceless figurine which turns out to be worthless lead.

In *Camino Real* Gutman carries on his wrist a white cockatoo named Aurora. In a flashback in *Casablanca* the bar which serves as meeting place for Bergman and Bogart is the Belle Aurore. Ferrari's bar in the film is called the Blue Parrot. In the play a character names the town's hotspots as "the Pink Flamingo, the Yellow Pelican, the Blue Heron, and the Prothonotary Warbler! They call it the Bird Circuit" (II, 469). And Greenstreet also has a white cockatoo in MGM's *Malaya* (1950), in which he plays a barkeeper named the Dutchman, who, despite the war in the Pacific, can manage deals with Americans and Japanese alike. Clearly Greenstreet has been an obsession with Williams—his one-act play *The Last of My Solid Gold Watches* is dedicated to the monumental actor (*27 Wagons*, p. 73); and the dramatist may even have had the actor in mind as he conceived *Cat*'s Big Daddy.

Still other echoes of *Casablanca* find their way into *Camino Real*. When Henreid leads the others in the singing of the "Marseillaise" to drown out the singing of "Wacht am Rhein," the German major orders the closing of Rick's cafe. In Williams' play, the Dreamer shouts the forbidden word—"*Hermano!*" and "The cry is repeated like springing fire and a loud murmur sweeps the crowd." Gutman says, "The word has disturbed the people and made it necessary to invoke martial law!" (II, 450–52). A monocled English gentleman has his wallet stolen in the film as he sits at an outdoor cafe with his wife; in the play, which contains the minor stereotyped characters of Lord and Lady Mulligan, a pickpocket lifts Kilroy's wallet (II, 459). Just as gendarmes seize Peter Lorre, who in the film breaks from them to plead for help from Rick, officers in the play press in on Kilroy, who gets away temporarily to dash into the theater, beseeching the audience to help him (II, 479–83). *Casablanca's* gendarmes, who round up suspects throughout the film, become, surrealistically, *Camino Real's* omnipresent Streetcleaners, waiting for the moment of death to pounce on their prey and cart them away.

Another Warner Brothers' film of the period, *Hold Back the Dawn* (1941), based on a Ketti Frings story with a screenplay by Charles Brackett and Billy Wilder, may also have contributed atmosphere and character to *Camino Real*. Within a flashback frame, *Hold Back the Dawn* tells the story of yet another European refugee waiting in still another limbo, a Mexican border town. Iscovescu, played by Charles Boyer, a former dancer, now a gigolo, manages to get a room at the seedy Esperanza Hotel, run by Flores, like Gutman a rotund proprietor in a white linen suit; the actor this time is Nestor Paiva, not Greenstreet. The room becomes available suddenly when its former occupant, another refugee waiting for entry into the United States, hangs himself. In Block Six of *Camino Real*, when Kilroy asks the proprietor of the rundown Ritz Men Only for a room, a voice is heard above: "*Stiff in number seven! Call the Streetclean-*

ers!" "Number seven is vacant," the proprietor tells Kilroy, "with absolutely no change in face or voice" (II, 476–77). Iscovescu, irresistible to women, exploits a naive schoolteacher played by Olivia de Havilland and marries her to gain access to the United States and freedom. *Camino Real*'s Iscovescu-like Casanova, however, in a further plot inversion is himself exploited by Marguerite Gautier. During an auto trip through the rain in *Hold Back the Dawn*, de Havilland listens to the sounds of the windshield wipers, which she likens to breathing, as she watches them arc away from each other to return again and again. Over and over she repeats the word "together." In *Camino Real* a defeated Marguerite returns to Casanova, and he comforts her: "and we are together, breathing quietly together, leaning together, quietly, quietly together, completely, sweetly together, not frightened, now, not alone, but completely quietly together" (II, 524–25).

While Williams has never publicly acknowledged a debt to either *Hold Back the Dawn* or *Casablanca*, he has himself conveniently supplied evidence that he has seen the latter—over and over again. Describing the early years of his career in a *Playboy* interview (April 1973, p. 80), Williams said, "In 1943, I was ushering at Broadway's Strand Theater for $17 a week. The attraction was *Casablanca* and for several months I was able to catch Dooley Wilson singing *As Time Goes By*." Memory plays curious tricks: *Casablanca* played the Strand for only five weeks, but that was long enough for the film to insinuate itself into the writer's unconscious. Williams' memory may even have tricked him into forgetting his own sleight of hand in transforming *Casablanca* into *Camino Real*.

III

More significant in Williams' development than his sometimes occasional, sometimes extensive borrowings, intentional or otherwise, from specific films is the studied use throughout his career of film techniques adapted to the stage. The production notes for *The Glass Menagerie* contain Williams' manifesto "for a new, plastic theatre which must take the place of the exhausted theatre of realistic conventions if the theatre is to resume vitality as a part of our culture" (I, 131). "When a play employs unconventional techniques," Williams writes, "it is not, or certainly shouldn't be, trying to escape its responsibility of dealing with reality, or interpreting experience, but is actually or should be attempting to find a closer approach, a more penetrating and vivid expression of things as they are." Such unconventional elements as the screen device, the music and the lighting techniques which Williams calls for in Menagerie are all borrowed from films past and present which provide a fluidity often lacking in the conventional fourth-wall realism of the modern theater.

While the screen device was rejected by Menagerie's first director, Eddie Dowling, and Williams has not attempted to employ it again, music plays a consistently important role in all the plays, establishing atmosphere as well as providing leitmotifs for various characters. At times the music has a realistic source; at times it is simply there, serving as background, as it does in most films. In Menagerie, for example, music comes from both the victrola which Laura plays and the bars and cafes in the vicinity of the Wingfield tenement. Essential to the play, however, is the single recurrent theme which has no obvious source, but weaves in and out of the scenes like distant circus music which "serves as a thread of connection and allusion between the narrator with his separate point in time and space and the subject of the story" (I, 133). Generally associated with Laura, the music provides, as does the background music of nearly every film of the first two decades following the introduction of sound, an "emotional emphasis to suitable passages."

In A Streetcar Named Desire music comes from the radio and from the bars of the French Quarter, but the recurring "Varsouviana" polka suggests Blanche's loosening hold on reality and is heard by her alone—and the audience (I, 376, 411, 414). The music in Battle of Angels has a realistic basis—a character plays a guitar, a juke box is heard. Even the religious chant which swells in exultation as the play ends, reminiscent of the many choirs of heavenly angels at the close of Hollywood films, comes from the church across the fields (I, 122). In Orpheus Descending, however, mandolin music fades in and out as Lady recalls her father's wine garden. Occasionally a "phrase of primitive music or percussion" is indicated (III, 239). A band of carollers provides an a cappella commentary on

The Mutilated (*Dragon Country*, p. 79) and sings of miracles as the play ends. One basic musical theme recurs in *Summer and Smoke* (II, 121), while *Suddenly Last Summer* employs music suggestive of the Encantadas (III, 367); and thematic music which Williams refers to as "The Lament" underscores *Sweet Bird of Youth* (IV, 9).

Some of the plays use unlocalized sounds in addition to background music. Echoing voices and jungle noises are also heard in *Suddenly Last Summer* along with harsh bird cries that come "in rhythmic waves like a savage chant" (III, 356). *The Milk Train Doesn't Stop Here Anymore* uses amplified heart beats to indicate Mrs. Goforth's agitation (V, 13), and wind chimes sound throughout *In the Bar of a Tokyo Hotel* (*Dragon Country*, p. 7).

While music and sound emanate from behind the scenes, the lighting of a play controls what the audience sees on the stage. The basic unit of a Williams play, like that of a film, is the scene rather than the act. The structures of *Menagerie, Streetcar, Summer and Smoke, The Rose Tattoo, Camino Real, Orpheus Descending, Milk Train* and *Kingdom of Earth* all depend on the juxtaposition and progressive effect of relatively short scenes. Of the unconventional techniques discussed in his *Menagerie* notes, the most significant in the structuring of his plays is the lighting, through which Williams achieves tension and its release. It is the adaptation to the stage of film transitions through lighting effects which provides the Williams play with its fluidity and cohesion.

A Williams play generally presents a set designer with an extraordinary challenge. All of the above named plays require settings which reveal at once more than one locale. Exteriors and interiors, at times on different levels, must all be on stage simultaneously. Occasionally the audience sees the full set; at times only one area remains in view. Williams, however, has nearly solved the designer's problem for him by indicating throughout how lighting controls the play's focus, just as the film camera controls what the eye may see. And he does so by borrowing from the movies such transitional devices as the iris, the fade in and fade out, the lap dissolve and the crosscut.

Effectively, albeit infrequently, Williams calls for a pinpoint of light to open or close a scene, just as Griffith used the iris in (the "gradual appearance of the scene through an expanding circle") [2] and the iris out (the "gradual disappearance of the scene through a contracting circle"). Williams directs the eye, as Griffith did, to a particular object or to a person—even a part of a human being. The dramatist's most telling iris in opens *You Touched Me!*, a play about a young girl's awakening, which inverts the Sleeping Beauty myth in the crucial scene in which Matilda touches Hadrian's forehead as he pretends to sleep. Williams prepares for the moment from the beginning of the play: "Before the full stage lights come up, a pin spot of light appears on a large piece of heavy silver and the hands of MATILDA moving dreamily over its surface with a polishing cloth. The light blooms gradually from this" (pp. 4–5).

Summer and Smoke, the play with the most elaborate lighting design, makes more extensive use of the iris effect. In scene four, for example, when John is drawn toward Alma—the soul—but embraces Rosa—the body—in front of the anatomy chart, "the light lingers on the chart as the interior dims out" (II, 187). After Rosa's father shoots Dr. Buchanan in scene seven, "everything dims out but a spot of light on Rosa standing against the chart . . . and light disappears from everything but the wings of the stone angel" (II, 216–17). Other scenes begin or end with a circle of light on either Alma or the angel representing eternity. *The Night of the Iguana* makes a single use of the iris out at the emotional peak which ends the second act: "A pure white flash of lightning reveals HANNAH and NONNO against the wall, behind SHANNON, and the electric globe suspended from the roof goes out, the power extinguished by the storm. A clear shaft of light stays on SHANNON's reaching-out hands till the stage curtain has fallen, slowly" (IV, 326). *Small Craft Warnings* also ends an act with the effect: "A pin-spot of light picks up Violet's tear-stained and tranced face at the otherwise dark table" as the curtain falls (V, 266).

A more usual transition in films—and also in Williams' plays— is a fade in or fade out. It is Williams' practice in all of his plays to separate individual scenes with lights dimming gradually, then coming up again. The curtain is used only to mark the ends of acts. Scene four of the second act of *Orpheus Descending* fades out with a backlighting effect before the curtain falls. As Lady goes to Val, she closes the curtain over the entrance to the alcove: "Its bizarre design

... is softly translucent with the bulb lighted behind it" (III, 305). Occasionally a fade in is accompanied and immediately preceded by a sound transition as in scene three of *Menagerie*: "Before the lights come up again, the violent voices of Tom and Amanda are heard" (I, 160). The technique, which suggests the sound-overlap of the movies, is repeated in *Summer and Smoke*: "Before the light comes up a soprano voice is heard singing ..." (II, 188).

The opening of *Menagerie* seems a development of the establishing shot which begins nearly every film. The audience learns where it is before subsequent scenes can be further localized. The Wingfield apartment is shown flanked by St. Louis alleys. Tom speaks to the audience as the alleys and the tenement wall fade away, and light comes up within the apartment. By means of a scrim, a lap dissolve—in film terms—is effected. The same technique opens *The Rose Tattoo*. Serafina's frame cottage is located within an environmental setting representing a Gulf Coast community. Scenes dissolve from exterior to interior as the play progresses.[3]

One side of the stage in *Summer and Smoke* represents the rectory, the realm of Alma and soul, a spiritual world; the other side of the stage is the doctor's office, the realm of John and body, a material world. Between them is a neutral area dominated by the statue of Eternity. The movement between the extremes is effected and their interrelationship revealed by the lighting transitions within and between the scenes. The lap dissolve repeatedly allows the light to diminish in one area as it increases in another. At times a light comes up on Alma in the rectory as John and Rosa play a scene in the already lit office. The structure of the play is a logical adaptation of D. W. Griffith's technique of crosscutting, which enables the audience to follow simultaneous action in two or more locales.

That the authors of *You Touched Me!*, written before *Summer and Smoke*, are aware of the possibilities of stage crosscutting is revealed in the second act when "a dual scene" is indicated with the Captain and Hadrian in one room and Emmie and Matilda overhearing them and reacting in another (p. 65). After *Summer and Smoke* Williams again effects crosscutting by the manipulation of lighting. The last scene of *Period of Adjustment* alternates between living room and bedroom. Ralph and Dorothea prepare for bed in the one room while Isabel and George prepare for bed in the other.

The opening and closing of the bathroom door directs the focus of attention as light enters the bedroom and is shut off again. The alternating action in the two rooms is obviously to be considered a simultaneous occurrence.

On two occasions in *Menagerie*, Amanda, alone on stage, telephones subscribers to women's magazines (I, 160, 177). As she speaks, a spotlight brings her face sharply into focus in scenes which are otherwise static. Williams uses lighting to blot out the rest of the playing area as Amanda is seen in the equivalent of the film close-up. Williams calls for the close-up again and again in quiet moments of little or no action in a number of his plays. If the amber follow-spots on the two players in *I Can't Imagine Tomorrow* (*Dragon Country*, p. 133) suggest the lighting of the opera, the ballet, or the outmoded stage of another era, Williams intends their use as did O'Neill in *Welded* to help an audience focus on faces and words, for the play is void of action. Gutman calls for a "follow-spot on the face of the ancient knight" at the end of *Camino Real* as Don Quixote takes out a pocket mirror and grooms his beard and moustache in preparation for a final journey into the unknown (II, 589). The static *In the Bar of a Tokyo Hotel* is played in a small area of intense light, and the sun brings the face of the dying D. H. Lawrence into close-up in *I Rise in Flame, Cried the Phoenix* (*Dragon Country*, pp. 3, 59). Throughout *Small Craft Warnings* as each character disengages himself from the others to speak to himself, "the light in the bar should dim, and a special spot should illuminate" him (V, 225). The latter part of the final scene in *Suddenly Last Summer* is virtually a monologue in which Catharine relates the horror of Sebastian's death. As her story progresses, the surrounding area dims out "and a hot white spot is focused on" her (III, 414). Catharine's revelation ends in a riveting close-up.

Lighting enables Williams to employ yet another film technique—the reaction shot, a variation of the close-up, which shows "the effect, on one or more characters, of something seen, heard, or otherwise realized" (Fulton, p. 310). Although he relies on it in several plays, the technique is most fully explained in *Menagerie*'s notes: "Shafts of light are focused on selected areas or actors, sometimes in contradistinction to what is the apparent center. For instance, in the quarrel scene between Tom and Amanda, in which Laura has no active part, the clearest pool of light is on her figure. This is also true of the supper scene, when her silent figure on the sofa should remain the visual center" (I, 133). Even the absent father has an opportunity to react in Menagerie as his photo lights up (I, 168). Throughout his plays lights come up and lights fade away as Williams views all his subjects through the eye of a camera.

IV

In addition to the various projections which, together with the captions, punctuate the action of Menagerie, Williams suggests the use of scenic projections in the form of stars, clouds, sea, palm trees and sunflowers on a cyclorama in Summer and Smoke, Sweet Bird of Youth and Out Cry. Of all his plays, however, only Sweet Bird calls for the actual projection of film onto the stage. In the entire Williams canon Sweet Bird is unique in one other respect—it is the only play in which Williams considers the possibility of films as works of art.

At the end of the second act of Sweet Bird, southern demagogue Boss Finley arrives at the Royal Palms Hotel for his nationally televised speech at a "Youth for Tom Finley" rally in the hotel ballroom. Although the setting for the scene is the adjacent cocktail lounge, "there suddenly appears on the big TV screen, which is the whole back wall of the stage, the image of BOSS FINLEY" (IV, 106), as Williams uses film to enlarge the scope of the stage. While Finley is pictured building toward the climax of his oft-repeated "Voice of God" speech, the voice of the heckler is heard, as the TV camera pans to reveal him at the back of the hall. The picture cuts to a reaction shot of Heavenly registering horror, then back again to the monstrous head of her politician father, as Finley quells the disturbance by reminding his audience that it is Easter and likening himself to the risen Christ. But Finley as savior is merely illusion on a flickering screen. In front of his image, counterpointing it, a gruesome scene is enacted. The heckler has been removed from the hall and is silently and systematically beaten by Finley's thugs, as Chance in a "tight intense follow spot beam" reacts to what he sees—the illusion of film, the reality of life (IV, 108).

While film was startlingly employed in Sweet Bird's Broadway production in 1959, it is possible to perform the scene—less effectively certainly—without film. The film portion was omitted in the Kennedy Center revival of the play for the American Bicentennial Theatre Series in 1975; only Finley's voice was heard, as the lighting suggested the rally taking place offstage.

What cannot be omitted from *Sweet Bird*, however, is the character of Alexandra del Lago as the soul of art—suffering, devouring, enduring, perhaps even triumphant. Alexandra, or the Princess Kosmonopolis as she calls herself while traveling incognito, is literary kin to the protagonist of Williams' 1950 novella *The Roman Spring of Mrs. Stone*. Mrs. Stone, a stage actress, finds solace in retirement in the arms of the beautiful Italian boy she buys. Friends urge her to attempt a comeback, but the actress knows it is, for her, too late. She had always been a presence, a personality, rather than an artist. Her career has faded with her beauty. By the time Williams' aging actress reappears in *Sweet Bird*, she has acquired the stylized grotesquerie of Norma Desmond, the has-been film goddess played by one-time film goddess Gloria Swanson in Charles Brackett and Billy Wilder's bizarre and compelling Paramount film *Sunset Boulevard* (1950). Desmond, determined to make a comeback, hires a failed script writer to polish the creaking vehicle she has fashioned for her return to the screen. Naively thinking he has the upper hand in their relationship, the writer, William Holden, is eventually destroyed as the actress succumbs to madness.

In another plot inversion, Williams' Alexandra del Lago, a conquering lady of the lake, has fled from the screening of her comeback film, which she thinks is a fiasco, into a sordid round of sex, drugs and drink. She is accompanied on her journey into oblivion by Chance Wayne, a no-longer-young young man, who has retained the only commodity he can offer the world, an incredible beauty that is fading. As Chance uses Alexandra to gain access to the glamorous world of Hollywood, she exploits him in turn—for art is a voracious mistress. Before Finley's men can literally castrate Chance, Alexandra has figuratively beaten them to it. For Alexandra is a survivor, and she goes off to enjoy a temporary triumph. Her comeback is no disaster; the "picture has broken box-office records. In New York and L.A.!" (IV, 118). Although she knows in her heart that her latest triumph may be her last, she at least has the strength to carry on. She is finally touched by Chance's plight; she has compassion for him and would rescue him if she could. But there is no hope,

Alexandra realizes, for Chance. His youth has gone; her art endures. "The screen's a very clear mirror," Alexandra tells Chance early in the play as she speaks of her career: "There's a thing called a close-up. The camera advances and you stand still and your head, your face, is caught in the frame of the picture with a light blazing on it and all your terrible history screams while you smile" (p. 34). Late in the play Williams demonstrates that the stage too can reflect the truth of life: "The PRINCESS moves out onto forestage; surrounding areas dim till nothing is clear behind her but the Palm Garden" (p. 115). By manipulating Alexandra into the stage equivalent of a screen close-up, Williams reveals conclusively that stage truth can be achieved through the adaptation of screen technique. In close-up, Alexandra, film star, recognizes herself as artist: "I seem to be standing in light with everything else dimmed out. He's in the dimmed-out background as if he'd never left the obscurity he was born in. I've taken the light again as a crown on my head to which I am suited by something in the cells of my blood and body from the time of my birth. It's mine, I was born to it" (pp. 115–16). When word comes that her comeback is successful, the artist accepts it, understands it: "Out of the passion and torment of my existence I have created a thing that I can unveil, a sculpture, almost heroic, that I can unveil, which is true" (p. 120). Significantly, the medium of her art is the movies.

In *Sweet Bird of Youth* a dramatist embraces the movies and proclaims them a valid form of art. There may be differences of opinion on the subject, but there can be no difference of opinion finally on the validity of Williams as artist. And Williams enhanced his art—at the Delta Brilliant.

Notes to Albert E. Kalson, "Tennessee
Williams at the Delta Brilliant"

1. Maria Ley-Piscator, *The Piscator Experiment: The Political Theatre* (New York: James H. Heineman, Inc., 1967), p. 236. Gerald Weales, *Tennessee Williams* (Minneapolis: University of Minnesota Press, 1965), p. 33, and Edward Murray, *The Cinematic Imagination* (New York: Frederick Ungar Publishing Co., 1972), pp. 49–50 note the relationships between the screen device, silent films and epic theater, as does George Brandt in an excellent seminal study, "Cinematic Structure in the Work of Tennessee Williams," *American Theatre*, ed. John Russell Brown and Bernard Harris (London: Edward Arnold Ltd., 1967), pp. 184–185.
2. Film terms are here defined as in "Glossary of Motion-Picture Terms," A. R.

Fulton, *Motion Pictures: The Development of an Art from Silent Films to the Age of Television* (Norman: University of Oklahoma Press, 1960), pp. 307–11.

3. Brandt, "Cinematic Structure," p. 169 points out that O'Neill, before Williams, "achieved a kind of cinematic flow" in the movement from exterior to interior and back again in *Desire Under the Elms*, and Travis Bogard, *Contour in Time* (New York: Oxford University Press, 1972), p. 344 suggests that the special curtain which shows the house as seen from the street at the opening of each part of O'Neill's trilogy, *Mourning Becomes Electra*, "is in cinematic terms a long shot, giving a perspective on the close-ups to follow."

Tennessee Williams' Dramatic Technique

NORMAN J. FEDDER

"T HE QUESTION NOW for Tennessee Williams," wrote Benjamin Nelson in 1961, "is what happens next? Has he come to the end of something and is he ready to set off in a new direction, or will he continue to explore his image of the universe which has hardened not only into a philosophical but an artistic commitment? His art is often so good that we find ourselves asking him for greater mastery, and deploring his loss of control. We tend to think less of what he has accomplished than what he could accomplish. We continually wonder if his art is great enough not only to sustain itself, but to develop further" (p. 294).

That statement seems sadly appropriate, looking back on it from the vantage point of the mid-seventies. For it was in 1961 that *The Night of the Iguana* opened in New York and became the last Williams work to date to "sustain itself" with the public and the critics. Since then, one play after another has either been kindly lamented or angrily deplored. We tend now to think on "what he has accomplished" and have given up on "what he could accomplish." Revival productions of his earlier works are received with rave notices, and he is again and again hailed as "America's greatest living playwright." But the hope of his sustaining himself in new plays, not to speak of "developing further," seems futile.

This may well be a foolishly premature judgment. Similar state-

229

ments had been made about O'Neill while he was at work on his greatest achievements. At the moment, however, we confront a playwright who seems, in the words of a current reviewer, "a flickering shadow of his former self" (from review of *The Red Devil Battery Sign* production, *Boston Globe*, quoted in *Time*, July 7, 1975, p. 29).

Has he perhaps "set off in a new direction"? This is Williams' view of the matter. "I am quite through with the kind of play that established my early and popular reputation," he explains in *Memoirs* (quotations from pp. xvii, xviii except as noted). "Since *The Night of the Iguana*, the circumstances of my life have demanded of me a continually less traditional style of dramatic writing." Yet, his life account provides nothing new, apart from its biographical candor, with respect to the playwright's basic premises: "many of the things which concerned me in the past continue to preoccupy me today." *Memoirs*, like the plays, focuses on his pervasive central theme "the need for understanding and tenderness and fortitude among individuals trapped by circumstance" (Barnett, p. 113). His beloved "freaks of the cosmic circus" (*Winter of Cities*, p. 91) frolic through its pages, and there is still the obsessive Williams emphasis on "That sensual music."

Has his *technique*, then, changed so radically? What the critics have deplored in his later writing has been evident enough in the earlier: discursive plotmaking, excessive theatricality, verbal superfluity. What has happened, I think, is not a change in style, but in emphasis—a bringing to stage center of that "loss of control" which has often marred his major plays and continually doomed his most recent.

To support this viewpoint I propose to examine Tennessee Williams' dramatic technique as it functions, in general, in his major plays through *The Night of the Iguana*—and as it alters, in particular, in each play since then. Technique is defined as the way in which a playwright employs *plot, theatricality* and *language* to establish tone, create character and express theme.

PLOT

The freakish vs. the conventional or normal; the delicate vs. the brutal or virile; the vital vs. the sterile or mechanical—Tom and Laura vs. Amanda and Jim; Blanche vs. Stanley; Maggie and Big

Daddy vs. Brick and Gooper. These are the essential dramatic con-
frontations in Williams' plays. The sharpness of the contrasts and
the consequent intensity of the struggles make for consistent tonal
power, but not always for successful character creation and thematic
statement.

For one thing the contrast may be made too simplistic or stark or
overlaid with more symbolic significance than is credible. Both *Battle of Angels* and *Orpheus Descending* portray a hero who is presumably a prototype of sexual and spiritual liberation—a fleshly Christ
who will redeem through self-sacrifice all womankind. Yet, his major
accomplishments seem to be the ability to "hold my breath three
minutes without passing out," go "all day without passing water,"
and "burn down" "any two-footed woman" (III, 264). In *You
Touched Me!* Hadrian not only effects Matilda's sexual liberation
but also her international self-consciousness. Williams imperfectly
attempts "to unite a personal and cosmic hero"—"to unite phallic
worship and a new league of nations" (Joseph Wood Krutch, review,
Nation, October 6, 1945).

On the other hand, the contrast can be lost in an attempt to
avoid oversimplification. Williams responded to the criticisms of
Summer and Smoke by rewriting it as *The Eccentricities of a Nightingale*. The conflict between John and Alma has been so scaled down
and subtlized that it is hardly a conflict at all, with the spirit vs. flesh
polarity a peripheral matter. The play has become distinctly un-
dramatic in comparison with its predecessor, however more credible
its plot.

Or the conflict can be dissipated in episodic or free associative
plotmaking. Williams has been criticized for being more a *scene
wright* than a playwright—of often losing his command of the central dramatic action by introducing tangential or repetitive situations
(Falk, p. 175). *Battle of Angels—Orpheus Descending* and *Camino
Real* are overwhelmed with superfluous characters and conflicts. The
focus of *The Glass Menagerie* wanders episodically among Amanda,
Tom, and Laura. The second-act confrontation between Brick and
Big Daddy is probably the finest scene in all Williams, but no version
of act three of *Cat on a Hot Tin Roof* adequately resolves Brick's
encounter with "mendacity." (Williams wrote a third version of the
act for a production in New England.) Although culminating in the

eloquent interchange between Shannon and Hannah, *The Night of the Iguana* is rather loosely structured around the former's nervous breakdown. That *A Streetcar Named Desire* is his greatest play is due in no small measure to his unswerving focus on Blanche's disintegration—making each scene contribute in rising tension to the climactic insanity. Blanche battles to the very end to maintain her values against an equally bellicose antagonist. The conflict is unified and progressive.

But often in Williams, as in the case of Shannon, the protagonist seems defeated before he even starts, or struggles half-heartedly, or faces opposition of minimal challenge. The most effective central characters in Williams, as in all plays, must earn their right to their dramatic destiny through unified and developing conflict with worthy antagonists. Otherwise, the plays go nowhere dramatically—and the consequent tone, characterization, and theme diminish in credibility, power, and magnitude.

Williams has written, for the most part, in the realistic mode, but always on the borderline of the fantastic—and, occasionally, right in the thick of it. The quality of Williams' plots—their essentially larger-than-life tonality— points readily beyond realism, leading him often to highly symbolic situations such as the Easter analogies in a number of plays or to outright Expressionism as in *Camino Real*.

This method easily spills over into comedy which thrives on incongruity and exaggeration. Much is comic in Amanda's idiosyncrasies, Stanley's mannerisms, Big Daddy's obscenities, Shannon's fantasies. *Camino Real* abounds in the farcical. *The Rose Tattoo* and *Period of Adjustment* are fully comic in tone. (Not to mention the early *You Touched Me!*)

Williams' comic technique helps to minimize the melodrama inherent in his grotesque situations, and have us laugh *with* him, not at him. It is rarely light comedy since it always derives from an essentially morbid situation which is never far from reach—the "American black comedy" which he claims to have invented (*Memoirs*, p. 212). And one wonders whether it isn't less successful in his comedies than in his tragedies—for the "happy endings" of the "light" plays seem to have been forced upon Williams by the genre.

Since his typical plot involves the defeat or destruction of a highly pitiable protagonist, the theme of compassion is omnipresent.

Often the antagonist is equally pathetic—Val and Lady, Amanda and
Laura, Chance and the Princess, Shannon and Hannah. And the
so-called strong men—Jim, Stanley, John—get their share of sympathy. Here Williams indulges in sentimentality—in demanding our
compassion for aberrant characters who have not at all earned it in
the action of the play. When, for example, Chance implores the
audience for "recognition of me in you," we have a right to reply,
"Says you, buddy; keep your sick head to yourself!" What compels
Chance's fall from stud to castrato is a mess of *his* making—and
hardly "the enemy, time, in us all" (IV, 124).

THEATRICALITY

"... a symbol in a play has only one legitimate purpose which is to
say a thing more directly and simply and beautifully than it could be
said in words. ... the incontinent blaze of a live theatre, a theatre
meant for seeing and for feeling ... the vulgarity of performance ...
The color, the grace and levitation, the structural pattern in motion,
the quick interplay of live beings, suspended like fitful lightning in
a cloud, these things are the play, not words on paper" (II, 421, 423).

Williams' employment of theatrical symbolism is a major aspect
of his dramatic technique. Setting, lighting, sound, costumes, props,
and movement are everywhere expressive of tone, character, and
theme. His sets always symbolize the values of the play. From the
start he cautioned designers against photographic likeness. He was
writing for "a new, plastic theatre which must take the place of the
exhausted theatre of realistic conventions" (I, 131): The drab mercantile store which becomes transformed into the attractive casino
in *Battle of Angels*; the rectory and the angel opposite the dispensary
and anatomy chart in *Summer and Smoke*; the jungle garden in
Suddenly Last Summer; the verandah with its separate cubicles in
The Night of the Iguana.

Some of the most effective aspects of a Williams production derive
from his theatricality: The theme of illusion vs. reality defined
through the breaking of a tiny glass animal or the shading of a light
bulb; characterization through old gowns and letters; the recurrent
counterpoint of off-stage sounds to enhance a world of moods and
meanings.

But frequently his love for the theatrical runs riot. *Orpheus*

Descending is overloaded with symbolic theatrics. Val Xavier, for example, plays music like Orpheus, wears a D. H. Lawrence snakeskin, and resembles J. Christ in portraiture and martyrdom. This symbolism works considerably against his credibility and evokes an unintended tone of ludicrousness. *Camino Real* is a forest of symbols for which one cannot see the trees! Archetypically costumed characters rush about a metaphorical set wielding prototypal props and shouting mythic verities. If and when the trees are discernible, they remain just such—wooden, not human. Excessive theatricalism overwhelms both *The Rose Tattoo* and *Sweet Bird of Youth*—in myriad roses and mammoth television images. As Signi Falk observes: "Williams often is more concerned with what is theatrical than with truth" (p. 175).

LANGUAGE

Williams' language has been unequaled in the American theater in its ability to be both conversationally idiomatic and poetically vivid—true to both the surface appearance and the inner truth. Williams has brought poetry back to the theater to a more significant degree than T. S. Eliot, Christopher Fry, and Maxwell Anderson, by hardly seeming to do so. Our perception of his vivid characters derives in great measure from their manner of expression:

The elaborate imagery of his delicate ladies—Blanche: "I shall die of eating an unwashed grape one day out on the ocean. . . . And I'll be buried at sea sewn up in a clean white sack and dropped overboard—at noon—in the blaze of summer—and into an ocean as blue as . . . my first lover's eyes!" (I, 410).

The earthy exuberance of his virile males—Big Daddy: "They say you got just so many and each one is numbered. Well, I got a few left in me, a few, and I'm going to pick me a good one to spend 'em on! I'm going to pick me a choice one, I don't care how much she costs, I'll smother her in—minks! Ha ha! I'll strip her naked and smother her in minks and choke her with diamonds! Ha ha! I'll strip her naked and choke her with diamonds and smother her with minks and hump her from hell to breakfast. *Ha aha ha ha ha!*" (III, 96).

The morbid eloquence of his decadent artists—The Princess: "There's nowhere else to retire to when you retire from an art, because, believe it or not, I really was once an artist. So I retired to the moon, but the atmosphere of the moon doesn't have any oxygen in it. I began to feel breathless, in that withered, withering country, of time coming after time not meant to come after" (IV, 33).

The graphic clichés of his solid burghers—Jim: "I believe in the future of television! . . . I wish to be ready to go right along with it. Therefore I'm planning to get in on the ground floor. In fact I've already made the right connections and all that remains is for industry itself to get under way! Full steam . . . Knowledge—Zzzzzp! Money—Zzzzzzp!—Power! That's the cycle democracy is built on!" (I, 222).

The right word, the right image, the right turn of phrase—to convey the sense of their uniqueness.

Williams has written some of the most memorable dialogues in all theater literature—building from encounter to confrontation to revelation to explosion. But he has also made use of the extended monologue and the choral interlude—with varying success. Tom's narrative comments are effective to a point, but they tend to inflation. Chance's lengthy apostrophes are purely hot air. The "cast of orators" in Camino Real compete in tedium. On the other hand, Catharine's mounting narrative of Sebastian's demise is dramatically perfect. The literary ladies in Summer and Smoke and The Rose Tattoo townsfolk are chorally relevant. The flower vendor belongs at Blanche's grave. The "no-neck monsters" interweave Brick's evasions in telling comic relief and contrast. However, who needs the "Heileluyah Chorus" of The Night of the Iguana?

Finally, Williams' words sound his favorite themes:

Psychological:

The liberating and humanizing qualities of uninhibited sexuality—Chance: "the great difference between people in this world is not between the rich and the poor or the good and the evil, the biggest of all differences in this world is between the ones that had or have pleasure in love and those that haven't and hadn't any pleasure in love, but just watched it with envy, sick envy" (IV, 50).

Romantic illusion as preferable to gross reality—Blanche: "I don't want realism. I want magic! . . . Yes, yes, magic! I try to give that to people. I misrepresent things to them. I don't tell truth, I tell what *ought* to be truth" (I, 385).

The need for compassion for the psychically maimed—Hannah: "Nothing human disgusts me unless it's unkind, violent" (IV, 363–4).

Social:

The lamentable decay of the old southern aristocracy—Amanda: "Well, in the South we had so many servants. Gone, gone, gone. All vestige of gracious living! Gone completely! I wasn't prepared for what the future brought me" (I, 204).

The dehumanizing qualities of industrial civilization—Serafina: "They make the life without glory. Instead of the heart they got the deep-freeze in the house" (II, 342).

The Romantic rebel as superhero confronting the enemy time—Byron: "lately, I've found myself listening to hired musicians behind a row of artificial palm trees—instead of the single —pure-stringed instrument of my heart . . .
Well, then, it's time to leave here!
—There's a time for departure even when there's no certain place to go!
. . . .
*Make voyages!—Attempt them!—*there's nothing else . . ." (II, 508).

Theological:

God viewed as a brutal predator in the classic Darwinian framework —Shannon: "the gospel of God as Lightning and Thunder . . . stray dogs vivisected" (IV, 305).

The depraved artist as sacrificial Christ figure—Frieda: "You can't stand Jesus Christ because he beat you to it. Oh, how you would have loved to suffer the *original* crucifixion! (*Dragon Country*, p. 62).

The essential loneliness of the human condition—Val: "We're all . . . sentenced to solitary confinement inside our own skins" (III, 271).

When these themes arise naturally from the plays as inferences derived from the behavior of the characters, they are convincing and persuasive. But too often they remain simplistically in the mouths of their spokesmen as gratuitous outbursts unrelated to the action. This "besetting sin"—as Eric Bentley puts it—of "fake philosophizing," "straining after big statements" (*What Is Theatre?* p. 63) is particularly obtrusive in the rhetoric of Val, Chance, and Shannon—and of nearly everybody in *Camino Real*.

Such is the essence of Williams' technique in the "traditional style of dramatic writing" (*Memoirs*, xviii) which he left behind with *The Night of the Iguana*—but only in degree, not kind. The plays which follow differ in technique only in the enlargement of these earlier tendencies. "Free associative in style," "undisguised in self-revelation," they anticipate the *Memoirs* (p. xviii) to come. Like his heroine in the first of these efforts, Williams now lets it all harangue out—if only for an audience of tape recorders.

The Milk Train Doesn't Stop Here Anymore (1963)

The play has a plot of sorts. Mrs. Goforth is in conflict with a number of characters—chiefly the Christlike Christopher Flanders whose presumed attempt to minister to her last hours constitutes the main line of action. But Chris is a negligible antagonist against the egomaniacal heroine who does him in at every turn, as she vanquishes all others in her way—and almost immediately. The result is hardly any sense of developing tension—and the structure of the play becomes not much more than an endless monologue as the dying old nympho records for posterity her every orgasm.

The plot recalls Val's awakening of the death-bound Lady in *Orpheus Descending* and its comic counterpart in Mangiacavallo's rejuvenation of the eternally mourning Serafina in *The Rose Tattoo*. And even more closely—the misalliance of the not-so-young-anymore would-be actor Chance with the aging not-so-famous-anymore movie actress The Princess in *Sweet Bird of Youth*. The retrospective structural method parallels the plot of *Suddenly Last Summer* where the heart of the play is the narrative revelation of the death of Sebastian by Catharine Holly. Yet, each of these plays has considerably more dramatic tension and power than this tedious version of them. Equally matched combatants appear in the earlier plays, and the conflicts build and develop in the course of the action. The sense of fait accompli comes only with the final curtain. Even in *Suddenly*, Catharine's story is told in defiance of hostile auditors who would cut out a piece of her brain to silence her. Her story is not simply a narrative but an invasion of the resistant illusions of Mrs. Venable. Goforth's tale, in contrast, is recorded—not resisted—goes nowhere dramatically—is merely boring.

The setting is replete with screens which two kabuki-style stage assistants move about to "gracefully" reveal and mask the various scenes. Instead, these and the numerous other theatrical elements— exotic costumes and settings, microphones connected to tape recorders, a mobile named "The Earth is a Wheel in a Great Big Gambling Casino"—do just the opposite: garishly reveal the structural aimlessness and mask the thematic integrity of the play. The excessive theatrics serve to call to attention the insubstantial meaning.

This meaning is largely conveyed through the speeches of Mrs. Goforth and Christopher rather than through the action. Thus, although her ribald ramblings and his messianic mumblings are true enough to type, they are hardly tenable as the universal truths the playwright speaks through them.

Slapstick Tragedy (1966)

The Mutilated

For the most part, this play is a series of cat fights between two floozies interacting with assorted types of equally mutilated humanity in no particular dramatic order and culminating in a wholly unmotivated tableau of Christian togetherness and a vision of "Our Lady." A chorus of carollers wanders in and out singing of pity for "the strange, the crazed, the queer" (*Dragon Country*, p. 81). This is, of course, the old Williams message—so admirably rendered in the fables of the mutilated Laura, Alma, Blanche. But *rendered*, through the valiant struggles of these blighted ladies against overwhelming dramatic odds—not merely *talked about* in the lengthy monologues which have, unfortunately, become Williams' chief method of character portrayal.

The set is to be "as delicate as Japanese line drawings"—"so spidery . . . that the audience will accept the nonrealistic style of the play"

(p. 80). Yet not the style is unacceptable but the substance—which is not enhanced in its credibility by an excess of visual and sound effects such as The Bird Girl and her glued-on chicken feathers, Jack In Black and the carollers, and the garishly costumed ladies. Such effects in themselves need not be distracting—as indeed they are not in A *Streetcar Named Desire*, where they everywhere contribute to the developing dramatic action rather than call attention to themselves. Finally, the bosom talk which defines Trinket and Celeste well enough serves only to enlarge their essential flatness—their mutilations of body and spirit reduced to a singletoned language of lust: Celeste's hooker argot, Trinket's whine of "LOVE!"

The Gnädiges Fräulein

There is a unified and developing action in the Fräulein's tragicomic struggle to outcatch the cocaloony birds as they tear away her costume, her eyes, her hair, her flesh—a struggle at which she continues to persist as the curtain falls. However, much of the plot is the accompanying commentary of the callous Polly and Molly, effective to a point as exposition and contrast, but entirely too long.

Is this Williams' black comic comment on his own career: determined to persist in creative endeavor—however transformed in talent or circumstance, however hostile the public and critics, however self-destructive the means? The quixotic struggle of the fantastic Fräulein is indeed evocative of such overtones. And it has been admired in a number of quarters in this regard. William Inge thought the "personal humor" "just marvelous" (Steen, p. 120). Williams calls it "my best work of the sixties" (*Memoirs*, Illustration 141).

More than in any play since *Camino Real*, the playwright has indulged his love for elaborate sights and sounds: a frame cottage as if Picasso had designed it—the pelican-hued Polly and Molly contrasted with the wild-colored Fräulein—the giant cocaloonies—a blond-bewigged Indian dancer—the singing heroine rushing off and on in successive states of undress and mutilation, until she is "transfigured as a saint under torture" (*Dragon Country*, p. 245). Much of this is integral to the theatrical conception, but one can't help feeling Williams could have spent more time in developing the character of the Fräulein and less on concocting all those fanciful fireworks. For the Gnädiges Fräulein is too one-dimensional to embody meanings much beyond her strange self, defined as she is through the words of others. Her inarticulateness reduces her complexity. The play is too much the discursive squawk of the pelican ladies rather than the compelling cry of the indomitable songbird.

Kingdom of Earth (1968)

Estelle Parsons (Myrtle in the Broadway production) speaks favorably of a critic's comment that "the play and Tennessee's later works had now a vertical quality where it wasn't so much the story line, but it was characters. The exploration of characters more than a story line" (Steen, p. 272). This remark well explains Williams' current structural approach. Again and again characters are depicted not by developing dramatic action but by loosely connected monologues and incidents. Yet, as Walter Kerr has observed, character divorced from situation is lifeless. Situation stirs the fires of creative characterization. Character is heightened by story because there is a correlation between "the range of a play's activity and the size of its characterization. . . . It takes a certain number of psychological responses to enable a man to stir a cup of tea. It takes a good many more to enable him to kill his father" (*How Not to Write a Play*, pp. 120–23).

And it is ironic that Miss Parsons should cite *Kingdom of Earth* as primarily a play of character. It has more of a story line than any of the later plays: the developing struggle of Chicken against Lot for the possession of their ancestral home through the allegiance of Myrtle. If we find these characters as "fascinating" as Miss Parsons does, it will be through our involvement with this story line.

But in fact these characters are less attractive than ever in a Williams fable—mindless, gross, abhorrent. Of course, this is nothing new in criticism of the playwright's subject matter. A score of critics condemn him for his "sewer mentality"—his "evil or disagreeable or deplorable characters" (Donahue, pp. 230–31).

Williams has answered them effectively. Morbidity in drama is not *his* invention. Evil appears in Shakespeare and Brecht. A writer must express the world as *he* sees it—however disreputable that world may be. "The magnitude . . . does not exist in the matter but in the manner" (Donahue, pp. 232–4). But it is in this respect that *Kingdom of Earth* is artistically wanting. The manner of the work diminishes the matter. Chicken, Lot, and Myrtle are considerably less compelling than Stanley, Blanche, and Stella.

It is a technical, not a thematic, question. The clash of the delicate and depraved (Lot) with the virile and depraved (Chicken and Myrtle), resulting in the destruction of the former and the union of the two latter, reminds us strongly of Blanche's tragic encounter with Stanley and Stella. But *Kingdom of Earth* seems to be a parody of *A Streetcar Named Desire*, largely because of the *manner* of writing: the *reduction* of the characters' sensibilities in the plot, theatricality, and language.

Too much of the plot is centered on the simplistic and contrived business of appropriating pieces of paper—the deed, the marriage license. The crotch-stroking Chicken, the bellowing Myrtle, the transvestite Lot are theatrically repellent. And the set of elegant bedroom over primitive kitchen for metaphorical ascending and descending is especially gauche. The characters speak low-level stuff—of barnyards and show biz and beauty parlors—when from nowhere Chicken wheels on the old "Big Bed Ex-Machina": "There's nothing in the world, in the whole kingdom of earth, that can compare with one thing . . . on the bed . . . a woman waiting" (V, 211) and wanting it. Chicken's kingdom of earth, like the play which promotes it, never gets off the ground.

In the Bar of a Tokyo Hotel (1969)

Structurally, the play consists of a sequence of two character scenes—mostly between Miriam and the barman—in which Miriam holds forth on her pathetic relationship with her artist husband and grabs for the barman's genitals. The husband is really the focus of the play. And he takes his place in Williams' gallery of neurasthenic artist-heroes—a male Gnädiges Fräulein in his last stages of dissolution: falling down without will, crawling naked over his canvases, convinced he has invented color—his dying breath a torrent of paranoid invective. But, again, we see more of the relatively bland wife and the barman than of the dynamic husband. And what we see of him is so highly sensational and one-dimensional as to render him abhorrent.

The theatrical environment is starkly realistic. It serves as both a frame for the coldness of encounter between wife and barman and as a contrast with the flamboyance of the artist's monologues. But despite the climactic costume and complexion change, the play's theatricality lies essentially in its language. The dialogue is consciously spare and strange. Williams has his characters follow the barman's unidiomatic English by clipping their sentences:

BARMAN: My instruction is. (*Dragon Country*, p. 5)
MIRIAM: The important idioms can be learned very. (p. 6)
MARK: I covered the floor with several sheets
of newspaper before I. (p. 14)

This effect of incompletion perhaps relates to the central image of faded brightness: "the circle of light is the approving look of God" (p. 53). Mark "thought that he could create his own circle of light" (p. 53). It is certainly expressive of this shadowy play, which falls far short of illuminating its fascinating subject.

Nothing is essentially wrong with the technique of making one character live through the language of another. The character, in fact, may become more vivid than if he were physically present. This is certainly the case in the brilliant evocation of the character of Sebastian in *Suddenly Last Summer*. But it is vital then that the one through whom we learn of that character be equally vivid and that description be given the proper focus and fullness in the body of the play. But Miriam—like Molly and Polly before her—is considerably less eloquent than Catharine in rendering the tragedy of her artist—and the artist is diminished accordingly.

Small Craft Warnings (1972)

The short play *Confessional* was expanded into this longer version. And "confessional" is an apt description of both its dramatic structure and its artistic failings. The plot consists of the assorted squabbles of a variety of barroom denizens: the raucous beautician Leona letting loose her ire against the phallic defection of her lover Bill with her friend Violet; the malpractice of a drunken, unlicensed doctor; the wornout homosexual Quentin warding off the tendered affection of the idealistic young Bobby. All this is presided over by Williams' alter ego, the bartender Monk, who speaks for the author in his sincere compassion for these blighted creatures. And each character is given the spotlight at one point to "confess" his raison d'etre.

The play seems closest of all Williams' work to the structural practice of the Chekhov whom he considers his major literary influence. Yet, the play lacks the through line of action which permeates even the most variegated of the Russian's dramas: Irena's and Masha's developing relationships with Tusenbach and Vershinin (*The Three Sisters*); Lopahin's growing struggle with Madame Ranevski (*The Cherry Orchard*). Moreover, the various subplots in Chekhov reinforce the main one in theme and tone; and the whole is of sufficient magnitude to have impact on an audience.

Any central conflict in *Small Craft Warnings* is Leona's. But she has already more or less decided to leave Bill. Rather than a dramatic encounter between the two, we have an endless stream of invective against Bill. Just at what point Leona will storm out for the curtain is anybody's guess. The central conflict lacks dramatic contour. Such is equally true of the sporadic actions of the other characters, attenuating the impact of the play. It is difficult to maintain much interest in the random behavior of a variety of screwballs, unless you're getting fifty dollars an hour.

The setting is adequate to the play, but invites comparison with the more successful barroom dramas, *The Time of Your Life* and *The Iceman Cometh*, which gather up their forgotten souls into a framework we long remember. There is a symbolic sailfish to which Quentin refers and a confessional spotlight. But this is the least theatrical Williams play, and closest to the photographic realism he deplores.

It is upon his characters' confessional eloquence that Williams depends in lieu of plot and theatricality. As Walter Kerr discerns: "Mr. Williams' gift for knowing how people think, feel, and speak reasserts itself at least enough to keep us fully attentive." Well, at least until intermission time. "*Small Craft Warnings* has no need at all of another act. . . . it grows heart-heavy with repetition, our own capacity for surprise wanes. The people have long since told us all we need to know, perhaps all there is to know, about them" (*New York Times*, April 16, 1972).

The play recalls Masters' poetic graveyard: a *Small Craft Anthology* of posthumous lives. But from this point of view these vessels were well warned. The one-act *Confessional* was the measure of their size. They are out of their depths in the longer version.

Out Cry (1973)

". . . about the play," Clare says in one version, "I wonder sometimes if it isn't a little too personal, too special, for most audiences. . . . it's more like an exercise in performance by two star performers, than like a play, a real play" (p. 62). Clare's perception of the structural quality of *Out Cry* is concurred with by her creator in his *Memoirs*. The play will not "hold," he writes, without "stars" playing Felice and Clare. And he accounted for the Broadway failure in just these terms—the lack of "name" and "stage presence" of Cara Duff-MacCormick (p. 233). But can a play so discursive in structure and private in content hold any audience except big name fans and advanced acting students? For Williams is more determined than ever to "confess all"—this time through the mouths of a sibling duo intent on performing their *Two-Character Play* of psychotic self-revelation.

Nothing is inherently esoteric or uninteresting about their story: their deranged father killing their mother and then himself—their increasingly frenetic and hopeless attempts to live down the tragedy against the derision and ostracism of the community—their loss of economic security—their ultimate mental breakdown.

Much recommends the dramatic method of telling that story through a Pirandelloesque structure of "two actors in search of an audience." Yet, rather than employ the highly suspenseful approach of increasingly more intense dramatic revelation—as in Catharine's story or Blanche's confessions—Williams resorts again to a free associative style, to the play's detriment.

The essential plot is the drive of Felice and Clare to render their story as actors in a theater. Ironically and ultimately they realize they are doomed forever to reenact that story in a theater they can never leave. The problems inherent in turning life into theater are fascinating, and Williams touches on them throughout the play—but he has made them only peripheral to his desire to reveal the rambling thoughts and moods of the two characters.

Yet, early in the play we know almost everything we need to know about them. All they do later is spin out verbal variations on their problems. Why return for act two? Moreover, although Felice is perhaps a little more aggressive than Clare, he is so much like her that there is relatively little dramatic contrast. They do conflict with one another even to the point of violence; but too often they merely exchange bon mots on their common mental states. Consequently, one gets the sense of having eavesdropped on a conversation between a couple of wonderfully articulate lunatics, which proves interesting for a while, but ultimately tedious.

The version of 1973 describes a "fragmentary set" in the "vault of a foreign theater"—"a huge, dark statue upstage, a work of great power and darkly subjective meaning . . . of things anguished and perverse"—"mechanical sounds suggesting an inhuman quality"— "Images . . . projected on the stage backdrop" of "a subjective quality, changing subtly with the mood of the play" (pp. 6–7). The theatrical environment is appropriate for this theatrical play—although the dark statue seems a pretentious addition, as do a number of seemingly gratuitous theatrical moments—the card under the door, the bubble blowing, the pillow smothering. They obtrude on, rather than derive from, the dialogue—having been apparently added to compensate for the talkiness. (In the revision for volume five of *The Theatre*, 1976, reentitled *The Two-Character Play*, Williams does manage to decrease the obtrusiveness of his statue.)

The talk is, nevertheless, the best part of the play. Interchangeable as are the speeches—in a sense a monologue broken up between two voices—these voices ring true in theme, character, and tone. They cry out brilliantly for as long as we can bear—not too long.

"There is nothing slap-dash about Williams' work. Although it often gives the appearance of having been done at breakneck speed, it is always the product of alterations and careful revisions. It is a mistake to view Williams as a literary anarchist although he often seems to abandon himself to impulse and emotion" (Nelson, pp. 181–2). Again Nelson's statement in 1961 is no less descriptive of Williams' current practice. As much as his *Memoirs* extol revolution, his approach to his art has not radically changed. Each of these later plays has developed from shorter versions through numerous drafts and try-out productions. His impulse to excess inheres in his vision, not his craft.

Williams well knows what his public wants—a technique in plot, theatricality, and language of control and balance—that "taut alliance" between release and restraint of the plays which made him famous (Nelson, pp. 291–2). But while wanting the approval and understanding of audiences, he insists on writing in keeping with *his* needs: "I have always written for deeper necessities than the term 'professional' implies, and I think this has sometimes been to the detriment of my career but more of the time to its advantage." (*Memoirs*, pp. xviii–xix). In light of the "detriment" of the last fifteen years, one might question the "advantage" of a dramatic technique which prefers self-indulgence to professionalism.

Williams in the Seventies:
Directions and Discontents

WILLIAM J. FREE

CRITICAL DISSATISFACTION over Tennessee Williams' plays of the seventies has been almost unanimous. Of the reviewers of *Out Cry* and *Small Craft Warnings*, only Clive Barnes found much virtue in either play, and his likings seemed more vague than directed. On the other hand, discontent with the plays was specifically directed and uniform. Harold Clurman's reviews in *The Nation* are fairly representative. Of *Small Craft Warnings*: "an *old* play . . . old in the sense that it repeats the mood and mode of much earlier work. Williams has been there before—and so have we" (24 April 1972, p. 540). Of *Out Cry*: "it is too limited in its symbolic imagery and construction . . . to hold us. . . . Williams has always held to the romantic idea of art as self-revelation, but in this instance the mask of an objective dramatic argument is so thin that there is hardly a separation between the mask and the face" (19 March 1973, p. 380).

Clurman's remarks typify two general themes in Williams criticism: the charge that Williams repeats himself by going over and over the same territory and the charge that his plays, for better or worse, are autobiographical. The latter theme has especially prevailed in academic criticism, which has always tended to read Williams allegorically. The fact that he has repeatedly, and as recently as a *New York Times* interview in December 1975, branded such attempts "ludicrous" has of course failed to deter anyone.

Both charges against Williams do his plays an injustice by failing to take them on their own terms. Deflection of our interest from an author's work to his life, particularly in Williams' case, too often reflects a taste for lurid sexual detail rather than for art. Furthermore, the artist's work relates not to the outer details of his life but to the inner world of his imagination, so to jump from an account of Williams' sexual preferences to an allegorization of his plays is to ignore an important middle step, as the publication of his *Memoirs* should clearly establish. Few artists of our century have been more delighted to detail their private lives or more reluctant to reveal the working of their imaginations than Williams. The few mentions of people from his life in relationship to his plays deny that any individual is the direct model for any character or that any situation from life relates directly to any dramatic event. Williams tells us in the *Memoirs* that the imagination is the only place in which the artist can live, but he continues to live there privately and secretly. Thus the temptations to identify Williams' emotional crack-up of the sixties too directly with the confinement and emotional hysteria of the brother and sister in *Out Cry*, and either to allegorize Doc in *Small Craft Warnings* (the role Williams himself played on stage and with which he says he most identifies in the play) as a description of Williams' sense of his own alienation from the contemporary theater or to consider Quentin's relationship with Bobby in the same play as simply a dramatization of the playwright's own middle-aged homosexuality, are too easy to have much value.

The charge of repeating himself, on the other hand, is perhaps more relevant if viewed in its proper context. True, the variety as well as the depth of an artist's imagination is a factor in his ultimate worth. On the other hand, even the writer who repeats himself, if by that we mean that each of his works is an analogue to the same narrow imaginative content, can be of great value provided each work makes us genuinely experience that content anew and delight in the experience. The real charge to be brought against *Out Cry* and *Small Craft Warnings* is not that they repeat Williams' earlier plays. Both plays, I believe, move into territory which Williams has not fully revealed to us in his earlier plays. But neither play succeeds

completely in revealing that territory. They are failures of dramatization rather than failures of theme. Their problem is not that they
are autobiographical or that they specifically repeat Williams' other
work but that they are inadequate expressions of whatever is in the
playwright's imagination.

Small Craft Warnings seems to me torn between two impulses,
neither of which gets fully realized. One is a theme relatively new
to Williams. The other is a stylistic device, the lyrical confession,
which isn't new, but which here neither becomes integrated with the
dramatization of theme nor works itself out fully.

In his most revealing comment about Small Craft Warnings, Williams says: "I have suddenly undertaken to correct what I've gradually come to recognize as the principal structural flaw in Small Craft
Warnings, the long monologue of the bartender Monk coming directly after the monologue of Quentin, the homosexual film-scripter,
which is much the most effective piece of writing in the play, and
since the play's values are so largely verbal, Quentin's speech is obviously the climax, at least of Act One" (Memoirs, p. 234). Quentin's speech is the source of the play's values, but the key to those
values perhaps comes less in the monologue than in the lines which
immediately precede it and which give it its meaningful context:

> QUENTIN: What is the thing that you mustn't lose in this world
> before you're ready to leave it? The one thing you mustn't lose ever?
> LEONA: . . . Love?
> (Quentin laughs.)
> BOBBY: Interest?
> QUENTIN: That's closer, much closer. Yes, that's almost it. The word
> that I had in mind is surprise, though. The capacity for being surprised.
> I've lost the capacity for being surprised, so completely lost it, that if
> I woke up in my bedroom late some night and saw that fantastic fish
> swimming right over my head, I wouldn't be really surprised.
>
> (V, 259–60)

Quentin goes on to relate his loss of surprise to his being a homosexual, too facilely perhaps. For what Quentin is describing is not
simply a homosexual experience but a world-weariness which comes
from realizing a lack of variety in essential human relationships. The
monologue functions to remove the theme from a narrow sexual
context to that of quasi-philosophical questioning:

I've asked all the questions, shouted them at deaf heaven, till I was hoarse in the voice box and blue in the face, and gotten no answer, not the whisper of one, nothing at all, you see, but the sun coming up each morning and going down that night, and the galaxies of the night sky trooping onstage like chorines, robot chorines: one, two, three, kick, one, two, three, kick . . . Repeat any question too often and what do you get, what's given? . . . A big carved rock by the desert, a . . . monumental symbol of wornout passion and bewilderment in you, a stupid stone paralyzed sphinx that knows no answers that you don't but comes on like the oracle of all time, waiting on her belly to give out some outcries of universal wisdom, and if she woke up some midnight at the edge of the desert and saw that fantastic fish swimming over her head . . . y'know what she'd say, too? She'd say: "Oh, well" . . . and go back to sleep for another five thousand years (V, 261).

The idea is not new, either in Williams or in Western culture. The universe has remained enigmatically silent to man for well over a century. Nor, unfortunately, are the metaphors particularly fresh, nor the philosophical musing particularly related to its dramatic context. The source of Quentin's mal d'esprit is not the world's refusal to answer the "big questions" but the dulling effect of the narrow repetitiousness of life's common experiences, a dilemma to which the homosexual has no special access, for it is universal.

The intensity of the boredom, however, is a new tone in Williams' work. This theme of dulling repetition provides a matrix within which we can understand his characters. Leona rages against it. Bill is too stupid and too centered on his penis to know it exists; Bobby too young to have experienced it yet. Doc can still wonder at the mystery of birth and death and can still see them through "this cloud of . . . irreverent . . . paraphernalia" (V, 250) thrown up by society and medical science. For Monk, providing a refuge for wanderers is enough to give life meaning. For Violet, only refuge itself matters. All are running from the loneliness and confinement of life. In one sense, the source of Quentin's values lies in all Williams' life and work. As he describes in his *Memoirs*, his life has always been a tentative bohemian existence characterized, as are practically all his plays, by the most fragile human contacts. Describing his early days in New Orleans, he expresses this obsession of his life in the metaphor which gives this play its title: "I knew and associated closely with a good many other young writers and/

or artists and all of us were disregarding the small craft warnings in the face of which we were continually sailing our small crafts, each with his crew of one, himself that crew and its captain. We were sailing along in our separate small crafts but we were in sight of each other and sometimes in touch, I mean like huddling in the same inlet of the rocky, storm-ridden shoreline, and this gave us a warm sense of community" (p. 2).

The need for, and the temporariness of, that inlet thematically pervades Williams' plays to the degree that the reader can find in all of them characters to whom the description applies: Laura, Blanche, Alma Winemiller, Brick, Chance Wayne, Shannon: everyone can supply his own list. The newness in *Small Craft Warnings* is the note of boredom and weariness with life, or, more accurately, a delicate tonal quality to that weariness seldom encountered before. Quentin is not, like Blanche, for example, destroyed by the callous indifference or downright brutality of others; he is simply deadened by the repetitiousness of the act of love and by his recognition of the essential sameness of life. Blanche and most of Williams' other characters long for the inlet and the sense of community; to Quentin, the sailing isn't worth it any more. And, however much the other characters in *Small Craft Warnings* may resist that sense of futility, it surrounds them all.

The central problem with *Small Craft Warnings* is that Williams does not find an adequate dramatic expression for the matrix within which his characters exist. Several reviewers have compared the play to O'Neill's *Iceman*. But the comparison is, I think, somewhat superficial. In *Iceman*, Hickey provides a dramatic center which sets the static lives of the other characters in motion; and although most of the residents of Harry Hope's Tavern return to their starting places, at least Hickey has sent them out into the street. O'Neill makes us see the simultaneous need for and futility of pipe dreams by the dramatic interaction of his characters and lets us observe and realize the ironic results. Williams' characters in *Small Craft Warnings*, on the other hand, are at their worst when they interact. The conflicts among them seem both trivial and irrelevant to the play's main theme. The sense of life in the play comes about instead in the monologues in which they reveal themselves and their positions within the thematic matrix Williams sets up. Each has his turn, and each plots his position. This side of the play is essentially lyrical rather than dramatic, and it exists almost separately from the parts of the play in which the characters interact.

A much more fruitful contrast for the play, I believe, is to Robert Patrick's *Kennedy's Children*. In a bar of social standing similar to Monk's, six characters reveal their involvement in and disillusionment with the sixties in a series of monologues, never speaking directly to one another or recognizing another's presence. The effect is that of a series of confessionals with the audience acting as priest. *Kennedy's Children* is not totally successful; perhaps no play completely devoid of dramatic interaction can be. But it is of a piece. Patrick has the courage to sustain his monologues. Williams loses his nerve and retreats into the familiar territory of Tennessee Williams' particular brand of romantic naturalism. It is in these retreats that we sense a traversing of familiar ground and feel that the other times over the terrain were much more interesting. The result is a division of focus in the play from which it cannot recover.

The comparison to *Kennedy's Children* reveals a further weakness in the style of Williams' monologues, a weakness in the poetry of his language. The problem becomes apparent when we compare Quentin's monologue with a speech of similar philosophical ennui, one of Clara's monologues from *Kennedy's Children*. Clara has set out to become the new Marilyn Monroe only to discover that no one wants a new Marilyn Monroe. "Weren't all the disguises and masks supposed to have been dropped? I mean, when Raquel Welch and a bunch of drag-queens are the current sex symbols—isn't there something wrong? What made them hate women? And men, what made them hate men? Is it just because there are so many people, and media and all have made them so much alike? Is that why everything keeps harking back to another era? Any other era? Any freak, any monster, anything different? Why don't we want anything beautiful? Why don't we want anything beautiful to be, to exist, to live? Is it overpopulation or what? Are we just instinctually avoiding reproduction? Stimulation, involvement, reproduction? Everybody's drunk, everybody's drugged, everybody's making TV commercials—where are the stars! What's wrong with them? What's wrong with me?" (in *Plays and Players*, 22, p. 48).

Although Patrick's language lacks the phonetic gracefulness of

Williams', Clara's monologue has something that Quentin's lacks.
It reverberates against a solid sense of reality and history. Quentin's
imagery never leaves the hot-house world of literary symbolism. It
is a free-floating imagery assembled in the writer's imagination but
lacking in substantial context. Its symbolism—the fish, the chorines,
the sphinx—reaches toward abstractions which are not located in
time and space, not even, as I indicated above, fully in Quentin's
own experience. Clara's imagery, though poorer as pure imagery,
is so situated. Its reverberations evoke the structure of our own experience with the sixties in a substantial context. This difference,
the abstractness of Williams' symbolism, contributes strongly to the
sense of repetition because the level of abstraction relates the words
to the entire modernist movement and leaves it essentially without
concrete location.

Out Cry is a more complex play than Small Craft Warnings and
in the long run a better play. But some of the same problems of
unity exist in it, too, and some of the same misunderstandings about
its basic nature exist in the criticism of it. Mel Gussow, writing in
the New York Times, contended that Out Cry is basically a monologue: "the two characters are too similar, not conflicting halves of
a personality as much as one person talking to himself, a feeling
that is intensified by the fact that each often finishes sentences for
the other" (11 March 1973, II, 1). The implication here, and in
other critics, is that the person doing the talking is really Tennessee
Williams. Such an interpretation, I believe, badly misunderstands
the play.

Structurally, Williams organizes Out Cry by enclosing its earlier
version, The Two-Character Play, in a play-within-a-play device.
Felice and Clare, brother and sister, are the surviving members of
a traveling theatrical company on tour in an unspecified foreign
country. After establishing their theatrical context, they perform
one of the familiar pieces in their repertory, The Two-Character
Play. As the play develops, the theater becomes a metaphor for their
loneliness and confinement and The Two-Character Play doubles
their situation by locating it in a fictional context in the southern
Gothic tradition familiar to all who know Williams. Their father,
a mystic of questionable sanity, has murdered their mother and
committed suicide. The psychological effect on them is to confine

them in their house, trapped by their fear of the outside world and by an unspecified morbidity at the core of their characters. The hint of dual suicide as a solution functions on both the levels of the outer structure and the play-within-a-play. But at the end, Clare and Felice find themselves locked in the theater, the cold and darkness closing in on them, and choose to continue the *Two-Character Play* to its end.

Critics of *Out Cry* have complained specifically about the overwhelming triteness of the dialogue and the personal subjectivity of the dramatic images. Clare herself wonders about their *Two-Character Play*, "if it isn't a little too personal, too special, for most audiences" (p. 62). Williams has acknowledged the play's thematic closeness to his own experience: "Confinement has always been the greatest dread of my life: that can be seen in my play *Out Cry*." (*Memoirs*, p. 233) Confinement is a legitimate fear and the playwright's subjective response a legitimate subject for drama. But here, Williams neither completely focuses his material nor makes it totally convincing.

The problem is not that the play is thinly veiled autobiography nor that the characters are merely superficial masks for the playwright. To assert, as does Gussow, that Felice and Clare are really the same personality is to ignore the rather considerable effort Williams goes to, particularly at the beginning of act one, to distinguish them. The *actors* Clare and Felice do not think alike and do not complete each other's lines. Their identities draw together only when they are portraying the *characters* Clare and Felice in the *Two-Character Play*. We are dealing not with a pair of static masks, but with a shifting pair of dynamic characters whose identities begin to merge as they perform their play. Williams' device of having them complete each other's lines does not indicate that their lines are really part of a monologue but that they are giving each other needed support in an emotionally difficult situation and that they are so familiar with their play that they are rushing toward its conclusion.

The true weakness of *Out Cry* lies in the relationship between the symbolism of the play-within-a-play device and the content of the *Two-Character Play*. Williams' theatrical symbolism is, of course, derivative from Pirandello and the playwrights of the absurd, perhaps too directly so to be effective. Clare and Felice are at the end of their rope. Only continuing the tour continues life; if the tour stops, they cease to exist. Furthermore, what Clare calls their "unexpected and—*unalterable—circumstance*" (p. 11) continues to narrow their possibilities until they are reduced to repeating the *Two-Character Play*.

The *Two-Character Play* forces on them a new level of confinement. The trauma of their father's act has stopped time. Clare is afraid to leave her house: "Suppose I came home alone, and in front of the house there was a collection of people around an ambulance or police car or both? We've had that happen before" (p. 34). Does her statement indicate that her life has morbidly stopped at a moment in her past and that she is doomed to live always suspended at that point, or does it indicate her fear that she might return to find that her brother has followed in his father's steps? Their circumstance has so confined them that their only alternatives seem to be death or separation and isolation in State Haven. Felice has apparently already experienced the latter alternative, as had their father, and both he and Clare find it unacceptable. Only in the safe harbor of their home can each find the human closeness necessary to sustain life. Thus, at least superficially, their confinement in their New Bethesda mansion seems equivalent to the confinement of the actors Clare and Felice in their theater and in the necessity of continuing their tour.

But only superficially. The theater metaphor draws upon the teatro del mundo tradition and, presumably, attempts to represent the total human condition. We, like they, have to continue our tours, even though "unexpected and unalterable circumstance" narrows our possibilities and confines us to smaller and smaller circumferences. The symbolism is shopworn and obvious, but clear. But we have much more difficulty accepting the characters in *Two-Character Play* as representative of the human condition. Rather, they are representative of neurotic, perhaps even psychotic, behavior. We see them not as images of ourselves but as psychopathic case histories observed from a distance.

The really telling difficulty is the existence of a world outside their mansion: the world of Grossman's market, the "Citizen's Relief" organization, the Reverend Wiley, whom Clare impulsively telephones. This world is hostile and confining only in their imaginations. Grossman even comes across as a somewhat patient man. Their confinement is not, then, representative of the human condition, as it is in the theater motif, but is a projection of their own warped imaginations, warped by an unusual circumstance in their lives rather than by the fundamental limitations of being human. Thus the relationship between the two levels of the play is not concentric but excentric, and our interest in the characters as case histories overpowers our ability to accept them as reflections of ourselves.

The use of theatrical symbolism is similarly unfocused. The burning rose in the carpet, the twin-headed sunflowers, and the statue which dominates the stage, "a work of great power and darkly subjective meaning" (p. 7), are either too obvious or too "darkly subjective" to exercise any controlling force over our responses. How subjective we can realize by comparing the statue in *Out Cry* to the stone angel which dominates the set of *Summer and Smoke*. In the earlier play, the angel provides us an unchanging frame of reference against which to see the progressive decline and narrowing of Alma Winemiller's life. As Alma undergoes her own unexpected and unalterable circumstances, the angel assumes a richer and richer meaning and somehow manages at the end to encapsule the pathos of her life. But the statue in *Out Cry* never gets charged with meaning. Whatever "anguished and perverse" (p. 7) things it supposedly represents never emerge from the play and attach themselves to it. It remains subjective in the worst sense of the word.

In both *Out Cry* and *Small Craft Warnings*, Williams' failure is neither self-repetition nor self-dramatization. It is an inability to fuse the disparate elements of his imagination into an effective whole. Too many times our interest is led outward on wild goose chases after a scattering of dramatic motifs which never really lead us back into the play. To cite only two examples: Doc's bungling complicity in the deaths of the mother and her infant and the question of Felice and Clare's father's religious mysticism. In a sense, perhaps, Doc's failure is an ironic bungling of his sense of the mystery of birth and death; but the triteness and melodrama of the drunken physician stereotype weaken its effectiveness as a characterizing device. The event stands out as an attempt to shock for the sake of shock. Similarly, the father's insane mysticism may be simply a motivational device to explain his actions and, perhaps, to suggest a hereditary morbidity in his children; but, if the former, it arouses interest disproportionate to its function and, if the latter, it simply further removes Clare and Felice from the universal human condition into psychopathological peculiarity. All these are missteps that the younger Williams did not commit.

Furthermore, I believe the dissatisfaction we feel with these plays comes at least in part from our subsconsciously placing them in the context of the theater of the sixties. Williams, having for all practical effect lost the decade of the sixties from his life, seems to be trying to create "Theatre of the Absurd" without knowing it has already been done. Others before him, particularly Samuel Beckett, have etched the experience of confinement so deeply into our sensibilities and have done so with such control of their dramatic medium that Williams' plays seem old hat in comparison. For example, I think the repetitious indecision about whether to go out to Grossman's Market must echo Hamm's and Clov's similar indecision in *Endgame*. But the differences in the two situations are startling. To Hamm and Clov the alternative to confinement is nothingness. Their confinement is absolute; so is their dependence on each other. There is nothing but mutual confinement, just as there are no more pap, pain killer, coffins, and nature. Even "what we call making an exit" (as Clov says) is a perpetual remaining on stage. True, Clare and Felice will also remain perpetually on stage, but because someone has locked the doors, not because the stage is all there is.

The experience of his crack-up and the encroachments of middle age have given Williams new insights into life and new thematic directions to his imagination. But if he is to make the richness of his imagination available to us again, he must find and control the means of dramatic expression better than he has done thus far in the seventies. Otherwise we will continue to feel (with sadness) the same discontents.

Since I completed the above article Williams has published, in *The Theatre of Tennessee Williams*, volume five, a considerably revised version of *Out Cry*, returning to his previous title, *The Two-Character Play*. The revision indicates not only that the play is of high personal value to Williams but, more importantly, that he is aware of its flaws and is in sufficient control of his talent to make headway in correcting them. Although the revised play may not stand as one of Williams' grander achievements, it demonstrates a surer grasp of dramatic technique than anything he has done in the seventies, and it deserves a new and impartial production.

The new *Two-Character Play* keeps the play-within-the-play relatively intact, but the scenes which enclose it have a tightness and energy lacking in *Out Cry*. In particular, the characters lose most of the rhetorical, introspective quality which so weakened them and which perhaps caused the impression that they were but mouthpieces for the author. Secondly, the excessive theatrical symbolism to which I objected above is largely gone.

Perhaps the single most noticeable improvement is in the toughness of Clare. Her first appearance suffices as illustration. In *Out Cry* Clare enters "falteringly, blindly" and encounters, fearfully, the statue which in that version dominates the stage. She quickly goes into a disjointed and somewhat insane (and symbol ridden) speech: "I forget—*unalterable circumstance*, but—Remember the time that destitute old—painter—invited us to tea on the—Viale—something— somewhere and when we arrived—the concierge said, suspiciously, 'Oh, him, huh, five flights up, not worth it!'—Five flights up, not worth it!—No, not exactly worth it, the old, old painter was seated in *rigor mortis* before a totally blank canvas, teakettle boiled dry on the—burner—under a skylight—that sort of light through a dirty winter skylight is—*unalterable—circumstance*—but there is no skylight here, I haven't noticed a window—Is this theater under the ground? Is this the subterranean— pleasure-dome of—Kabla—Kubla —Koon? . . .—Sacred river must be—frozen over—(She collides with something: a startled cry.) *Felice!*" (p. 11).

The speech illustrates one of the great problems with *Out Cry*: the characters are so drugged or so on the edge of hysteria that they are unable to follow the train of their own thought and speak in phrases punctuated by pauses, yet they are able to construct elaborate and somewhat coherent patterns of poetic symbolism. To produce such a speech at the beginning of the play gives away too much by connecting the theater, death, and their circumstances before the mood of the *Two-Character Play* has a chance to work on the audience.

In the revised version, Clare is somewhat nervous, but far from the outer edge of self control. Her "fear" is of her own shadow, not the "monstrous aberration" (p. 9) of the previous version, and she can talk rather playfully about it. She enters, not to protest that she can't go on, but to encounter a press reception, and her reaction to learning that it has been cancelled reveals a different Clare from the character in *Out Cry*: "No press reception? Artists' Management guaranteed, Magnus personally promised, no opening without maximum press coverage on this fucking junket into the boondocks.— Jesus, you know I'm wonderful with the press . . ." (V, 312). The Clare of *Out Cry* would never have been "wonderful with the press."

The hardening of Clare's character improves the play in two important ways. First, it etches more sharply the individuality of the characters of the brother and sister, further obviating the contention that they are a single character. Felice becomes the softer and more sensitive of the two and Clare the more businesslike and direct. Their outlines are distinct and the conflicts between them more believable. Secondly, by causing Clare to be less neurotic, Williams strengthens the possibility of our accepting her condition as normal rather than exceptional. She comes across not as an embodiment of vague poetry but as an actress on a two-bit tour and somewhat at the end of her rope. This improvement does not completely eliminate the discrepancy between the two layers of the drama, but it makes a major stride in that direction.

Perhaps the most striking improvement in the play is the reduction of the dramatic symbolism. The grotesque statue which Williams wanted to dominate *Out Cry* has practically disappeared as a motive for dialogue and, more importantly, has lost all its sinister and mysterious connotations to become merely a papier-mâché giant. Although the sunflower symbolism remains, it seems less obtrusive because it no longer has to compete with the emotionally charged set. The set as Williams now describes it is obviously a theater, not the demonic figment of someone's imagination described in *Out Cry*.

Williams' revisions of *The Two-Character Play* may not reverse the verdict against *Out Cry*, but they do reopen the case. More importantly, they do demonstrate a recapturing both of dramatic control and of objectivity in Williams' work. Perhaps the unburdening of himself in the *Memoirs* will enable Williams to escape the obsessions which have plagued his imagination during the last decade and enable him, in his twilight years, to regain his position as our most eminent living dramatist.

Reflections on Moon Lake:
The Presences of the Playwright

DONALD PEASE

ENNESSEE WILLIAMS' recent publication of his autobiography has resulted in an increased concern over the relationship
between his art and his life. Williams uses his art as an organizing
principle for his life, but it remains unclear whether he sees his plays
as pretexts for his self-revelations or his life as merely a context for
his art. The central figure in the *Memoirs* is neither Williams the
man nor Williams the playwright but Williams the actor who plays
a part in an Off Broadway production of one of Williams' own plays.
While acting in the play, Williams remembers the past as a series of
disconnected incidents that cannot be integrated into his role within
the play.

An analysis of the *Memoirs* would obviously merit a paper in itself, but even these surface observations make it clear that the autobiography emphasizes the complicated relationship between the life
and the work. In so doing, the *Memoirs* only continues a familiar
Williams concern. In a sense the *Memoirs* can be described as extended forewords, for in the New Directions edition of his plays Williams wrote forewords that present the disparity between the world
of his plays and his personal life. Since the forewords appear *before*
the plays, the reader must begin Williams' dramatic enterprise with
a rendition of personal difficulties that necessitated the creation
of the plays. On occasion these difficulties shadow rather than intro-

261

duce the drama, for while Williams continually asserts the successful transformation of his being into the acts of the play, he does so
in a way that suggests the impossibility of the conversion: "It is
amazing and frightening how completely one's whole being becomes absorbed in the making of a play. It is almost as if you were
frantically constructing another world while the world that you live
in dissolves beneath your feet, and that your survival depends on
completing this construction at least one second before the old
habitation collapses" (II, 419).

It seems that Williams placed these forewords at the beginning of
the plays so that his plays might be seen not only to originate in and
transform but also to replace his individual life. In the forewords he
provides personal background not to clarify his plays but to dramatize his life. He constructs his forewords out of the worldly struggles
of Tennessee Williams the man, so that this man might become an
actor in the *"world without time"* (II, 260) of his plays. Once Williams can be seen as frightened of his mortality, the timeless world
of the play can likewise be seen to emanate from and displace this
fear.

The forewords prepare the reader to view the plays as the conversion of the frustration of Williams' life into the immortal struggles
of the plays. Williams even implies that, after juxtaposing his life
and his art, his act of writing itself constitutes a moral code that he
cannot help casting in dramatic terms: "The great and only possible
dignity of man lies in his power deliberately to choose certain moral
values by which to live as steadfastly as if he, too, like a character in
a play, were immured against the corrupting rush of time" (II, 262).

However, the very description of this project reveals the impossibility of success. What is the reader left with after reading the forewords but the memory of a life that needs to be transformed but
cannot be? The very separation of the play and the forewords into
two discrete forms implies that while the life can be dramatically
narrated it cannot be fully dramatized. The narration can dramatize,
but only as narration not as drama. The forewords reveal that behind
the playwright who finds his great subject in unfulfillable desire
stands a man who is tragically unable to fulfill his own desire to turn
his life into drama. Williams is condemned to write forewords that

expose a wish that can never come true. In this light, the overdrama-
tized outbursts in the forewords seem the shadowy, unassimilable,
unregenerate origins of the plays. Almost all the forewords record the
tragic separation of the man from his plays, and they reveal the
plays to be the projection and elaboration of this alienation.

Yet the forewords are not limited to the narration of failures.
While Williams cannot be transformed into the world of the play,
the reader sees that his need to be can turn him into a playwright.
The same Williams who cannot be turned into a figure in the play
can be absorbed into the act of making plays. And when Williams
acts as a playwright he exists between the mortal world measured by
time and the timeless world of the play. From this perspective the
forewords constitute a narrative interlude wherein Williams is inspired by the threat of his own mortality. According to the time
logic implicit in the forewords, Williams as playwright exists between
the world of time and the world without time; as playwright he dwells
in a world undefined by time.

Through the forewords the reader begins Williams' plays by witnessing the unfulfillable desire that leads to the making of the playwright. Moreover the forewords invite the reader to consider the
inevitable loss implicit in Williams' motive for becoming a playwright: unless Williams can remain a perpetual playwright, he must
once again confront his mortality. As soon as he finishes a play, he
must once again become a man limited by time.

All these implications suggest that Williams cannot see himself as
a successful playwright until he can find a play wherein he can abide
as playwright. If most of the finished plays separate him from his
desire to be the eternal playwright, one of his plays manages to unite
him with this desire. In the foreword and notes to *Cat on a Hot Tin
Roof*, Williams the man is completely absorbed into the role of
Williams the playwright. In failing to have the play produced in the
version he wished, the playwright himself succeeds in becoming a
Tennessee Williams hero.

Before Williams can be seen as a hero still another foreword is
necessary. Some preliminary survey of what constitutes a Tennessee
Williams hero must precede any discussion of Williams as hero. But
this discussion of the forewords is not meant to be merely intro-

ductory, for a discussion of Williams' early plays in terms of the forewords can be illuminating. Indeed many of these plays seem to reenact the struggle narrated in the forewords.

Just as Williams begins his plays with forewords that dramatize the writer's wish to become part of his play, so Williams the writer actually began his dramatic career with the invention of the writer as his hero. Nor is it surprising that in his first full-length play written for Broadway production, *Battle of Angels*, the hero should become a writer in order to express his inability to fulfill his desire. Valentine Xavier becomes a writer on the day he discovers that making love cannot fulfill his wish or answer his questions of the universe. He wants to know the answer to the "why" of this world. Lovemaking only causes the question to disappear momentarily. He becomes a writer in order to let the secrets of the world abide within him. Williams, who fears the world outside the play, invents as his first "real" character a writer whose motivating impulse is to bring the world within himself. Valentine Xavier hopes to make his consciousness expansive enough to hold within it the creative center of the universe. But he discovers that creative center to be a reflection of his own nature, for in becoming a writer Val discovers the secret for the continuation of the universe to be frustrated desire. When Val writes he becomes the means whereby desire can reenact the conditions of its own frustration.

The orphan Valentine was dispossessed of the land. As a result he was free to roam the world with an awareness as expansive as the globe's. As a wanderer, he temporalizes the desire to know the secret impulses of the world. He can express his desire only as the flight of longing, for flight is the eternal expression of unfulfillable desire. When he rests on his journey he awakens the desire of those he meets. Valentine Xavier becomes an angel of light who awakens the world into freedom by putting it back in touch with its desires. "Valentine" loves and "Xavier" cures through an erotic touch, for the erotic is the universal expression of desire. However, each character Val awakens comes to the perception that he or she is trapped. Valentine remains free only because he stands outside the world as a man dispossessed who wishes to hold within himself the secret creative impulses of the world. Moreover, his freedom becomes the stage upon which the characters act out their lack of freedom. When Val touches these characters he invariably reminds them of some world of innocence and fulfilled desire that they lost. Ironically the angel of light calls forth an angel of darkness who becomes violent in his inability to get what he wants.

For example, when Val embraces Vee Talbott while he fits her for shoes, he liberates her erotic instinct and thereby enables her to fulfill her lifelong goal to paint the savior. When she paints the savior, he turns out to be an image of Valentine Xavier. Xavier's *painted* eyes accuse her with the look of a desire she must keep suppressed to remain a respectable member of the community. Her art becomes the revelation of her alienated desire. Her embodiment of that desire as Val confirms Val in the role of displaced or dispossessed desire. Valentine is the incarnation of society's repressed desire. In this role Valentine polarizes individuals and the society as a whole.

If Vee Talbott sees Valentine as the simultaneous release and accusation of desire, Myra Torrance sees him as both an angel of light and an angel of darkness. For Myra, Val seems the replication of her lost love David Anderson, who loved her at Moon Lake but left her to marry a wealthy planter's daughter. As such Val represents both fulfilled and unfulfilled desire.

After David abandoned her for the planter's daughter, Myra conceived of herself as a barren piece of land; so she sold herself to the merchant Jabe Torrance. Yet all the time she lived with Jabe, she remained engaged to David Anderson in her dream life. Jabe gave her the social standing that would make her David's social equal, but he also forced her to see barrenness as the cost of that equality. When Valentine arrives he frees her from the barren land to return her to her dream world at Moon Lake. Val's search for life's meaning reminds Myra of her love for David. Val becomes a reincarnation of David who motivates her to separate herself from the waste land incorporated in the "mercantile store" and attach herself to the idyllic world of Moon Lake, which she recreates in her decorations of the confectionery store. But almost as soon as Myra regains her dream world through Val and the confectionery store, she is condemned to lose it again. When Val arrived, Myra had tried to turn him into David. She did not see Val as Val, but as her lost love, David, reincarnated. She treats Val as the vehicle for a lost memory; he is not valuable in himself but only for what he represents. Likewise, the confectionery store is not Moon Lake, but only an attempt at a restoration of Moon Lake—the confectionery store can only signify loss; it cannot regain for Myra what she lost. Myra has not rediscovered love; she has only merchandised it. She has treated Valentine just as she feels Jabe has treated her, for she has tried to trap him within the confines of her world. She has attempted to enclose him within the skin of her secret world. Val cannot inaugurate her reunion with David, but after she traps Val he can repeat her loss of David by running away. By the end of the play Myra realizes that even the child she conceived with Val reproduces the death and not the regeneration of the Moon Lake world. Myra wanted to destroy Jabe's world, for she felt it was destroying her. Instead Jabe's world did destroy *her*; destructive impulses caused her to become an agent of the world she wished to destroy. Myra became a replica of the woman from Waco, Texas, who accused Val of rape because he could not be bought.

Once Val releases the frustrated desires of Vee and Myra, he becomes the symbolic expression for the town of everything it must destroy to survive. Valentine Xavier's primitive, elemental passion mirrors the interior the townspeople had to alienate once they became orderly and ordinary citizens. He is burned to death with a blowtorch on Good Friday as the expression of the town's internal conflagration. The people could not choose a more fitting instrument for the immolation of the passion they wish to alienate than a blowtorch, which itself represents an exteriorization of repressed emotion. Immediately after the deaths of the major characters, the townspeople convert the mercantile store into a museum where they can view the remnants of a world they had to destroy.

But, as with all worlds that come to an end on Good Friday, this one rises again as the play *Battle of Angels*. If Val the writer wished that the secrets of the world could take life within him, the play fulfills his wish, for his snakeskin literally becomes the curtain for the world of the play which exposes the creative secret of the world to be perpetual loss. Of course Val's wish reflects Williams' desires to convert the real world into his interior, created world. Poetry only partially fulfills that desire, for Williams' poetry only lyricizes the individual interior world. "Personal lyricism is the outcry of prisoner to prisoner from the cell in solitary where each is confined for the duration of his life" (III, 3). Personal lyricism must master "its necessary trick of rising above the singular to the plural concern, from personal to general import" (III, 4), and the way to this mastery involves the metamorphosis of lyric poetry into drama. Only drama can satisfy a writer who thinks "of writing as something more organic than words, something closer to being and action" (III, 5). Usually when a lyric poet writes in a more public setting, he devises a setting that coincides with his lyrical vision of the world—the setting becomes an idyllic world where every character and every object fulfills the longing of the lyricist. Tennessee Williams' settings do not satisfy the desires of the lyric poet so much as they repeat them. Whereas the lyrical world always reminds the poet of his separation from a world that cannot fulfill him, it also always deludes him into trying to be lyrical. Tennessee Williams invents a dramatic world that publicizes his private one. His dramatic world is not a place of fulfilled desire, but one which dramatizes and immortalizes the impossibility of ever fulfilling desire. Williams overcomes personal loneliness by inventing a dramatic world that becomes the dream space for every man's loneliness. Like Val he converts his interior world into the world's interior. When he does so, his plays themselves become mankind's expression of the separation between desire and act, wish and reality. Perversely, Williams fulfills the dream of the lyric poet by inventing a dramatic world in which desire cannot be fulfilled.

Once such a world is invented, the wish becomes one of reunion with a real world. A world orginating in frustration is bound to be prone to catastrophe. Such catastrophes coincide with the disasters Williams' life is heir to. In fact Williams conceives of his plays as his disasters, and when the world rejects them as disasters the actual world replicates the invented world. After Boston enthusiastically rejected Battle of Angels, Williams re-formed the incident into a dramatic event where he becomes Val and Boston becomes the incensed town of his play: "As we crossed the Common there was a series of loud reports like gunfire from the street that we were approaching, and one of us said, 'My God, they're shooting at us!' " (III, 219). However, while the dramatic rendering embodies Williams' wish to unite the two worlds, his humor exposes their irreconcilable separation.

These two worlds did not remain separated indefinitely. The public accepted *The Glass Menagerie* with almost as much ardor as it exercised in rejecting *Battle of Angels*. In *The Glass Menagerie* the writer Valentine Xavier, who was a fugitive, becomes the writer Tom Wingfield, who dreams of running away from the imprisoning world ruled by his mother, where he must replace his fugitive father as the family's means of support. Tom lives for the future, while everyone else in the house dwells in the past. Once the present fails to satisfy longing, the past projects itself into the memory as a tempting idyllic world of contentment, but such a world is always an evasion of the present—a wish not to be. In *The Glass Menagerie*, Myra's memories of David at Moon Lake become the lost world of the Old South peopled by Amanda Wingfield's gentlemen callers. Both Myra's and Amanda's worlds are tombs masquerading as pastoral settings, for both worlds are attempts to forget the betrayals that destroyed Myra and Amanda. Laura Wingfield conflates the idyll and the museum into a glass menagerie that houses glass animals whose substance consists of Laura's sympathy and compassion. Since Laura is crippled, she cannot temporalize her longing through flight; so she memorializes it in her glass animals.

These memorabilia expose and shatter Amanda's self-deceiving memories when she attempts to relive her past through her daughter. When Tom invites Jim O'Connor as a guest for dinner, he invites a man who is a living piece of memorabilia, for he is a relic from Laura's past. In high school, Jim was a great success, but since then he lost his status. Success for him would inhere in recapturing his former status. While Jim seems only a ghost of his former self he embodies the deepest wish of every member of the Wingfield house. As the substitute father, he would allow Tom to escape by replacing him; as the gentleman caller, he would return Amanda to the glories of the South; as her dream lover come true, he would turn Laura's glass menagerie back into the real world. In fact Jim does momentarily change the Wingfield apartment into a heavenly paradise when he seems truly to love Laura. However, he leaves it a haunted house peopled by shattered dreams after it becomes clear that he has only used Laura as a proving ground for his powers of persuasion. When he talks with Laura, his dream of success collides with her dream of love. When his dream of success takes him back in memory to his past success in high school, both dreams combine to make the present reality seem ghostly. Jim reinstates Laura in her glass menagerie world by replacing her dream of love with the image of his dream girl. Hence the gentleman caller reenacts the original crisis of each character. When he abandons them, he becomes Laura's father and Amanda's husband. Far from replacing Tom as family provider, he previews Tom's following in his father's footsteps.

Battle of Angels used violence to unveil Val's interior; *The Glass Menagerie* reveals Tom's interior world to be one inhabited by two women confined to live with their dreams of escape. Unable to run away, Laura must stabilize her escape within the glass menagerie. Through this world Laura can recall the impossibility of ever realizing her dream. While Amanda tries to suppress the beastly instincts of the members of her household, Laura knows that each person is a transparent beast whose interior can be filled only with the light of a shared longing. Laura's failure with Jim strangely reunites her with her mother, for Laura has duplicated Amanda's loss of her gentleman caller. They now share a common experience of loss. When we last see Amanda, she bends over Laura and treats her with the sympathy Laura reserves for her glass animals. Moreover, Laura's failure constitutes the substance of Tom's quest. When he flees home to see the world, Tom sees it through Laura's eyes. The entire world becomes a glass menagerie made transparent through the intensity of longing. Laura's glass menagerie has become the essence not merely of Tom's world, but of the entire world, and Laura abides in Tom as his soul. All his efforts to flee from home result in his understanding that all the world suffers from the same disease as his home. Paradoxically, whereas Tom could not accept his home as his world, on leaving home he sees all the world's frustrations in terms of his home. The world seems only an expanded version of his home. When Tom writes, the world of his play becomes the living record of the world he would escape. By extension, the actual world's essence is revealed as its desire to escape from itself.

The Glass Menagerie domesticates the violent world of *Battle of Angels*. Tom Wingfield writes a play that illuminates two significant elements in Williams' dramatic world. Tom writes a play that instead of becoming an escape from his family becomes an expression of his family's and all America's need to escape from a world of unfulfilled desire. The play displaces the individual desire to run away by universalizing that desire. Moreover, Tom's narration of this play about unfulfilled desire reflects Williams' narration of his own unfulfillable desire in forewords.

Was the success of *The Glass Menagerie* the world's revenge on Tennessee Williams? Financial success made it possible for Williams to get everything he wanted out of the world—but that was precisely what Williams did not want. Worldly success separated him from the source of his poetic creation. It threatened to strip him of the need for his dream by offering him the opportunity to live the American myth of success. Success put Williams in possession of everything that his dramatic world proscribed. As a result the world threatened to dispossess him of his need to create. Williams responded by seeing the success of *The Glass Menagerie* as a catastrophe. His preface to the New Directions edition of *The Glass Menagerie* was originally entitled "The Catastrophe of Success." In this essay Williams pits his former way of life against the effete existence success threatened to provide: "The sort of life that I had had previous to this popular success was one that required endurance, a life of clawing and scratching along a sheer surface and holding on tight with raw fingers to every inch of rock higher than the one caught hold of before, but it was a good life because it was the sort of life for which the human organism is created" (I, 136). External success causes him to feel part of this world, but such a feeling dislocates him from the spiritual world of his creation. To defend himself from this sense of spiritual dismemberment, he develops a feeling of enmity for his play and so hears all praise of it as a manifestation of hypocrisy. That play threatened to be his last because it returned him to a world from which he had to feel displaced in order to create. Williams finally developed a saving strategy. He entered the hospital to have his fourth eye operation. Once his eye was operated on, he did not have to *see* this world, but his world would have to see him as disabled. People once again sounded sincere. Williams cannot hear compliments—they are all evasions for him, because they imply that a man works out of self-possession; but he does hear concern and worry, for they are expressions of loss. In essence, Williams cures himself of the disease of success by abandoning his public self with all of its "vanities and conceits and laxities" (I, 140) and exchanging it for "the only somebody worth being . . . the solitary and unseen you that existed from your first breath and which is the sum of your actions and so is constantly in a state of becoming under your own violation" (I, 140). Yet as we have seen, Williams can realize this "solitary and unseen" personality only through the act of writing a play, and the play world replaces the public ego with the world of a play; for it "is only in his work that an artist can find reality and satisfaction, for the actual world is less intense than the world of his invention and consequently his life, without resource to violent disorder, does not seem very substantial" (I, 138). Predictably, as a final act of spiritual restoration, Tennessee Williams overcomes success by writing a play also destined to be successful, A Streetcar Named Desire.

In Battle of Angels, the writer was the savior who became the symbol of everyone's lost love; in The Glass Menagerie, the writer mediated between the lost world and everyday reality; but in A Streetcar Named Desire, the writer himself embodied the lost world. As Allan Grey, he is not the substitute but the actual beloved who was betrayed. Love letters and poems secreted at the bottom of Blanche's suitcase are all that remains of Allan. These writings beg Blanche to help Allan regain hold on the world. Blanche was to be Allan's center of being in the world; she was to be his hold on reality. But Blanche betrayed her mission when she discovered that she could not be Allan's sole object of desire. Finding Allan alone in a room with an older man, she goes with him to the place where all dreams begin and are shattered in Williams' plays, Moon Lake, and there she tells Allan that his actions disgusted her. After Allan shoots himself out of shame, Blanche leads her life as an effort to regain Allan. When she becomes the prostitute for all the soldiers, she becomes the desired object she was not for Allan. If Blanche can satisfy the soldiers' desires as Allan's, perhaps she can remake Allan after the image of a soldier. Likewise, she seduces the seventeen year old boy both to regain Allan through him and to fashion for herself a reputation as bad as Allan's.

Interestingly, Allan Grey signals a turning point in Williams' conception of the character of the writer, for Allan Grey is not the primitive become writer but the writer become the polar opposite of the primitive. Stanley Kowalski possesses all the brutal instincts that Allan Grey lacked. Whereas the writer now appears as a figure whose desire could neither fulfill nor be fulfilled, Stanley Kowalski manages to live in a world where his dream can flourish. It is revealing that such a disjunction in Williams' characters should appear *after* the success of *The Glass Menagerie*. In fact the doubling of the role of writer/primitive into a dead writer and a flourishing primitive seems an appropriate response from a playwright who feels that the writer was almost destroyed by the vanity and insincerity that appeared with success. The changed level of Kowalski's desire and his capacity for insensitivity and brutality mirror Williams' reactions after the success of *The Glass Menagerie*. Stanley Kowalski lives in a world uninformed by the transforming power of art, and this world became Tennessee Williams' spectral reality after the writer in him was almost destroyed through the creation of a successful play.

When Tennessee Williams flees to the elemental world of Mexico, he writes a play in which the world he flees not only reappears but prevails. A *Streetcar Named Desire* makes it clear that for Williams the act of fleeing always becomes the act of re-living the past. Flight forces the presence of the past on his characters as the presence of what they attempt to flee. Flight only intensifies the presence of the past. When Blanche DuBois runs away from Laurel and Belle Reve, she does not leave that world behind but instead transports it to the Elysian Fields of Stanley Kowalski. Blanche flies from the world of her past to begin a new life, but Stanley forces her to re-enact the scene in her past that she attempts to flee, her destruction of her love, Allan. Stanley becomes her nemesis, for he responds to her with the same brutal frankness she directed at Allan on the night he destroyed himself. Conversely, Blanche exposes Stanley's apparently idyllic world as a museum of the spirit. Long before Blanche, Stella abandoned the world of Belle Reve in exchange for a dream world of sexual fulfilment with Stanley. When she stepped down from her mansion Stella gave Stanley's world its power and its magic, for his world needs Stella's acquiescence to remain a reality. Stanley can maintain the illusion of kingship in his world only by repeatedly pillaging Stella's mansion. After Blanche arrives, Stanley's world is threatened because Blanche can see it as a dream. She can see through his dream because she is conscious of her own need to invent a false world.

To Stanley, Blanche's dream represents the tenuous unreality of his life. Blanche has tried to return his wife to the world of Belle Reve, so Stanley must repossess his dream world by ravaging Blanche's. Stanley causes the world to see Blanche's dream for a lie and his own dream for the truth. His world depends on the destruction of everything Blanche's world represents. By revealing her reputation as a prostitute, he forces Blanche back into her past. As we have seen, Blanche's promiscuity was an expression of her loss. When Stanley labels her a whore, he turns this expression of her loss of love into her essence.

However, Stanley does not take her as he would a whore; he rapes her as an embodiment of Belle Reve. Through Blanche he re-enacts his initial triumph with Stella. By raping Blanche, Stanley once again pillages Belle Reve. Stanley must ravage Blanche, for he can regain the supremacy of his illusion only after he has reduced Belle Reve to ruins. After he rapes Blanche, her dream changes from the vision of a new life to the reverie of dying at sea. At play's end Blanche's desire has become one with its opposite—death.

This brief discussion of Williams' early plays indicates that the central action for his artistic work is transformation. If Myra sees Val as the metamorphosis of David, and Amanda discovers Jim O'Connor to be her gentleman callers returned, Blanche DuBois recovers her lost love in Mitch. Once she learns that Mitch has remained devoted to a girl who died, she can easily convert him into a representative of her lost love. The image that emphasizes this action is the moth or bird that leaves behind the abandoned cocoon or the broken shell to fly in a nighttime world. Since such metamorphoses involve an element of conflict, it is not surprising that Williams sets many of his transformation scenes against an open sky that itself turns cloudy or stormy as a projection of the inward sky of the characters. Williams' sets are the exteriorizations of the dream worlds envisioned by his characters, and they change *as* his characters change mood. All these transformations find their origin in the characters' need to evade some past event. In *Battle of Angels* and *The Glass Menagerie*, it was the loss of love; in *Streetcar Named*

Desire it was the brutalization of love. Are these past events within the plays themselves shadowy images of Williams' need to transform his "public self" (I, 138) into the world of a play? Is the loss that Williams sees his life to be the original loss that all his plays look back to? Are not his forewords the residue, the broken shell of a life that has failed to be transformed? These forewords express Williams' life somehow as a betrayal of his dream. They shadow the plays with such renditions of Williams' mortality as: "Whether or not we admit it to ourselves, we are all haunted by a truly awful sense of impermanence. I have always had a particularly keen sense of this at New York cocktail parties, and perhaps that is why I drink the martinis almost as fast as I can snatch them from the tray" (II, 261). The plays overshadow this fear by dramatizing Williams' fear of mortality, and once the mortality is dramatized it is immortalized in the world of the play in which time is arrested: "The diminishing influence of life's destroyer, time, must be somehow worked into the context of his play. . . . almost surely, unless he contrives in some way to relate the dimensions of his tragedy to the dimensions of a world in which time is *included*—he will be left among his magnificent debris on a dark stage, muttering to himself, 'Those fools'" (II, 264). Whereas time reduces Williams' life to debris, the plays use that debris as the setting for the timeless world of the play. In this play world, Williams wishes to bring all the members of the audience within the unifying warmth of a re-created shell, the transformed remnants of the shell of the world formerly shattered. Williams can feel at home only within his theater: "Our hearts are wrung by recognition and pity, so that the dusky shell of the auditorium where we are gathered anonymously together is flooded with an almost liquid warmth of unchecked human sympathies, relieved of self-consciousness, allowed to function . . ." (II, 262).

The forewords reveal the distance between Williams' art and a life that cannot be rendered into art but can only be the precondition for such a rendering. Even the accounts of incidents from his life remain merely forgettable incidents and not the events which become immortal once charged with the remarkable tensions in his drama. Only in *Cat on a Hot Tin Roof* does Williams manage to bridge the chasm between the world of his forewords and that of his plays.

In the New Directions edition, *Williams'* version of the play becomes a foreword to the performed version of it. Williams wrote two versions of *Cat on a Hot Tin Roof*. He preferred his first version but rewrote it because the director, Elia Kazan, felt a rewritten version of the second and third acts would make better dramatic sense. Williams had to rewrite the entire third act of this play because he was afraid to lose his director, Elia Kazan. To satisfy the demands of his director, Williams compromised his own vision of the play. It was Kazan's version and not Williams' which won the Pulitzer Prize and the New York Drama Critics' award, and the success of Kazan's play meant the failure of Williams' art. Whereas in his previous plays, the disaster of Williams' life was the necessary precedent for the creation of a play, now the failure of his art became an event in his life—an event which he could transcribe as part of his printed edition of the play. When a director reads this edition, he must choose between Williams and Kazan. As a result Williams has translated himself from an abandoned cocoon into an *act* of choice. Moreover, this act makes it clear that once one chooses Williams or Kazan, one chooses Williams *transformed into* the third act of his play. If his previous play turned Williams' life into art, *Cat on a Hot Tin Roof* turned his art into an event in his life and then enabled that event to be seen as the failure of his art.

In the foreword to this play, "Person-to-Person," Williams outlines the boundaries of this failure. After noticing that an artist's plays invariably find themselves rooted in the deeply personal, emotional life of the artist, he asserts that his own plays constitute his effort to break through the lonely walls of himself to reach out and embrace another. Williams lays bare the personal dimension of his play and the desperate attempt at communication to let the reader see its failure to communicate as a personal failure. In this play, which focuses on the difference between truth and reality, Williams is forced to lie just as is his central character Maggie.

Like Myra, Amanda and Blanche, Maggie the cat finds herself backed into a trap and she must claw her way out. Unlike Myra and Amanda, but like Blanche, Maggie married her dream lover, Brick. And like Blanche, she discovered that her lover did not love her as much as he did another. Brick devised a way of coping with the problem of human mortality that mirrored Williams' own. He tried to remain eternally young by playing the game of his youth with his youthful companion as long as he could. While Brick played football, he remained in a play world outside the parameters of human history. He and Skipper could maintain the illusion of youth by the authority of the illusory world of games.

Complications resulted when Maggie tried to get as close to Brick as Skipper was. Unable to achieve such intimacy in the bedroom, she tried to love Brick through the man to whom he was devoted. She tried to attract Brick's desire by forcing Skipper to confess to Brick that he was a homosexual and in love with Brick. Brick did not want to enter human time. He attempted to remain outside time through a game that was his idealization of the world. Skipper's phoned admission of his homosexuality distorted and profaned that ideal world and so made it part of the historical world. Brick could not accept the truth of that statement and remain Skipper's friend; so Brick answered Skipper's confession with silence. Just as Blanche's disgust led to Allan's suicide, Brick's disgust with Skipper ended in Skipper's death. If Blanche tried to atone for Allan's death by becoming the object of desire for every soldier in Laurel, Brick makes amends to Skipper by trying to drink himself into Skipper's grave. Alcoholism replaces football as the idealized form of their atemporal relationship. Brick drinks until he hears the "click" of the telephone receiver he slammed on Skipper's confession just as Blanche drinks until she hears Allan fire the gun at the Moon Lake Casino.

Brick lives as Skipper's principle of death. Not a rebirth but a second death, Brick lives his life as a form of Skipper's dying. Ironically Brick's father, who is afraid he is about to die, sees in Brick the emblem of his own life. When Big Daddy tries to reform Brick's life, he does so because he sees Brick as the objectification of the life he is about to lose. In their second-act confrontation scene, Big Daddy forces Brick to confess that it was his own mendacity, his inability to face his disgust for Skipper's desire that led to Skipper's death. Whereas Big Daddy had hoped that such a recognition of the truth would lead to Brick's reformation, Brick takes the scene as a revelation of the mortality and degeneracy of human existence. Big Daddy began this scene with Brick because he needed to talk with someone. He has just been told he did not have the cancer he feared. All the animal screams of terror he had suppressed when he struggled with his fear of death, he turned into a *conversion* sermon when he talked with Brick. Brick is the younger version of himself. Since Big Daddy had just conquered death within himself, he wished to conquer death in the exterior version of himself. However, Brick reconverts the scene when he tells the father the truth of his condition. Big Daddy had compelled Brick to face the truth of his mendacity. Now Brick forces his father to confront the truth of his own mortality when he tells him the doctor lied. Brick speaks as Big Daddy's own fear that diagnoses his disease to be terminal intestinal cancer.

In the second act both Big Daddy and Brick have attempted to evade the truth. Brick used alcohol, while his father tried a more subtle form of self-deception. Big Daddy tried to escape from his knowledge that man is the beast who must die, by resolving to live his newly recovered life *as if* he were starting life again. That is why he must reject Big Mama. She represents his past life which now has revealed itself to be mortal. He must replace her with some fantasized woman even though Big Mama remains as faithful to him as his rich Delta plantation.

While the second act reveals the truth that life is death for both Brick and Big Daddy, the first and third acts suggest that Maggie's lie can come true. Maggie tries to regain Brick in the first act by offering him a part in her game of love, but after he rejects this ploy, she regains him as her loss in the third act. After Mae and Gooper tell Big Mama that Big Daddy will die of cancer, she tries to evade this truth by begging Brick to father a child and thereby a second Big Daddy. She hopes to remember Big Daddy through Brick. Although Brick ignores her plea, Maggie tries desperately to remain in the game by announcing that she and Brick will have a child. Brick neither agrees nor disagrees, for by this time he listens only to the "click" that will give him the peace of Skipper's death. Williams' version of the third act climaxes in a remarkable tour de force wherein Maggie literally draws life from death. Unlike David Anderson, Jim O'Connor, or Allan Grey, Brick is the living memory of lost love, and what is more he is the abiding image of a dead man. Not a substitute but the dying version of the man Maggie loves, Brick haunts Maggie with the presence of a past love. Refusing to be defeated by the death that haunts Big Daddy and Brick, Maggie takes this man in her arms and literally conceives a child out of Brick's death. She makes love to Brick as she probably made love to Skipper, and when she whispers her devotion to Brick they resonate as words she might have originally whispered to Brick that night when she made love to him as Skipper. Now that Brick has become the alcoholic and dying version of Skipper, Maggie can repeat those words, "Oh, you weak people, you weak, beautiful people!—who give up.—What you want is someone to—take hold of you.—Gently, gently, with love! And—I *do* love you, Brick, I *do*" (III, 165–6). While Maggie remarries her husband as death, Brick does not begin to reform himself, but begins to perfect his slow ritual of dying. Big Daddy's second act dissertation on man as the beast who must die, which itself was a sublimation of his fear of death, now reverts to the beastly howl of the beast who knows he faces death. In the third act Big Daddy is transformed into the animal howl he earlier repressed.

In the performed version of the play, Brick tries to reform himself, and Big Daddy actually reappears on the stage. These two events belong together because Williams has secretly converted Kazan's directorial imperatives into another of Big Daddy's orders. Once Tennessee Williams presents a reformed Brick, he compromises Brick's fidelity to the death of his friend, but he affirms Brick's obedience to Big Daddy's second act command to reform himself. Brick lies to his own truth and acts as if Big Daddy's *wish* for immortality concealed in his attempt at Brick's rehabilitation could come true. Big Daddy also lies, for he now sees Maggie as the dream woman he fantasized as a promise of immortality. After Maggie announces that she will have a child, he picks her up off the floor and agrees that she does indeed have life in her. However, he feels this life as the erotic life he desires. In helping to make Maggie's lie seem true, Brick and Big Daddy betray the truths they discovered in the second act and seem compromised victims of self-deception. In Williams' version Brick's decision to remain an alcoholic seemed the decision of a man who remained strong in his devotion to a dead friend. Alcoholism was his prayer of devotion. That strength gave Maggie's final action a certain stature. But in the performed version Maggie does not conceive life with death but only manages a hysterical union with a weak man.

Not the characters but Tennessee Williams himself emerges as the real victim in this play, for he exists in this third act as a betrayed presence. His printed version of the play dramatizes Williams' victimization by a director whose drive for success has made a catastrophe out of one of Williams' most intimate plays. The performed version of the play was a success, but the price of this success was the destruction of Williams' version. *Cat on a Hot Tin Roof* marks the high point in Williams' career for it not only enables him to see the success of his play as a personal disaster but it enables his reader to see it as well. The printed version of this play itself becomes a dramatic representation of the author's central dramatic metaphor, for it dramatizes the destruction of Williams' personal vision and its resurrection by the world as a distorted image of the original. When the reader looks at the order of the printed version of *Cat*, he can see the successful version as an unsuccessful replica, as the loss of the vision Williams had earlier attained. When the reader can see this he can see that this work represents the play as itself a repetition of the eternal loss that always haunts and motivates Tennessee Williams.

Williams' play world has come full circle and duplicated his original reason for writing plays. He could see his version of the play as the world of Moon Lake betrayed and distorted by a Jabe Torrance figure who tried to merchandise and take possession of this dream world. The play has descended into reality, for the successful version performs the absence and not the presence of Williams' vision. Yet this failure in the midst of success extirpates and focuses Williams' need to be a playwright.

Bibliographical Note

The primary sources are those from which quotations are taken for this volume. Students of Williams know that bibliographical information is very complex because of revisions, title changes and unpublished manuscripts. For example, *Kingdom of Earth* is listed below because it is sometimes quoted in the text of the book, while a revision appearing in *The Theatre of Tennessee Williams* is also quoted.

The following list of both primary and secondary materials is intended only to supplement the abbreviated internal documentation. In addition to the bibliographies listed in the books on Williams, see Delma E. Presley, "Tennessee Williams: 25 Years of Criticism," *Bulletin of Bibliography and Magazine Notes* 30: 1 (January-March 1973), 21–29.

The interview published in *Life* is listed as Barnett, Lincoln. *Vogue* of 15 March 1951 published an essay by Williams on *The Rose Tattoo*. The interview in *Playboy* is listed as Jennings, Robert.

SECONDARY MATERIAL

Adler, Jacob H. "*Night of the Iguana*, a New Tennessee Williams?" *Ramparts* 1, November 1962), 59–68.

Barnett, Lincoln. "Tennessee Williams." *Life* 24 (February 16, 1948), 113–14.

Brooks, Charles. "The Comic Tennessee Williams." *The Quarterly Journal of Speech* 44: 3 (October 1958), 275–284.

Callaghan, Barry. "Tennessee Williams and the Cocaloony Birds." *Tamarack Review* (Toronto) 39 (1966), 52–58.

Campbell, Joseph. *The Hero with a Thousand Faces.* New York: Meridian Books, 1956.

Cash, W. J. *The Mind of the South.* New York: Random House, Vintage, 1941.

Cohn, Ruby. *Dialogue in American Drama.* Bloomington: Indiana University Press, 1971.

Donahue, Francis. *The Dramatic World of Tennessee Williams.* New York: Unger Publishing Co., 1964.

Edinger, Edward F. *Ego and Archetype: Individuation and the Religious Function of the Psyche.* Baltimore: Penguin Books, 1973.

Falk, Signi. *Tennessee Williams.* New Haven: College and University Press, 1961.

Frazer, Sir James G. *The New Golden Bough.* Ed. Theodor H. Gaster. New York: Criterion Books, 1959.

Fritscher, John J. "Some Attitudes and a Posture: Religious Metaphor and Ritual in Tennessee Williams' Query of the American God." *Modern Drama* 13 (September 1970), 201–215.

Funke, Lewis and Booth, John E. "Williams on Williams." *Theatre Arts* 46 (January 1962), 17–19, 72–73.

Ganz, Arthur. "The Desperate Morality of the Plays of Tennessee Williams." *American Scholar* 31 (Spring 1962), 278–294.

Hays, Peter L. "Tennessee Williams' Use of Myth in *Sweet Bird of Youth.*" *Educational Theatre Journal* 18 (1966), 255–258.

Jackson, Esther Merle. *The Broken World of Tennessee Williams.* Madison: University of Wisconsin Press, 1965.

Jennings, Robert. "Tennessee Williams: A Candid Conversation with the Brilliant, Anguished Playwright." *Playboy*, April 1973, pp. 69–84.

McCarthy, Mary Therese. "A Streetcar Called Success." *Sights and Spectacles.* New York: Farrar, Straus and Cudahy, 1956.

Nelson, Benjamin. *Tennessee Williams: His Life and Work.* New York: Ivan Obolensky, 1961.

Popkin, Henry. "The Plays of Tennessee Williams." *Tulane Drama Review* 4: 3 (1960), 45–64.

Reck, Tom S. "The Short Stories of Tennessee Williams: Nucleus for His Drama." *Tennessee Studies in Literature* 16 (1971), 141–154.

Skloot, Robert. "Submitting Self to Flame: The Artist's Quest in Tennessee Williams, 1935–1954." *Educational Theatre Journal* 25 (May 1973), 199–206.

Steen, Mike. *A Look at Tennessee Williams*. New York: Hawthorn Books, 1969.

Tischler, Nancy. *Tennessee Williams: Rebellious Puritan*. New York: Citadel Press, 1961.

Weales, Gerald C. *Tennessee Williams*. Minneapolis: University of Minnesota Press, 1965.

Contributors

Charles B. Brooks is professor of English at California State University at Long Beach.

Leonard Casper is professor of English at Boston College, Boston, Massachusetts.

Glenn Embrey was a lecturer in literature and writing at UCLA.

Norman J. Fedder is associate professor of theater and director of the playwright's workshop in the speech department at Kansas State University, Manhattan.

William J. Free is associate professor of English at the University of Georgia, Athens.

Albert E. Kalson is associate professor of English at Purdue University, Lafayette, Indiana.

John MacNicholas is associate professor of English at the University of South Carolina, Columbia.

Charles E. May is professor of English and chairman of the department at California State University, Long Beach.

George Niesen is an English instructor and program administrator for the Hartnell College program at Soledad Correctional Facility, California.

Donald Pease is associate professor of English at Dartmouth College, Hanover, New Hampshire.

Peggy W. Prenshaw is Honors Professor of English at the University of Southern Mississippi, Hattiesburg.

Leonard Quirino is professor of English at Western Connecticut State College, Danbury.

Judith J. Thompson is an assistant instructor at the University of Kansas, Lawrence.

285

Index

This list refers to some of the significant observations about the works. Main characters will of course usually be mentioned thereabouts, as will themes and techniques.

DATE DUE

1-3-84			
"RESERVE"			
Amer			
Drama			
APR 8 1985			
OCT 1 5 1985			
OCT 2 1 1985			
OCT 2 3 1985			
OCT 2 8 1985			
NOV 1 4 1985			
DEC 1 5 1985			
DEC 1 6 1987			
OCT 2 7 1988			
APR 1 1 1993			
MAR 2 8 1995			
APR 1 0 1995			
GAYLORD			PRINTED IN U.S.A.